T0261964

Progress and Applications of Mobile Computing

Progress and Applications of Mobile Computing

Edited by **Adam Houle**

CLANRYE INTERNATIONAL

New Jersey

Published by Clanrye International,
55 Van Reypen Street,
Jersey City, NJ 07306, USA
www.clanryeinternational.com

Progress and Applications of Mobile Computing
Edited by Adam Houle

International Standard Book Number: 978-1-63240-420-6 (Hardback)

Contents

Preface

In my initial years as a student, I used to run to the library at every possible instance to grab a book and learn something new. Books were my primary source of knowledge and I would not have come such a long way without all that I learnt from them. Thus, when I was approached to edit this book; I became understandably nostalgic. It was an absolute honor to be considered worthy of guiding the current generation as well as those to come. I put all my knowledge and hard work into making this book most beneficial for its readers.

Mobile Computing is an umbrella term used to refer to various devices that enable people to access information and data from anywhere. This book gives directions on how mobile software services simplify the mobile users' lives. The main contribution of this book is improving mobile software application in development stages as analysis, design, development and test as well as topics such as recent mobile network technologies like algorithms, decreasing energy consumption in mobile network, and fault tolerance in distributed mobile computing. It also deals with mobile software life cycles, human computer interaction discussing mobile device handset design strategies, and mobile application testing strategies. This book also discusses mobile applications as service, covering various mobile solutions and distinct application sectors.

I wish to thank my publisher for supporting me at every step. I would also like to thank all the authors who have contributed their researches in this book. I hope this book will be a valuable contribution to the progress of the field.

Editor

Part 1

Mobile Network Technologies

Algorithms of Mobile Network Development Using Software-Defined Radio Technology

Larysa Globa and Vasyl Kurdecha

National Technical University of Ukraine "Kyiv Polytechnic Institute"
Ukraine

1. Introduction

According to the World Forum for Research in Wireless Communications (Wireless World Research Forum, WWRF) it is expected that in 2015 the volume of traffic around the world will be 23 exabytes[1]. The existing division of the radio spectrum has serious limitations for this growth.

Today there are many standards, mixed wireless networks and mobile devices with many standards. The operators develop heterogeneous wireless networks to provide access to many services. The mobile devices with many standards use several active applications simultaneously to work with the different networks or the network recourses. Functioning of such mobile devices requires coordination and control of the capacity efficient using of the radio resource and the radio access networks.

The rapid development of means and wireless communication systems is ahead the processes of standardization and leads to the problems of interaction and compatibility. So, there are the problems: 1) significant growth of mobile traffic in the conditions of limited range; 2) lack of coordination and control of the capacity efficient using of the radio resource and the radio access networks; 3) actual lack of common standards for radio systems with the possibility of reconfiguration. According these problems it is needed to find solutions in this area. The decision of all this problems can be find by using software-defined radio (SDR) technology which requires the development of special algorithms for software updating and adapting. In this paper the algorithms of mobile network development using software-defined radio technology are proposed.

2. Algorithms for SDR BS software modification

Currently, SDR is widely used in cellular communications, where real-time support of the different changing radio protocols is required. In receive mode SDR can provide higher efficiency than "traditional" techniques. In digital signal processing their filtering is more closed to the ideal. In addition, by using software algorithms can be implemented functions, which are very difficult to get in analog processing.

---

[1]Tafazolli R. Technologies for the Wireless Future, volume 2.Wireless World Research Forum, (WWRF) / R. Tafazolli. – Oxford: Wiley, 2006. – 520 p.

2.1 Mobile cellular network based on SDR

Software-defined radio is a radio communication system which used software for modulation and demodulation operations of the radio signals. SDR change the priorities, and the processing unit becomes the core of radio system.

When using the SDR almost all operations for the signal processing are shifted on software that runs on hardware of the mobile or cellular base station. So, the operation control of some specific specialized microprocessor is designed for this signal processing. The aim of this approach is to develop the flexible and adaptive system. Such kind of the system can send and receive all radio signals using SDR.

The ideal implementation of SDR-receiver is the antenna connection directly to an analog-digital converter (ADC) which is connected to a powerful processor unit. In this case, the software running on processor unit provides processing of the incoming data stream and converts them into the desired format. The ideal SDR-transmitter would operate similarly. The software would form a data stream that would be transferred to a digital-analog converter (DAC) connected to the antenna.

Most of the radio equipment used in the networks is based on the hardware or hardware and software modules that allow upgrading it only under a single standard. For example, most GSM base stations, which are operated at present, can only be upgraded under the GSM standard, but the transition to other technologies require the hardware replacement. With the spread of the radio multiple standards - 2G/3G/4G and various technologies - GERAN, UTRAN, WIMAX and LTE becomes necessary cost savings and efficient using of the base stations in a longer life cycle, evolving to the new standards, speed, quality of service and environmental improvements. These problems force operators to look for the new solutions to reduce the unit capital and operating costs, to develop the networks quickly and efficiently.

In multi-channel and RF systems, the hardware defined radio (Fig.1) implementations require a significant amount of analog signal processing for every channel, leading to larger board size, increased analog design complexity, limited flexibility, and RF interference susceptibility.

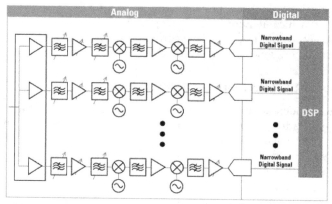

Fig. 1. Schema of the traditional Hardware Defined Radio

With the Software Defined Radio (SDR) approach (Fig. 2), signal processing is moved to the digital domain—providing various benefits[2]:

- Low Analog Complexity
- Less susceptibility for RF interference
- Unlimited flexibility
- Analog power does not increase with increased Rx channels

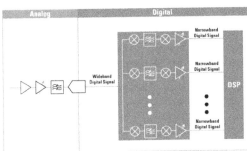

Fig. 2. Schema of Software Defined Radio

The flexibility possible with software-defined radios (SDRs) is the key to the future of the wireless communication systems. Wireless devices relied on highly customized, application-specific hardware with little emphasis on future-proofing or adaptation to new standards. This design approach generally yielded power- and performance-optimized solutions at the expense of flexibility and interoperability.

Wireless device developers, as well as service providers and end users, can upgrade or reconfigure SDRs continually as new versions of the wireless standards are released. Furthermore, SDR devices can adapt continually to changes in the spectral or network environment, including modulation schemes, channel coding, and bandwidth. They can use be used to establish and maintain ad hoc networks[3].

Technology Software Defined Radio (SDR), which are started to be used by advanced base stations equipment vendors for radio access network (RAN), becomes more relevant and an effective solution to these problems. New radio systems are known by various marketing names: Single RAN, Uni-BTS, Multi-RAN and Multi-standard Radio. But they all mean essentially the same thing - a relatively simple mechanism of modernization, which allows one base station to support simultaneously several different radio technologies.

Despite the marketing statements of new equipment RAN developers concerning its capabilities and, in particular, on the application in its SDR and the advantages that gives them using a technology offered by the base stations new platform vendors, there is no possibility for the operators to develop advanced multiprotocol and multifrequency

[2] National Semiconductors. Software Defined Radio (SDR) Solutions
http://www.national.com/en/adc/sdr.html
[3] Kevin W. Rudd and Chris Anderson. June 2010 Software-Defined Radio
http://www.computer.org/portal/web/computingnow/archive/june2010

networks based on them. Obviously, though the operator can use the same base station equipment, reprogramming it to support other standards, it's still need to add additional radio-frequency devices and antenna-feeder cells or replace them with universal multi-standard systems. Also, not so much technology used in base stations is limited to such a transition, but the existing infrastructure with its system of frequencies using regulation, the lack of standards and wide spreading of the terminal equipment capable of supporting these multifunctionality don't allow it to do at this stage.

But a phased transition is still possible, and the mobile operators already can choose available software-modifiable equipment for the evolution of their networks.

2.2 Development of an optimal architecture for network upgrade

Possible way for the development of mobile networks may be in the next direction of radio access networks modernization with using the transition to LTE technology (Fig.3).

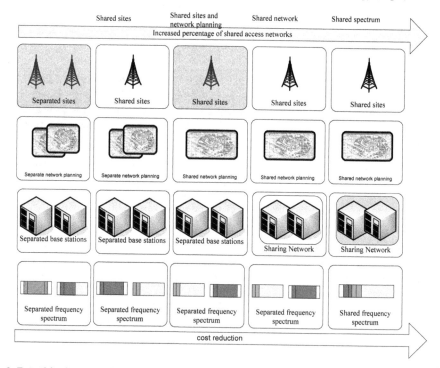

Fig. 3. Possible direction for network modernization

LTE technology for the service providers (operators) reduces the network cost of owning and operating allowing them to have some of the core network (MME, SGW, PDN Gw), but RAN divide for sharing. This can be achieved by flexible program mechanism allowing each base station to be connected to multiple CN nodes of the different operators. When the mobile terminal included in the operator's network, it connects to the corresponding node CN, based on the service provider identifier sent from the mobile terminal. RAN sharing as a concept was proposed by Orange and T-Mobile in the UK, and could become a model for many operators in their migration to 4G [5].The operators have already invested large amounts in obtaining licenses for 3G frequency spectrum and 4G, and to realize the return on these investments in the future they will have to follow the model of sharing the radio access network, providing operators the necessary requirements of the network. In this case the transition occurs from a fully separate networks (separate: sites, the network planning, base stations and spectrum) to the most optimal variant of the full radio access network sharing, spectrum, and overall planning. And in this case, for base stations the SDR technology is very easy to allow the gradual such functioning equipment upgrading by program way without significant additional investment in equipment.

LTE technology will allow for the higher frequency bands to create sufficient capacity for the transmission of multimedia traffic, and the lower - to ensure wide coverage, albeit with some damage to the bandwidth. LTE is able to work in a large number of frequency bands. When bandwidth is 1.4 MHz, LTE allows three times more efficient to utilize frequency resources than the cellular networks of second generation. Efficiency is determined by the number of bits that can be sent at 1 KHz allocated frequencies.

With the appearance of LTE technology, the scale of using SDR technology is expanded and it's possible to say that main suppliers are increasingly inclined to use it as a new platform to their radio sites and support its key importance in the conditions of standardized solutions. Standardization in the reconfiguration of mobile networks plays today the most important role, as new projects require a sufficient large investment from operators and developers of equipment and for this investment must be no assurance that equipment from different vendors to be integrated into existing networks and will work in a multivendor environment. Standardization of Reconfigurable Radio Systems (RRS) deals with a number of forums and organizations, such as: 3GPP TSG RAN, ETSI, Cognitive Networking Alliance (CogNeA), European Communications Office (ECO) SE43, IEEE, ITU-R, Joint Research Centre (JRC), Object Management Group (OMG), SDR Forum. Today, the standards (IEEE 802.18, 802.19, 802.21, 802.22, WAPECS, 1900) groups are developed in the various research organizations, which aim to create recommendations for improving spectrum management processes. Due to their implementation it's expected to obtain an additional gain in spectral efficiency and, consequently, in a radio service quality. In Europe, standardization in this area recently was engaged ETSI, which defined the concept of reconfigurable radio systems. This concept is based on technologies such as Software Defined Radio (SDR) and Cognitive Radio (CR), whose systems use radio and reconfigurable networks capabilities for self-adapt to the dynamically changing environment.

2.2.1 Basic requirements for base stations with the possibility of reconfiguration

The ability of reconfiguration is needed for: modulation and bandwidth, frequency allocation, including existing and upcoming bands, power levels, duplex mode, capabilities of the network architecture modification and other functions.

Basic requirements for base stations with the possibility of reconfiguration are given in Table 1.

General requirements for base stations	Requirements for the purposes of operators	Requirements for hardware manufacturers
Using of the several standards and transition between them	The possibility of rapid network planning and modernization including the necessary capacity and coverage	Compliance with the customer conditions
Frequency rearrangement	Rapid network deployment, which justifies the cost	Reducing the equipment number through effective control of them
The opportunity to participate in the dynamic spectrum allocation;	Flexible network performance, especially taking into account technology migration	The ability to update and modify the equipment functionality, the ability to increase its capacity through software updates
The opportunity of the spectrum re-using	Spectrum reusing and optimization; this requires total control of two or more systems that temporarily coexist geographically	RBS technical ability of spectrum reusing
The channel capacity dynamic optimization depending on the network load	Dynamic control of the hardware resources specified for the existing network and the new generation systems	The equipment certification;
Antennas tuning	-	3GPP standards compliance, to guarantee the full equipment compatibility
Reconfiguring of the transport network for plane architecture	-	The equipment reliability

Table 1. Basic requirements for the RBS with the possibility of reconfiguration

2.2.2 The network architecture for a base station with the possibility of reconfiguration and requirements for its functional blocks

Based on specified requirements, the simplest mobile SDR-network can be as follows – Fig.4.

Taking into account defined in paragraph 2.2.1 requirements, RBS optimal architecture can be offered (Fig. 5).

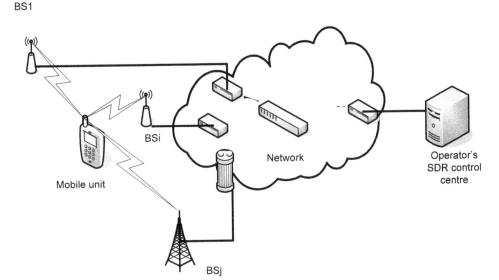

Fig. 4. The simple SDR mobile network.

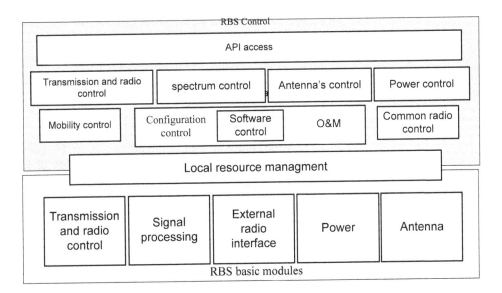

Fig. 5. Architecture of the base station with the possibility of reconfiguration

There are general requirements for functional units with the possibility of RBS reconfiguration (Table 2).

The functional unit of RBS	Requirements to block / function
Configuration Management Unit	software interface to start operations of reconfiguration;
	ensure of continuous agreed operation of all RBS units;
	If it's necessary to add the function Software Management (SW) into the operation of the reconfiguration;
	Transaction return;
	Rapid response in case of breakage or failure in the RBS (e.g., reorganization in damaged equipment).

The RBS functional unit	Requirements to block / function
Software Control Unit	The software download procedure execution
	Has to know what software is installed in every block;
	Has to know the potential interaction of software modules;
	The opportunity to activate / deactivate the software in RBS;
	RBS software process as an integral unit or as an independent application
	Flexibility of using different approaches to software management
O&M (technical service) Unit	Access to all important parameters of RBS configuration;
	Activation / deactivation of measurement control;
	Collecting and summarizing the results of measurements (collection and the summation scheme should be flexible and);
	Clients should be able to sign for delivery of measurements and / or configuration parameters results (delivery scheme should be flexible and reconfiguration);
	Servicing of internal and external clients;
	RBS defense from too many requests.
Transmission Control Unit	Servicing of internal and external clients;
	Having the following physical layer configuration: gigabit Ethernet, copper, optical, SDH, μwave, (multiple connections with a link to the supported standards);
	Having the following logic level configuration: TCP / IP, SDH-Frame, S1/X2 Association (referring to the supported standards);
	Supporting the internal configuration of the standard algorithms to RRM (Radio Resource Management) algorithms for autonomous fine-tuning.
Spectrum Management Unit	Supporting the separation of the spectrum bands and rules for their using;
	Planning / control of spectrum using in a supported cells (if enabled): algorithms, the period of appointment, thresholds, interference between the cells;;
	Supporting functions of cognitive radio.

Capacity Control Unit	Providing maximum transmitter power, a change of power in accordance with the RAT specifications for the cells, antennas, etc.;
	Providing specific power schemes management (in the daytime, at night, depending on events, saving power, etc.);
	Providing the effectiveness measuring to coordinate with RAT specifications
The functional unit RBS	Requirements to block / function
Mobility Management Unit	Providing handover parameters configuration (thresholds, timers, etc.);
	Horizontal handover providing (hard, soft, etc.);
	Vertical handover providing (3GPP-WiFi-WiMAX, etc.).
Radio Resource Control Unit	Supporting the choice of terminal equipment access based on: The required quality of service (bandwidth, maximum delay, real time / unreal time); Radio conditions; User preference; Network policies; Information about a neighbor cell; Cell location (latitude / longitude), its radius and capacity; Cell capabilities (supporting services to the real / unreal time); Dynamic data such as current cell load.
Antenna Control Unit	Providing radiation pattern of antennas, the antenna directed action coefficient, antenna direction;
	Sector configuration providing (3x1, 1x1, etc.);
	Supporting of different physical types of antennas (Multi-pad, MIMO, SIMO);
	Using of heterogeneity receivers / transmitters, according to the separate antenna cable structure;
	Providing mechanical rotation / tilt, electrical rotation, modified rotation / tilt, azimuth direction.

Table 2. Requirements for the RBS functional units with the possibility of reconfiguration

Based on the proposed network architecture for the effective network operation it is necessary to realize the method of SDR network reconfiguration.

2.3 The method of radio access network reconfiguration

The method of the base station reconfiguration uses graph of the base station software states, flowchart of the base station software upgrading sequence, the scheme of the software modification and block diagram of the control objects in the base station with the possibility of reconfiguration.

2.3.1 System description

To consider the software as a set of simultaneously operating and interacting programs in all hardware and software modules of the basic station, this provides general functional operation for all applications and supporting programs. This software includes basic functional blocks: the functions of maintenance and hardware and software modules control, functions in SDR signal processors (execution programs of generation radio interface, antenna beam control, etc.). Let's consider the program blocks and functional elements to be the subject of reconfiguration for SDR-technology.

2.3.2 Functional elements with combined program blocks

Combined software units managing of the functional elements are run as well in a main processor of a functional module as in processors of devices (e.g., SDR signal processors). The program management object can be configured to perform at one or more functional elements, and presented as several program blocks in the same loaded unit of the functional module. How the program can be structured is shown in Fig.6. The program unit associated with the management object - functional element in a functional module, has the same attributes as the functional element and is included in the same restart group. For example, if a functional element is restarted, then all software units belonging to this functional element are restarted too. Other blocks will not be affected.

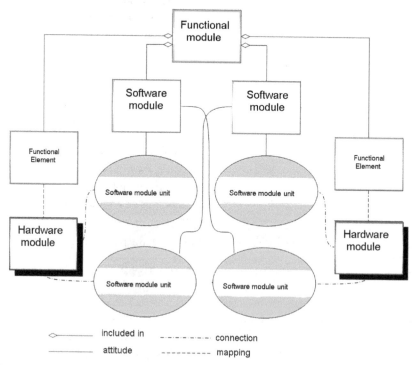

Fig. 6. The management object structure of the functional module with combined program blocks

2.3.3 Functional elements with connected program blocks

In this case software blocks are run in the functional element directly, as it is shown in fig. 7. Software blocks are configured with indicating, how software blocks are distributed and which functional element they are run on. The attributes that are linked with the name of the block in the software management object cannot be used to connect the software block to management objects - functional elements. The attribute of the restart group is not being used at this time. If a functional module is restarted, then all program blocks in this module are restarted.

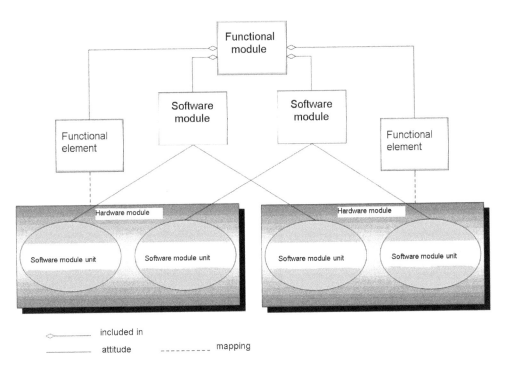

Fig. 7. The management object structure of the functional module with connected program blocks

2.3.4 State phases of the BS software

The graph of the BS software states is shown on the fig. 8.

If one considers the base station software as a single management object or as one application, then it is possible to define the main phases of its operation, a transition to which is executed at the certain events that occur during operation of the base station (increasing the number of software failures, necessary to perform action on a particular schedule, etc.), and in case of the commands, written in Man-Machine Language (MML). These commands come from the outside. They are:

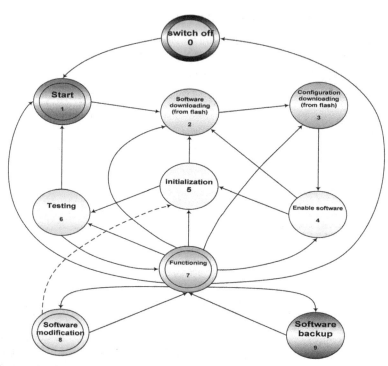

Fig. 8. The graph of the BS software states with the possibility of reconfiguration

- Phase 0 "Off"

In this phase the base station is in the standby mode and the software isn't loaded into processor RAM of the functional modules and O&M. The external power is connected to the base station, but the internal power supply off. Thus, all functional modules and functional elements of the BS are inactive except for independent software module of BS power management. This module should provide an opportunity to remote turn on and off the internal power sources for BS by sending MML command from OSS or from the control element(O&M terminal). Switching to the Phase 0 is executed from the Phase 7 by remote external MML command or emergency in the case of forced power interruption from any phase. Passing from Phase 0 to Phase 1 is executed at the event of its successful completion.

- Phase 1 "Start"

In this phase the synchronized and consistent (in a strictly fixed order) turning on the internal power supply of the BS hardware modules and activation of the boot modules , the management interface of BS internal resources are carried out. In fact, the boot modules have to be located in processors ROM of the BS modules, and boot programs have be activated immediately after power-on to the processor modules.

Also, switching to Phase 1 is executed from phase 6 in the case of unsuccessful testing of functional modules after software initialization or from the phase 7 by remote external MML command. Passing from Phase 1 to Phase 2 is executed at its successful completion event.

- Phase 2 "Downloading software from flash"

In this phase the parallel software download from the flash memory modules into the RAM of the BS main O&M module and all regional processors that provide the work of functional modules and the BS functional elements. Also, passing to Phase 2 is executed from phase 5 in the case of unsuccessful software initialization or from the phase 7 by remote external MML command. Passing from Phase 2 to Phase 3 is executed by its successful completion event.

- Phase 3 "Downloading configuration from flash"

In this phase the parallel download of the BS configuration files from the flash memory modules into the RAM of the main O&M BS module and all regional processors to provide of the functional modules and functional BS elements is executed. Passing to Phase 3 is executed also from phase 7 by remote external MML command. Passing from Phase 3 to Phase 4 is executed by its successful completion event.

- Phase 4 "Running software"

In this phase it is executed the synchronous and consistent running (in a strictly fixed order) of the downloaded software modules in the main O&M processor and later in regional processor functional modules, under the management of O & M module. Passing to Phase 4 is executed also from phase 7 by remote external MML command. Passing from Phase 4 to Phase 5 is executed at its successful completion event.

- Phase 5 "Initialization"

In this phase it is executed synchronous and consistent initialization of all program modules and blocks with the initial set of these blocks variables, and configuration of software complex for programs support, defined by configuration files, and the actual bringing of all working modules to an active state, ready for testing BS applications. Passing to Phase 5 is also executed from Phase 7 and Phase 8 by remote external MML commands. Passing from Phase 5 to Phase 6 is executed by its successful completion event, in case of unsuccessful completion of Phase 5,passing to Phase 2 is executed for restarting software in some or all BS modules.

- Phase 6 "Testing"

In this phase it's executed parallel independent testing of all the hardware and software modules correct functioning according to the performance algorithm. Then testing is executed of the all modules collaboration within the application, specified by configuration data. Passing to Phase 6 is executed also from phase 7 by remote external MML command. Passing from Phase 6 to Phase 7 is executed by the its successful completion event, in the case of unsuccessful completion of Phase 6, passing is executed to Phase 1 for the initial start, or if necessary - repair execution.

- Phase 7 "Functioning"

This is the main phase, in which the functioning of the base station is executed. It provides execution of all applications, defined by the BS configuration data and its resources control, configuration and providing of its interaction with other elements of the mobile network: Radio Network Controller (RNC), Base Station Controller (BSC), Operational Support Systems

(OSS), etc. Switching to Phase 7 is also executed from Phase 8 and Phase 9 after their completion. Passing from Phase 7 to Phase 8 is executed by external MML command when software upgrade is requested. Passing from Phase 7 to Phase 9 is executed by the external MML command when software backup is requested. Passing from Phase 7 to Phase 6 is executed by external MML command when regular or compulsory testing is requested. Passing from Phase 7 to Phase 5 is executed by external MML command for restarting the software modules. Passing from Phase 7 to Phase 4 is executed by external MML command or in the case of detecting software failure. Passing from Phase 7 to Phase 3 is executed by external MML command, or in the case of detection configuration data failure to reload configuration files from flash memory. Passing from Phase 7 to Phase 2 is executed by external MML command, or in the case of detection of non-revolving by means of restarting crashing software for reloading of the software module from flash memory. Passing from Phase 7 to Phase 0 is executed by external MML command to switch off internal power supply BS.

- Phase 8 "Software modification"

In this Phase 3 main functions of software modification are executed:

Correction of software block

Software update of the functional module and the functional element

Software upgrade of the base station

Return from Phase 8 to Phase 7 is executed by external MML commands at the completion of software correction or update. Passing from Phase 8 to Phase 5 is executed by external MML commands when the software upgrade function is completed.

- Phase 9 "Software backup"

In this phase it is executed backup of all software modules, memory modules, data blocks and links of the program modules and blocks from the main O&M module, the functional blocks and functional elements in structured DUMP, that includes 3 files: programs, data and references, which are stored in the flash memory of O&M main module. Return from Phase 9 to Phase 7 is executed after completion of backup Phase.

2.3.5 The general scheme of the operation sequence of the base station with the ability to modify software

Fig.9 presents general diagram of the operation sequence of the base station with the ability to modify the software. It describes the basic steps which must be completed in the states phases on the BS management objects level, according to diagram in the Fig.6.

In the off state in the standby mode BS receives a command to power up independently from the site or remotely with OSS or O&M terminal. Standalone the BS power management software module generates signals internal power supply on of the BS modules in software defined sequence. After time-out power on at all functional modules, their power on are controlled.

In case of hardware inactivity of any of the modules, BS indicates "accident of powering" on the power supplies on the scoreboard display and informs about the accident through the O&M interface (in OSS or control element).

On successful completion of powering on in all functional modules boot software modules are activated. They are located in the processor ROM of the each module.

Loading modules activate the internal interface of local resources management, total control of which is done by the main O&M module. O&M module makes a request to the software download in the processor RAM of the modules from local flash memory devices, guided by these processors.

After the timeout software downloads into all functional modules, the load control is executed using responses which confirm loading of these modules.

If not all modules verified the software downloading from the local device flash memory, O&M module activates the emergency software module download from the active backup, located in the flash memory of O&M module.

Later on a load test of software is done and if unsuccessful downloading some of the modules, BS indicates "accident of the software downloading" on the scoreboard display and informs about the accident through the O&M interface (in OSS or control element).

On successful completion of software loading into all modules, O&M module initiates the loading of the configuration settings from a BS configuration file in all custom function modules, functional elements (blocks of software).After a timeout boot parameters in blocks of software the loading and configuration are controlled by responding units of software downloads.

If not all blocks verified download of the configuration parameters the BS indicates "accident of configuration" on the scoreboard display and informs about the accident through the O&M interface (in OSS or control element).On successful completion of parameters loading in the software blocks and BS configuration BS the initial start (or restart) of all modules and software blocks is executed with the main O&M module in all functional modules. They in its turn initiate the restart of software units in functional elements.

After the waiting times of restart in all functional modules complete the monitoring the restart completion is executed from all software blocks.

In case, if not all software blocks confirmed restart complete, it is executed the cycle restarts test. If reset phase was performed twice or more times in a short time interval and if the restart was cyclic, then the BS indicates "accident of cyclic restart" on the scoreboard display and informs about the accident through the O&M interface (in OSS or control element).

If the restart was not cyclical, the attempt is made to restart the software of restart module correctly with an active backup. If restart of the all software modules and blocks was successful it is executed the initializing of the all applications, followed-up – applications modules start, of all modules and applications functioning, the synchronization of signaling protocols, further tuning antenna system by successive queries from basic O M module. After a timeout the BS and all applications readiness are controlled confirmation of readiness. If the BS is not ready, the message "Accident of Start applications" indicates on the scoreboard display through O&M interface (in OSS or control element) and the attempt is made to restart the software modules with an active backup.

When BS is ready full operational command interface is run what allows to continue working with BC as a complete part of the network through signaling protocols and O&M

interface, to interact with other network elements: RNC, BSC, Mobility Management Entity (MME) and the control system (OSS)

Then BS is functioning into test functionality mode.

After testing timeout BS executes control of the testing end completion. If the test result is unsuccessful, then "accident Test BS" is indicated on the scoreboard display through O&M interface (or in OSS) and attempt to re-start is made. On successful completion of testing, the BS goes into full operation mode. Operational command interface further allows executing the BS management via O&M interface with the control system (OSS, the control element or the terminal O&M).

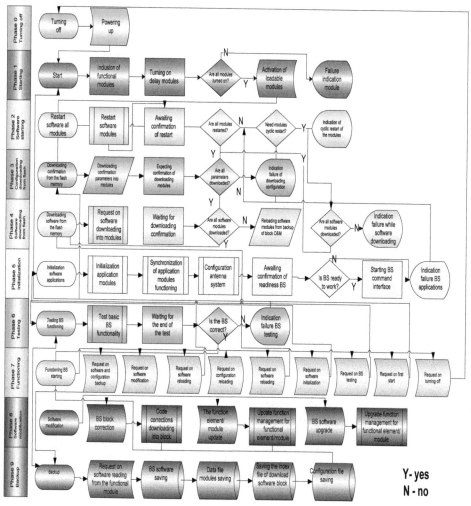

Fig. 9. Block diagram of the operation sequence of the base station with the ability to modify software

The base station receives the following basic commands:

- Request for software and configuration backup;
- Request for the software modification;
- Request for the software reload;
- Request for the configuration reload;
- Request for the software restart;
- Request for initialization of the applications;
- Request for BS testing;
- Request for the BS initial start;
- Request for the BS turning off.

In addition to these requests BS has to receive and process a lot of other requests, associated with applications functioning, the definition of different settings, etc. But they are not associated with software modification.

On command of software and configuration backup main O&M module sends a request to the functional modules for reading and backup of all software modules, memory modules and data blocks, links on blocks and software modules structured DUMP, that includes 3 files: programs, data and links as well as the configuration file stored in flash memory of the main module O&M. After the backup it is executed returning back to operation phase. It should be noted that in the phase of Backup BS continues normal operation only with some restrictions of O&M functions.

The commands to modify the software perform:

- Correction of the software block;
- Update of the function modules or functional element software;
- Upgrade of the base station software.

After upgrading the software of the function Upgrade the initial start (or restart) all software modules and blocks is executed. In two other cases, the software modifying it is executed returning to the operation stage. When the software modifying, BS continues normal operation only with some restrictions of O&M functions too.

2.4 Software modification of the base station with the possibility of the reconfiguration

The process of corrections downloading into the software block should be done in the running block, so it may be cause of the unplanned failure of the BS operation and even break it down. Therefore, this operation has been carefully checked before performing. This will allow making software management very flexible and in some cases to avoid serious loss of traffic connected with the Upgrade functions and maintenance costs for software Update.

2.4.1 Sequence description of corrections loading operations into the base station software block

On the command from OSS, the control element or O&M terminal (0-7) executes direct loading of corrections (commands codes) into correction space of the program in processor

RAM of the functional module (fig.10).Further corrections are activated by setting navigation in the correction workspace from the points of corrections installation and returning into the next program point from the correction workspace into the software workspace. It also set a mark in the links memory of the software block about the block correction and its status (active / passive).The variables and constants used by software block can be changed directly in the processor RAM of the functional module too. In this case, the correction activation will be consisted of only installing the correction marks in the software block.

The unit is executed the functionality test of the software block with the special tests. If the software block is wrong functioning it is executed the corrections deactivation and retuning the software block into its initial state before corrections with the corrections removal from the correctional workspace.

Further, the commands are send to OSS, the control element or the O&M terminal, with indication of downloading correction error into the software block and then the correction function of the software block is completed. If successful testing of the block with installed correction, the correction function of the software block is completed successfully.

2.4.2 The sequence description for the Update function of the functional module/BS element software

The Update function of the functional modules or elements software should be executed with the ability to transfer all variable data and parameters associated with the block that is modified, into the new modified software module. This function is needed for reducing the cost of BS characteristics redefinition after modification.

On the OSS command the control element or the O&M terminal executes the regional processors separation of the functional module. At the same time working (EX) processor continues to execute the program of the functional module or the functional element, and backup (SB) processor will be used to transfer data into the new module from EX processor. Then it is made direct download software of the new module into SB processor. Then the table of the functional data transfer is downloaded into the EX processor. Interface of data transferring between the EX and the SB processor is activated.

Next step is the data transfer of the software blocks of the functional modified module or the functional element from the EX processor into the SB processor. After data transfer is executed the software of the modified module in SB processor is restarted. Then it is made checking of the new software correct functioning of the module. When work is incorrect the command is sent to OSS, the control element or O&M terminal, and the function Update error of the functional modules or the functional element (0-5) is indicated and then the software Update function in OSS, the control element or the O&M terminal are ended.

On the side of the functional module the SB&EX processors are transferred in parallel operation with the software of the Update function shut downing, and, an actual, loss of the modified software in SB processor.

When new software is executed correct it is made switching the EX&SB processors of the functional module with software restart. Then new software of the functional module or functional element begins to work.

Further if necessary it is made saving the copy of the modified software from the EX processor into the internal flash memory of the functional module. Then EX&SB processors are transferred in parallel operation with the successful completion of the software Update function.

2.4.3 Description of operations for the software of the base station modernization/update

The update function of base station software should be made with the possibility of the all variable data and parameters of all BS software blocks transfer during the transition to a new release of software within a single standard. This function is needed to reduce the cost of the BS character is tics redefinition after modification. When replacing the base station software to another standard, data transfer should be not carried out if new software blocks are not hereditary. In this case, the preparation of new software applications is executed by applications of the radio network scheduler and OSS. Then downloading of the new software into the flash memory of the O&M basic module, its activation, reboot of the function modules and restart are executed.

On command from the OSS, when the Upgrade function with a data transfer is used, the control element or the O&M terminal downloads the new software into flash memory of the main O&M module. At the same time working (EX) processor continues to execute the program of the O&M module and backup (SB) processor will be used to transfer data into the new software blocks from the EX processor. The structure universality of the processor modules should allow software modification of the all functional modules using only the processors of the O&M module.

Then it is made the new software direct downloading of the all modules into SB processor and the BS configuration file loading. After that the tables of functional data transfer of all modules into the EX processor are downloaded and the interface of data transferring between the EX and SB processors is activated.

At the next step the data transfer of all software blocks of all functional modules and functional elements and the configuration file transfer into the base station new software blocks are done.

After the transfer have already done it is executed the BS software restart in the SB processor of the O&M module and checking the correctness of the new software blocks functioning. When the functioning is incorrect the command is sent to OSS, the control element or O&M terminal, which indicates the software error of the BS function Upgrade and then the software of the Upgrade function in OSS, the control element or the O&M terminal completes. On the side of the BS O&M module, the EX and SB processors are transferred into parallel operation to complete the software of the Upgrade function and, as a fact, to loss of the modified software in SB processor.

If operation of new software blocks is correct it is executed modified software backup from EX processor into flash memory of the O&M module with the notes installation to mark the BS active software for further BS software restart after the transfer of the Upgrade function data will be completed.

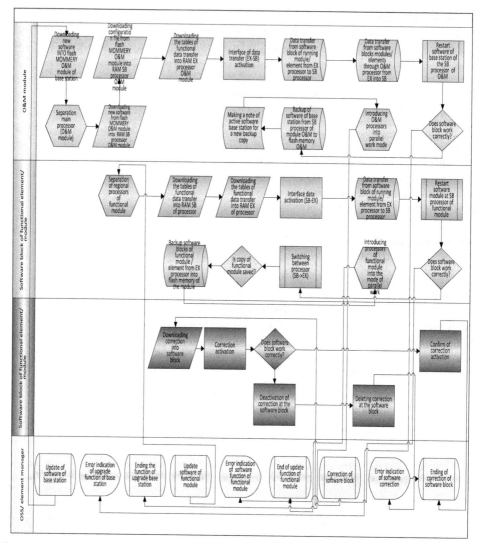

Fig. 10. The block- diagram of the operations sequence for the BS software modification

Then EX and SB processors are transferred into parallel functioning and the software data of the Upgrade function are transmitted successfully. After the software of Upgrade function completion it is executed the software initial start (or restart) of the all modules and blocks.

There is the block diagram of the operations sequence for software modification which has three main modifications functions:

- Software blocks correction;
- Software Update of the function modules or the functional element;
- Software Upgrade of the base station.

The block diagram of the operations sequence for software modification is shown on fig. 10.

2.4.4 The general control scheme of the software modification

Fig.11 shows the diagram of the software modification control. The software modification control is executed with OSS using software named "Software Manager", which executes:

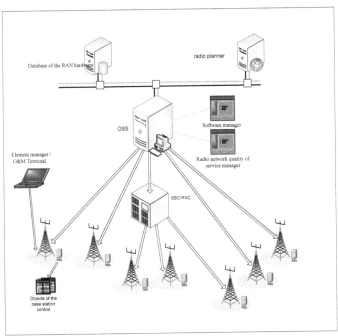

Fig. 11. The general scheme of the software modification control

- The loading and activation of the correction in units of BS software;
- Downloading the package for the function "Software Update" of a functional module or a functional element and execution of the update software function;
- Downloading the new release of software for execution of the base station software upgrade function.

The correctness control of the control objects and the whole base station functioning after software modernization is made by the manager of the radio network quality control.

There is proposed to use the radio network scheduler (located on a separate server) for computing the all radio network parameters and preparing upgrading packages for each network element when the radio access network is upgrading and using the new standards or combining the different standards. The scheduler will use the separate database of installed radio access network equipment. Prepared by the scheduler packages of BS modernization with all settings of the parameters are loaded in the certain sequence through OSS to BS. In this case it can be involved BSC /RNC. The control element or the O&M terminal is also used for the local software upgrades on a separate BS.

Fig. 12 shows the processor modules of the BS control objects. The main O&M module is represented by two processors working in parallel mode in the normal operation phase, or in the mode of the separation for Upgrade function. This module is executed the information interchange with the network via O&M interface, and also controls other BS functional modules via control of the local resources. He has flash memory that backup copies of the BS software and the software of the O&M module are stored. RAM is also used for software loading and for the subsequent software start.

The each functional element is also represented by two regional processors functioning in parallel mode in the normal operation phase or in the mode of separation for Upgrade function. The each functional element has its flash memory and RAM. Data exchange with the main O&M unit is run using the control interface of the local resources.

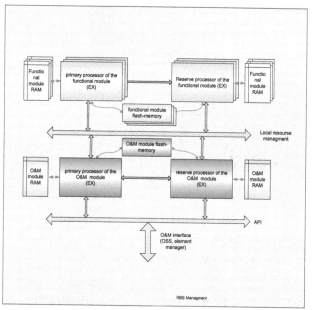

Fig. 12. Block diagram of BS control objects with the possibility of reconfiguration

3. Conclusion

Thus, it is considered a new concept of development a multi-standard mobile network. It includes the architecture of the base station development with the requirements for its functional units and the method of reconfiguration of the radio access network. The method of reconfiguration is based on the state graph of the base station functioning, the block diagram of an operations sequence of base station functioning, the block diagram of an operations sequence of the base station software upgrade, the principle of the software modifications control and structural pattern of the BS control objects with the reconfiguration ability. This allows to development a radio network that is different from existing single standard mobile radio networks by the reconfiguration opportunity without changing the hardware of the radio access network. It also gives the ability to support many radio standards based on the one universal base station platform with flexible antenna systems and using SDR technology.

The next stage of research will be:

- Simulation of the proposed algorithms,
- Development of the software updating and adaptation algorithms for the mobile terminals functioning in SDR network,
- To propose the recommendations for using of all this algorithms in the mobile SDR-network development.

4. Acknowledgment

The authors are grateful to Ericsson-Ukraine for sponsorship, which enabled them to publish the results of their scientific research in this book.

5. References

Tafazolli R. Technologies for the Wireless Future, volume 2.Wireless World Research Forum, (WWRF) / R. Tafazolli. – Oxford: Wiley, 2006. – 520 p.

Dillinger B. Software defined radio : architectures, systems, and functions/ B. Dillinger, S. Madani. – New York: Wiley, 2003. – 454 p.

WiMAX Infrastructure Solutions from Texas Instruments [Internet resource] // http://www.ti.com/wimaxwi Wednesday, 14 October 2009 22: 08:14.

Globa L. S., Kurdecha V. V., Zingaeva N. A. Using of SDR-solutions in reconfigured mobile systems// Scientific and industrial collected articles "Scientific Notes of the Ukrainian Research Institute of Communications" № 1(17) 2011 p. // http://www.nbuv.gov.ua/portal/natural/Nzundiz/2011_1/Index.htm

Kurdecha V. V., Zingaeva N. A The optimal architecture of reconfigurable base stations (RBS) and the requirements for RBS / 21th International Crimean Conference "Microwave & Telecommunication Technology" (Crimico'2011), Sevastopol, 12-16 of September 2011: Collected articles of the Conference – Sevastopol: Veber, 2011, p. 465

Accelerating WiMAX System Design with FPGAs [Internet resource] // http://www.altera.com/literature/wp/wp_wimax Wednesday, 14 October 2009

Xilinx Solutions for WiMAX/WiBro System Design [Internet resource] // http://www.xilinx.com/esp/wireless/bfwa/ieee_802_16.htm Sunday, 18 October 2009

National Semiconductors. Software Defined Radio (SDR) Solutions http://www.national.com/en/adc/sdr.html

Kevin W. Rudd and Chris Anderson • June 2010 Software-Defined Radio http://www.computer.org/portal/web/computingnow/archive/june2010

Bruce F. Cognitive Radio Technology / F. Bruce. – Boston: Newnes, 2006. – 656 p.

ETSI TR 102 680 V1.1.1 Reconfigurable Radio Systems (RRS); SDR Reference Architecture for Mobile Device // (2009-03).

ETSI TR 102 681 V1.1.1 Reconfigurable Radio Systems (RRS); Radio Base Station (RBS) Software Defined Radio (SDR) status, implementations and costs aspects, including future possibilities // (2009-06).

ETSI TR 102 683 V1.1.1 Reconfigurable Radio Systems (RRS); Cognitive Pilot Channel (CPC) // (2009-09)

ETSI TR 102 745 V1.1.1 Reconfigurable Radio Systems (RRS); User Requirements for Public Safety // (2009-10)

ETSI TR 102 838 V1.1.1 (2009-10) Reconfigurable Radio Systems (RRS); Summary of feasibility studies and potential standardization topics // (2009-10)

2

A Low-Overhead Non-Block Check Pointing and Recovery Approach for Mobile Computing Environment

Bidyut Gupta[1], Ziping Liu[2] and Sindoora Koneru[1]
[1]Computer Science Department, Southern Illinois University, Carbondale,
[2]Computer Science Department, Southeast Missouri State University, Cape Girardeau,
USA

1. Introduction

Check pointing/rollback-recovery strategy is used for providing fault-tolerance to distributed applications (Y.M. Wang, 1997; M. Singhal & N. G. Shivaratri, 1994; R. E. Strom and S. Yemini 1985; R. Koo & S. Toueg, 1987; S. Venkatesan et al.,1997; G. Cao & M. Singhal, 1998; D. Manivannan & M. Singhal, 1999). A checkpoint is a snapshot of the local state of a process, saved on local nonvolatile storage to survive process failures. A global checkpoint of an n-process distributed system consists of n checkpoints (local) such that each of these n checkpoints corresponds uniquely to one of the n processes. A global checkpoint M is defined as a consistent global checkpoint if no message is sent after a checkpoint of M and received before another checkpoint of M (Y.M. Wang, 1997). The checkpoints belonging to a consistent global checkpoint are called globally consistent checkpoints (GCCs). The set of such checkpoints is also known as recovery line.

There are two fundamental approaches for checkpointing and recovery. One is the asynchronous approach and the other one is the synchronous approach (D. K. Pradhan and N. H. Vaidya 1994; R. Baldoni et al. 1999; R. Koo & S. Toueg, 1987; S. Venkatesan et al.,1997; G. Cao & M. Singhal, 1998; D. Manivannan & M. Singhal, 1999).

Synchronous approach assumes that a single process invokes the algorithm periodically to take checkpoints. This process is known as the initiator process. This scheme is termed as synchronous since the processes involved coordinate their local check pointing actions such that the set of all recent checkpoints in the system is guaranteed to be consistent. The scheme assumes that no site involved in the distributed computing fails during the execution of the check pointing scheme. In its most fundamental form, it works in two phases as follows.

In the first phase the initiator process takes a tentative checkpoint and requests all other processes to take their respective tentative checkpoints. Each process informs the initiator process that it has taken it.

In the second phase, after receiving such information from all processes the initiator process asks each process to convert its tentative checkpoint to a permanent one. That is, each process saves its checkpoint in nonvolatile storage. During the execution of the scheme each process suspends its underlying computation related to an application. Thus, each process remains blocked each time the algorithm is executed. The set of checkpoints so taken are globally consistent checkpoints, because there is no orphan message with respect to any two checkpoints. It may be noted that a message is an orphan with respect to the recent checkpoints of two processes if its receiving event is recorded in the recent checkpoint of the receiver of the message, but its sending event is not recorded in the recent checkpoint of its sender.

This synchronous approach has the following two major drawbacks. First, The coordination among processes while taking checkpoints is actually achieved through the exchange of additional (control) messages, for example the requests from the initiator and the replies to the initiator. It causes some delay (known as synchronization delay) during normal operation. The second drawback is that processes remain blocked during check pointing. It contributes significantly to the amount of delay during normal operation. However, the main advantage is that the set of the checkpoints taken periodically by the different processes always represents a consistent global checkpoint. So, after the system recovers from a failure, each process knows where to rollback for restarting its computation again. In fact, the restarting state will always be the most recent consistent global checkpoint. Therefore, recovery is very simple. On the other hand, if failures rarely occur between successive checkpoints, then the synchronous approach places unnecessary burden on the system in the form of additional messages and delay. Hence, compared to the asynchronous approach, taking checkpoints is more complex while recovery is much simpler. Observe that synchronous approach is free from any domino effect (B. Randell, 1979).

In the asynchronous approach, processes take their checkpoints independently. So, taking checkpoints is very simple as there is no coordination needed among processes while taking checkpoints. Obviously, there is no blocking of the processes while taking checkpoints unlike in the synchronous approach. After a failure occurs, a procedure for rollback-recovery attempts to build a consistent global checkpoint. However, in this approach because of the absence of any coordination among the processes there may not exist a recent consistent global checkpoint which may cause a rollback of the computation. This is known as domino effect (B. Randell, 1975; K. Venkatesh et al., 1987). Observe that the cause for domino effect is the existence of orphan messages. In the worst case of the domino effect, after the system recovers from a failure all processes may have to roll back to their respective initial states to restart their computation again. In general, to minimize the amount of computation undone during a rollback, all messages need to be saved (logged) at each process.

Besides these two fundamental approaches there is another approach known as communication induced check pointing approach (J. Tsai et al., 1998; R. Baldoni et al., 1997; J. M. Helary et al., 2000). In this approach processes coordinate to take checkpoints via piggybacking some control information on application messages. However this coordination does not guarantee that a recent global checkpoint will be consistent. This means that this approach also suffers from the domino effect. Therefore, a recovery algorithm has to search for a consistent global checkpoint before the processes can restart their computation after recovery from a failure. In this approach taking checkpoints is simpler than synchronous approach while the recovery process is more complex.

B. Gupta et al., 2002 have proposed a simple and fast roll-forward check pointing scheme that can also be used in distributed mobile computing environment. The direct-dependency concept used in the communication-induced check pointing scheme has been applied to basic checkpoints (the ones taken asynchronously) to design a simple algorithm to find a consistent global checkpoint. Both blocking and non-blocking schemes have been proposed. In the blocking approach direct-dependency concept is implemented without piggybacking any extra information with the application messages. The use of the concept of forced checkpoints ensures a small re-execution time after recovery from a failure. The proposed approach offers the main advantages of both the synchronous and the asynchronous approaches, i.e. simple recovery and simple way to create checkpoints. Besides, the algorithm produces reduced number of checkpoints. To achieve these, the algorithm uses very simple data structure per process, that is, each process maintains only a Boolean flag and an integer variable. Since each process independently takes its decision whether to take a forced checkpoint or not, it makes the algorithm simple, fast, and efficient. The advantages stated above also ensure that the algorithm can work efficiently in mobile computing environment.

There also exist some other efficient non-blocking algorithms (G. Cao & M. Singhal, 2001; E. N. Elnozahy et al., 1992; L. M. Silva & J. G. Silva, 1992); however they require significant number of control (system) messages to determine a consistent global checkpoint of the system. In (G. Cao & M. Singhal, 2001), the authors have proposed an efficient non-blocking coordinated check pointing scheme that offers minimum number of check points. They have introduced the concept of mutable checkpoint which is neither a tentative checkpoint nor a permanent checkpoint to design their check pointing scheme for mobile computing environment. Mutable checkpoints can be saved either in the main memory or local disks. It has been shown that the idea of mutable checkpoints helps in the efficient utilization of wireless bandwidth of the mobile environment. In general, it may be stated that the ideas of non-blocking check pointing, reduction in the number of checkpoints to be taken, and using less number of system messages may offer significant advantage particularly in case of mobile computing, because it helps in the efficient use of the limited resources of mobile computing environment, viz. limited wireless bandwidth, and mobile hosts' limited battery power and memory.

In this context, note that after recovery from a failure even if the processes restart from their respective checkpoints belonging to a recovery line, still it not necessarily ensures correctness of computation. To achieve it, any application message that may become a lost message because of the failure must be identified and resent to the appropriate receiving process. The responsibility of the receiving process is that it must execute all such lost messages following the order of their arrival before the occurrence of the failure (D. B. Johnson & W. Zwaenepoel, 1987; M. L. Powell & D. L. Presotto, 1983; L. Alvisi & K. Marzullo, 1995).

An example of a lost message is shown in Fig. 1. In this figure, after the system recovers from the failure f, if the two processes P_i and P_j restart from their respective checkpoints C_i and C_j, then message m will be treated as a lost message. The reason is that process P_j does not have a record of the receiving event of the message m whereas process P_i has the record of sending it in its checkpoint C_i. Therefore when the processes restart, P_i will not send message m again to P_j since it knows that it already sent it once. However this will lead to wrong computation, because P_j aftet its roll back to its last checkpoint needs the message m for its computation. In such a situation, for correct computation this lost message m has to be identified and process P_i must resend it to process P_j after the system restarts.

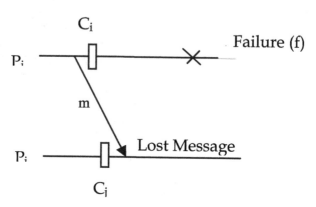

Fig. 1. Message m is a lost message

The objective of this work, is to design a check pointing and recovery scheme for distributed computing environment which is also very suitable for distributed mobile computing environment. It considers both determination of a recovery line and resending of all lost messages to ensure correctness of computation. First, a fast recovery algorithm is presented that determines a recovery line that guarantees the absence of any orphan message with respect to the checkpoints belonging to the recovery line. Then the existing idea on sender-based message logging approach for distributed computing (D. B. Johnson & W. Zwaenepoel, 1987) is applied to identify and resend any lost messages. It helps a receiving process, after it restarts, to process these messages following the order of their arrival before the occurrence of the failure. Thus taking into account both orphan messages and lost messages will ensure correctness of computation.

The presented check pointing algorithm is a non-blocking synchronous algorithm. It means application processes are not suspended during check pointing. The non-blocking algorithm does not require that all processes take their checkpoints; rather only those processes that have sent some message(s) after their last check points will take checkpoints during check pointing. It is shown that this algorithm outperforms the one in (G. Cao & M. Singhal, 2001) mainly from the viewpoint of using much less number of system (control) messages. As pointed out earlier that non-blocking check pointing along with the reduced number of checkpoints to be taken and less number of system messages may offer significant advantage particularly in case of mobile computing, because it helps in the efficient use of the limited resources of mobile computing environment, viz. limited wireless bandwidth, and mobile hosts' limited battery power and memory.

This work is organized as follows: in Sections 2 and 3 we have stated the system model and the necessary data structures respectively. In Section 4, using an example we have explained the main idea about when a process needs to take a checkpoint by using some very simple data structures. We have stated some simple observations necessary to design the algorithm. In Section 5 we have presented the non blocking check pointing algorithm along with its performance, and presented a scheme for handling lost messages. In Section 6 we have discussed its suitability for mobile computing systems. Section 7 draws the conclusions.

2. System model

The distributed system has the following characteristics (R. Koo & S. Toueg, 1987; S. Venkatesan et al.,1997; P. Jalote, 1998): Processes do not share memory and communicate via messages sent through channels Channels can lose messages. However, they are made virtually lossless and order of the messages is preserved by some end-to-end transmission protocol. Message sequence numbers may be used to preserve the order. When a process fails, all other processes are notified of the failure in finite time. We also assume that no further processor (process) failures occur during the execution of the algorithm. In fact, the algorithm may be restarted if there are further failures. Processes are piecewise deterministic in the sense that from the same state, if given the same inputs, a process executes the same sequence of instructions.

3. Data structures

Let us consider a set of n processes, $\{P_0, P_1,..., P_{n-1}\}$ involved in the execution of a distributed algorithm. Each process P_i maintains a Boolean flag c_i. The flag is initially set at zero. It is set at 1 only when process P_i sends its first application message after its latest checkpoint. It is reset to 0 again when process P_i takes a checkpoint. Flag c_i is stored in local RAM of the processor running process P_i. A message sent by P_i will be denoted as m_i.

As in the classical synchronous approach (M. Singhal & N. G. Shivaratri, 1994), we assume that an initiator process initiates the check pointing algorithm. It helps the n processes to take their individual checkpoints synchronously, i.e. the checkpoints taken will be globally consistent checkpoints. We further assume that any process in the system can initiate the check pointing algorithm. This can be done in a round-robin way among the processes. To implement it, each process P_i maintains a variable CLK_i initialized at 0. It also maintains a variable, $counter_i$ which is initially set to 0 and is incremented by 1 each time process P_i initiates the algorithm. In addition, process P_i maintains an integer variable N_i which is initially set at 0 and is incremented by 1 each time the algorithm is invoked. Note the difference between the variables $counter_i$ and N_i. A control (request) message M_c is broadcasted by a process initiating the check pointing algorithm to the other (n-1) processes asking them to take checkpoints if necessary.

In the next section, we explain with an illustration the idea we have applied to reduce the number of checkpoints to be created in the non blocking synchronous check pointing scheme proposed in the work.

4. An illustration

In synchronous check pointing scheme, all involved processes take checkpoints periodically which are mutually consistent. However, in reality, not all the processes may need to take checkpoints to determine a set of the GCCs.

The main objective of this work is to design a simple scheme that helps the n processes to decide easily and independently whether to take a checkpoint when the check pointing algorithm is invoked. If a process decides that it does not need to take a checkpoint, it can resume its computation immediately. This results in faster execution of the distributed algorithm. Below we illustrate with an example how a process decides whether to take a checkpoint or not.

Consider the following scenario of a distributed system of two processes P_i and P_j only. It is shown in Fig. 2. Assume that their initial checkpoints are C_i^0 and C_j^0 respectively. According to the synchronous approach, P_i and P_j have to take checkpoints periodically. Suppose that the time period is T. Before time T, P_i has sent an application message m_1 to P_j. Now at time T, an initiator process sends the message M_c asking both P_i and P_j to take their checkpoints, which must have to be consistent.

Process P_i checks its flag and finds that $c_i = 1$. Therefore P_i decides to take its checkpoint C_i^1. Thus because of the presence of C_i^1, message m_1 can never be an orphan. Also, at the same time P_j checks if its flag $c_j = 1$. Since it is not, therefore process P_j decides that it does not need to take any checkpoint. The reason is obvious. This illustrates the basic idea about how to reduce the number of checkpoints to be taken. Now we observe that checkpoints C_j^0 and C_i^1 are mutually consistent.

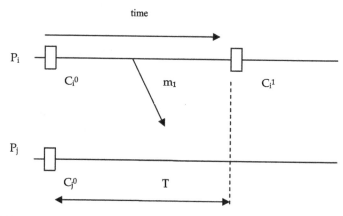

Fig. 2. C_i^1 and C_j^0 are mutually consistent

The above discussion shows the simplicity involved in taking a decision about whether to take a checkpoint or not. Note that the decision taken by a process P_j whether it needs to take a checkpoint is independent of the similar decision taken by the other process. It may be noted that keeping a copy of each of the flags c_i and c_j in the respective local RAMs of the processors running P_i and P_j can save some time as it is more time consuming to fetch them if they are stored in stable storage than to fetch them from the respective local RAMs.

Below we state some simple but important observations used in the proposed algorithm.

Theorem1: Consider a system of n processes. If $c_j = 1$, where C_j^k is the latest checkpoint of process P_j , then some message(s) sent by P_j to other processes may become orphan.

Proof: The flag c_j is reset to 0 at every checkpoint. It can have the value 1 only between two successive checkpoints of any process P_j if and only if process P_j sends at least one message m between the checkpoints. Therefore, $c_j = 1$ means that P_j is yet to take its next checkpoint following C_j^k. Therefore, the message (s) sent by P_j after its latest checkpoint C_j^k are not yet recorded. Now if some process P_m receives one or more of these messages sent by P_j and then takes its latest checkpoint before process P_j takes its next checkpoint C_j^{k+1}, then these received messages will become orphan. Hence the proof follows.

Theorem 2: If at any given time t, $c_j = 0$ for process P_j with C_j^{k+1} being its latest checkpoint, then none of the messages sent by P_j remains an orphan at time t.

Proof: Flag c_j can have the value 1 between two successive checkpoints, say C_j^k and C_j^{k+1}, of a process P_j if and only if process P_j has sent at least one message m between these two checkpoints. It can also be 1 if P_j has sent at least a message after taking its latest checkpoint. It is reset to 0 at each checkpoint. On the other hand, it will have the value 0 either between two successive checkpoints, say C_j^k and C_j^{k+1}, if process P_j has not sent any message between these checkpoints, or P_j has not sent any message after its latest checkpoint. Therefore, $c_j = 0$ at time t means either of the following two: (i) $c_j = 0$ at C_j^{k+1} and this checkpoint has been taken at time t. It means that any message m sent by P_j (if any) to any other process P_m between C_j^k and C_j^{k+1} must have been recorded by the sending process P_j at the checkpoint C_j^{k+1}. So the message m can not be an orphan. (ii) $c_j = 0$ at time t and P_j has taken its latest checkpoint C_j^{k+1} before time t. It means that process P_j has not sent any message after its latest checkpoint C_j^{k+1} till time t. Hence at time t there does not exist any orphan message sent by P_j after its latest checkpoint.

5. Problems associated with non-blocking approach

We explain first the problems associated with non-blocking approach. After that we will state a solution. The following discussion although considers only two processes, still the arguments given are valid for any number of processes. Consider a system of two processes P_i and P_j as shown in Fig. 3. Assume that the check pointing algorithm has been initiated by process P_i and it has sent the request message M_c to P_j asking it to take a checkpoint if necessary. As pointed earlier that both processes will act independently, therefore P_i takes its checkpoint C_i^1 because its flag $c_i = 1$. Let us assume that P_i now immediately sends an application message m_i to P_j. Suppose at time $(T + \epsilon)$, where ϵ is very small with respect to T, P_j receives m_i. Still P_j has not received M_c from the initiator process. So, P_j processes the message. Now the request message M_c from P_i arrives at P_j. Process P_j finds that its $c_j = 1$. So it decides to take a checkpoint C_j^1. We find that message m_i has become an orphan due to the checkpoint C_j^1. Hence, C_i^1 and C_j^1 cannot be consistent.

5.1 Solution

To solve this problem, we propose that a process be allowed to send both piggybacked and non –piggybacked application messages. We explain the idea below.

Each process P_i maintains an integer variable N_i, initially set at 0 and is incremented by 1 each time process P_i receives the request message M_c from the initiator process. In the event that process P_i itself is the initiator, then also it increments N_i by 1 immediately after the initiation of the algorithm. That is, the variable N_i represents how many times the check pointing algorithm has been executed including the current one (according to the knowledge of the process P_i). Note that at any given time t, for any two processes P_i and P_j, their corresponding variables N_i and N_j may not have the same values. It depends on which process has received the request message M_c first. However it is obvious that $| N_i - N_j |$ is either 0 or 1.

Below we state the solution for a two process system. The idea used in this solution is similarly applicable for an n process system as well.

Consider a distributed system of two processes P_i and P_j only. Without any loss of generality assume that P_i initiates the algorithm by sending the message M_c to process P_j and it is the the kth execution of the algorithm, that is, $N_i = k$. We also assume that process P_i now has taken its decision whether to take a checkpoint or not, and then has taken appropriate action to implement its decision. Suppose P_i now wants to send an application message m_i for the first time to P_j after it has finished participating in the kth execution of the check pointing algorithm. Observe that P_i has no idea whether P_j has received the message M_c corresponding to this k^{th} execution of the algorithm and has already implemented its check pointing decision or not. To make sure that the message m_i can never be an orphan, P_i piggybacks m_i with the variable N_i. Process P_j receives the piggybacked message <m_i , N_i > from P_i. We now explain below why the message m_i can never been an orphan. Note that N_i = k ; i.e. it is the kth execution of the algorithm that process P_i has last been involved with. It means the following to the receiver P_j of this message:

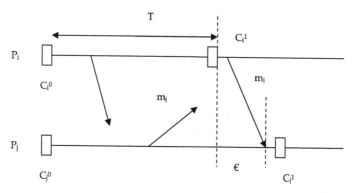

Fig. 3. C_i^1 and C_j^1 are not mutually consistent

1. process P_i has already received M_c from the initiator process for the kth execution of the algorithm,
2. P_i has taken a decision whether to take a checkpoint or not and has taken appropriate action to implement its decision,
3. P_i has resumed its normal operation and then has sent this piggybacked application message m_i.
4. the sending event of message m_i has not yet been recorded by P_i.

Since the message contains the variable N_i, process P_j compares N_i and N_j to determine if it has to wait to receive the request message M_c. Based on the results of the comparison process P_j takes one of the following three actions (so that no message received by it is an orphan), as stated below in the form of the following three observations:

Observation 1: If N_i (= k) > N_j (= k-1), process P_j now knows that the kth execution of the check pointing algorithm has already begun and so very soon it will also receive the message M_c from the initiator process associated with this execution. So instead of waiting for M_c to arrive, it decides if it needs to take a checkpoint and implements its decision, and then processes the message m_i. After a little while when it receives the message M_c it just ignores it. Therefore, message m_i can never be an orphan.

Observation 2: If $N_i = N_j = k$, like process P_i, process P_j also has received already the message M_c associated with the latest execution (k^{th}) of the check pointing algorithm and has taken its check pointing decision and has already implemented that decision. Therefore, process P_j now processes the message m_i. It ensures that message m_i can never be an orphan, because both the sending and the receiving events of message m_i have not been recorded by the sender P_i and the receiver P_j respectively.

Observation 3: Process P_i does no more need to piggyback any application message to P_j till the $(k+1)^{th}$ invocation (next) of the algorithm. The reason is that after receiving the piggybacked message $<m_i, N_i>$, P_j has already implemented its decision whether to take a checkpoint or not before processing the message m_i. If it has taken a checkpoint, then all messages it receives from P_i starting with the message m_i can not be orphan. So it processes the received messages. Also if P_j did not need to take a checkpoint during the kth execution of the algorithm, then obviously the messages sent by P_i to P_j staring with the message m_i till the next invocation of the algorithm can not be orphan. So it processes the messages.

Therefore, for an n process distributed system, a process P_i piggybacks only its first application message sent (after it has implemented its check pointing decision for the current execution of the algorithm and before its next participation in the algorithm) to a process P_j, where $j \neq i$, and $0 \leq j \leq n-1$.

5.2 Algorithm non-blocking

Below we describe the algorithm. It is a single phase algorithm since an initiator process interacts with the other processes only once via the control message M_c.

```
At each process P_i(1≤ i ≤n)
  if CLK_i = (i+ (counter_i * n) ) * T   //when its turn to initiate the checkpointing procedure
    counter_i = counter_i + 1;
    N_i = N_i + 1;
    broadcasts M_c to (n-1) other processes;

    if c_i = 1 //at least one message it has sent after its last checkpoint
      takes checkpointC_i;
      c_i = 0;
      continues its normal operation;

    else //if it decides not to take a checkpoint
      continues its normal operation;
  else if P_i receives M_c
    N_i = N_i + 1;
    if c_i = 1 //at least one message it has sent after its last checkpoint
      takes checkpointC_i;
      c_i = 0;
      continues its normal operation;
    else
      continues its normal operation;
```

```
else if   P_i receives a piggybackedmessage < m_j, N_j > && P_i has not yet received M_c for the
          current execution of the check pointing procedure

     N_i = N_i + 1;

     if c_i = 1 //at least one message it has sent after its last checkpoint
        c_i = 0;
        takes checkpointC_i without waiting for M_c;
        processes the received message m_j;
        continues its normal operation and ignores M_c, when received for the
        current execution of the checkpointing procedure;

     else
        processes any received message m_j;
        continues its normal operation and ignores M_c, when received for the
        current execution of the check pointing procedure;
else
        continues its normal operation;
```

Proof of Correctness : In the first 'if else' and 'else if' blocks of the pseudo code, each process P_i decides based on the value of its flag c_i whether it needs to take a checkpoint. If it has to take a checkpoint, it resets c_i to 0. Therefore, in other words, each process P_i makes sure using the logic of Theorem 2 that none of the messages, if any, it has sent since its last checkpoint can be an orphan. On the other hand, if P_i does not take a checkpoint, it means that it has not sent any message since its previous checkpoint.

In the second 'else if' block each process P_i follows the logic of Observations 1, 2, and 3, which ever is appropriate for a particular situation so that any application message (piggybacked or not) received by P_i before it receives the request message M_c can not be an orphan. Besides none of its sent messages, if any, since its last checkpoint can be an orphan as well (following the logic of Theorems 1 and 2).

Since Theorem 2, and Observations 1, 2, and 3 guarantee that no sent or received message by any process P_i since its previous checkpoint can be an orphan and since it is true for all participating processes, therefore, the algorithm guarantees that the latest checkpoints taken during the current execution of the algorithm and the previous checkpoints (if any) of those processes that did not need to take checkpoints during the current execution of the algorithm are globally consistent checkpoints.

5.3 Performance

We use the following notations (and some of the analysis from (G. Cao & M. Singhal, 2001) to compare our algorithm with some of the most notable algorithms in this area of research, namely (R. Koo & S. Toueg, 1987; G. Cao & M. Singhal, 2001; E. N. Elnozahy et al., 1992). The analytical comparison is given in Table 1.

In this Table:

C_{air} is cost of sending a message from one process to another process;
C_{broad} is cost of broadcasting a message to all processes;
n_{min} is the number of processes that need to take checkpoints.
n is the total number of processes in the system;
n_{dep} is the average number of processes on which a process depends;
T_{ch} is the check pointing time;

Algorithm	Blocking time	Messages	Distributed
Koo-Toueg [3]	$n_{min} * T_{ch}$	$3 * n_{min} * n_{dep} * C_{air}$	Yes
Elnozahy [8]	0	$2 * C_{broad} + n * C_{air}$	No
Cao-Singhal [7]	0	$\approx 2 * n_{min} * C_{air} + min(n_{min} * C_{air}, C_{broad})$	Yes
Our Algorithm	0	C_{broad}	Yes

Table 1. System Performance

Figs. 4 and 5 illustrate how the number of control messages (system messages) sent and received by processes is affected by the increase in the number of the processes in the system.

In Fig. 4, n_{dep} factor is considered being 5% of the total number of processes in the system and C_{broad} is equal to C_{air} (assuming that special hardware is used to facilitate broadcasting – which is not the case most of the times). As Fig. 4 shows, the number of messages does not increase with the increase of the number of the processes in our approach unlike other approaches.

In Fig. 5 we have considered absence of any special hardware for broadcasting and therefore assumed C_{broad} to be equal to n * C_{air}. In this case, although the number of messages does increase in our approach, but it stays smaller compared to other approaches when the number of the processes is higher than 7 (which is the case most of the time).

5.4 Handling of lost messages

The sender-based message logging scheme proposed for distributed computing (D. B. Johnson & W. Zwaenepoel, 1987) to identify and resend lost messages is used in this work. This scheme has been the choice since it does not require message ordering, and message logging is done asynchronously. We apply it in the following way.

When a sending process, say P_i sends a message m to a process P_k, the message m is piggybacked with a send sequence number (SSN) which represents the number of messages sent by this process. The sender also logs the message m and its SSN in its local log. The receiving process P_k will assign a receive sequence number (RSN) to the message m, which represents the number of messages received by P_k. The RSN is incremented each time P_k receives a message. It then sends the RSN back to the sender P_i. After receiving the RSN corresponding to m, the sender records the RSN with the log of the message m. Thus message m is called a fully logged message. This local log is saved in stable storage when P_i takes its next checkpoint. Process P_i then sends an acknowledgement, ack to the receiver. In the meantime after sending the RSN to P_i, process P_k continues its execution, but cannot send any message until it has received the ack. Note that if the receiver fails before sending the RSN of the message m, the log of m does not have the RSN. In such a situation message m is called partially logged.

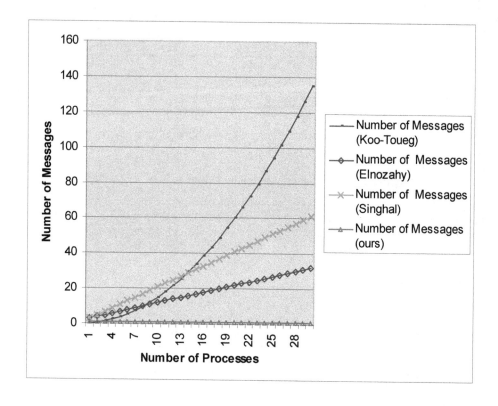

Fig. 4. Number of messages vs. number of processes for four different approaches when $C_{broad} = C_{air}$

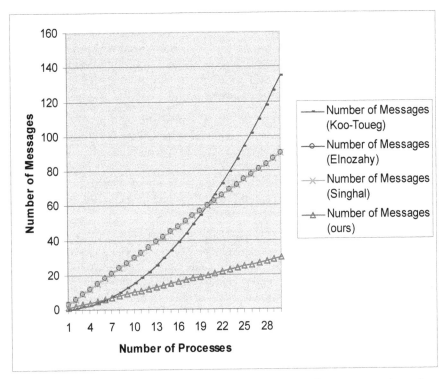

Fig. 5. Number of messages vs. number of processes for four different approaches when $C_{broad} = n * C_{air}$

Recovery is performed when P_k fails. It restarts from its checkpoint that belongs to the recovery line as determined by the check pointing algorithm. Now P_k looks for those (if any) messages such that their sending events have already been recorded in the respective senders' checkpoints and the receiving events have not been recorded in P_k's checkpoint belonging to the recovery line. These are the lost messages. To get back these messages, the receiver broadcasts a request to all processes for resending the lost messages. At this time the receiver also sends the value of the SSNs for different sender processes. Every sender then resends only those messages with a higher SSN that were sent to P_k before the failure.

The messages received by P_k from the senders are consumed by P_k in the order of their RSNs. Since the messages that were assigned an RSN by the receiver form a total order, therefore process P_k gets the same sequence of messages as it did before the failure and therefore executes the same sequence of instructions as it did before the failure.

Next, P_k receives the partially logged messages following the fully logged ones. These partially logged messages do not have any RSN values attached to them. So there is no total ordering imposed on them by P_k. However, according to the work in (D. B. Johnson & W. Zwaenepoel, 1987) the receiver was constrained from communicating with any process if the ack for any message it received is pending. Therefore any order in which these partially logged messages are resent to P_k is acceptable (D. B. Johnson & W. Zwaenepoel, 1987).

Observe that in our approach there does not exist any orphan message between any two checkpoints belonging to the recovery line. Hence the mechanism to handle orphan messages in (D. B. Johnson & W. Zwaenepoel, 1987) is not needed in our approach. Thus absence of any orphan and lost messages ensures correctness of computation.

6. Suitability for mobile computing environment

Consider a distributed mobile computing environment. In such an environment, only limited wireless bandwidth is available for communication among the computing processes. Besides, the mobile hosts (MH) have limited battery power and limited memory. Therefore, it is required that, any distributed application P running in such an environment must make efficient use of the limited wireless bandwidth, and mobile hosts' limited battery power and memory. Below we show that the proposed algorithm satisfies all the above three requirements.

1. The first requirement about the efficient use of the bandwidth is satisfied by our check pointing algorithm, because the presented algorithm is a single phase algorithm unlike any other existing algorithms (R. Koo & S. Toueg, 1987; D. Manivannan & M. Singhal, 1999; L. M. Silva & J. G. Silva, 1992). That is, the initiator process requests any other process to take a checkpoint by broadcasting only the control message (M_c) during any invocation of the algorithm. There is no other control message used. So our algorithm ensures effective utilization of the limited wireless bandwidth. In this context, it may be noted that our algorithm needs much less number of the system messages than in (R. Koo & S. Toueg, 1987; G. Cao & M. Singhal, 2001; E. N. Elnozahy et al., 1992; R. Ahmed & A. Khaliq, 2003).

2. The second requirement about the efficient use of the mobile host's battery power is satisfied, because (1) each MH is interrupted only once by the control message M_c, as our algorithm is a single phase one. It saves time since interrupt handling time cannot be ignored. Note that in other approaches (G. Cao & M. Singhal, 2001; R. Ahmed & A. Khaliq, 2003) it is more than one; and (2) each process P_i only checks if its $c_i = 1$ in order to decide if it needs to take a checkpoint. This is the only computation that an MH is involved with while participating in the algorithm.

3. The third requirement about the efficient use of the mobile host's memory is satisfied, because the data structure used in our algorithm is very simple. Only four variables are needed by each process P_i. These are: three integer variables, viz. N_i, counter$_i$, CLK_i, and one Boolean variable c_i. The amount of data structures stated above is much less than the same in the related works (G. Cao & M. Singhal, 2001; R. Ahmed & A. Khaliq, 2003).

7. Conclusions

In this work, we have presented a non-blocking synchronous check pointing approach to determine globally consistent checkpoints. In the present work only those processes that have sent some message(s) after their last checkpoints, take checkpoints during check pointing; thereby reducing the number of checkpoints to be taken. This approach offers advantage particularly in case of mobile computing systems where both non-block check pointing and reduction in the number of checkpoints help in the efficient use of the limited resources of mobile computing environment.

Also, the presented non-blocking approach uses minimum interaction (only once) between the initiator process and the system of n processes and there is no synchronization delay. This is particularly useful for mobile computing environment because of less number of interrupts caused by the initiator process to mobile processes, which results in better utilization of the limited resources (limited battery power of mobile machines and wireless bandwidth) of mobile environment. To achieve this we have used very simple data structures, viz., three integer variables and one Boolean variable per process. Another advantage of the proposed algorithm is that each process takes its check pointing decision independently which may become helpful for mobile computing. The advantages mentioned above make the proposed algorithms simple, efficient, and suitable for mobile computing environment.

The check pointing algorithm ensures that there is no orphan message between ant two checkpoints belonging to the recovery line. However, absence of orphan messages alone cannot guarantee correctness of the underlying distributed application. To ensure correct computation all lost messages at the time of failure have to be identified and resent to the appropriate receiving processes when the system restarts. The presented recovery approach handles the lost messages using the idea of sender-based message logging to ensure correctness of computation.

8. References

Y.M. Wang, (1997). Consistent Global Checkpoints that Contain a Given Set of Local Checkpoints, *IEEE Transactions on Computers*, vol. 46, No.4, pp. (456-468).

M. Singhal and N. G. Shivaratri. (1994). In: *Advanced Concepts in Operating Systems*, McGraw-Hill.

R. Koo and S. Toueg, (1987). Checkpointing and Rollback-Recovery for Distributed Systems, *IEEE Transactions on Software Engineering*, vol.13, No.1, pp. (23-31).

S. Venkatesan, T. T-Y. Juang, and S. Alagar, (1997). Optimistic Crash Recovery without Changing Application Messages, *IEEE Transactions on Parallel and Distributed Systems*, vol. 8, No. 3, pp. (263-271).

G. Cao and M. Singhal, (1998). Coordinated Checkpointing in Distributed Systems, *IEEE Transactions on Parallel and Distributed Systems*, vol. 9, No.12, pp. (1213-1225).

D. Manivannan and M. Singhal, (1999). Quasi-Synchronous Checkpointing: Models, Characterization, and Classification, *IEEE Transactions on Parallel and Distributed Systems*, vol.10, No.7, pp. (703-713).

G. Cao and M. Singhal, (2001). Mutable Checkpoints: A New Checkpointing Approach for Mobile Computing Systems, *IEEE Transactions on Parallel and Distributed Systems*, vol.12, No. 2, pp. (157 – 172).

E. N. Elnozahy, D. B. Johnson, and W. Zwaenepoel, (1992). The Performance of Consistent Checkpointing, *Proceedings. 11th Symp. of Reliable Distributed Systems*. October, 1992.

L. M. Silva and J. G. Silva, (1992). Global Checkpointing for Distributed Programs, *Proceedings, 11th Symp. of Reliable Distributed Systems*, October, 1992.

P. Jalote, (1998). Fault Tolerance in Distributed Systems. *PTR Prentice Hall*, (1994), *Addison-Wesley*, (1998).

R. Ahmed and A. Khaliq, (2003). A Low-Overhead Checkpointing Protocol for Mobile Networks, *IEEE CCECE 2003*, vol. 3, pg. (4 – 7), May 2003.

D. B. Johnson and W. Zwaenepoel, (1987). Sender-Based Message Logging, *Proceedings of 17th Intl. Symposium on Fault Tolerant Computing Systems*, Pittsburgh, 1987.

M. L. Powell and D. L. Presotto, (1983). Publishing: A Reliable Broadcast Communication Mechanism, *Proceedings of 9th ACM Symposium on Operating Systems*.

L. Alvisi and K. Marzullo, (1995). Message Logging: Pessimistic, Optimistic, and Causal, *Proceedings of 15th IEEE Intl. Conference on Distributed Computing Systems*.

B. Randell, (1975). System Structure for Software Fault Tolerance, *IEEE Transactions on Software Engineering*, vol. 1, pp. (226 - 232).

R. E. Strom, S. Yemini (1985). Optimistic Recovery in Distributed Systems, *IEEE Transactions on Software Engineering*, vol. 3, No. 3. pp. (204 - 226).

K. Venkatesh, T. Radhakrishnan, and H. F. Li, ((1987). Optimal Check Pointing and Local Recording for Domino-Free Rollback Recovery, *Information Processing Letters*, vol. 25, No. 5, pp. (295 - 304).

B. Gupta, S. K. Banerjee, and B. Liu, (2002). Design of New Roll-Forward Recovery Approach for Distributed Systems, *IEE Proceedings - Comput. Digit. Tech.*, vol. 149, No. 3, pp. (105 -112).

J. Tsai, S-Y Kuo., and Y-M Wang, (1998). Theoretical Analysis for Communication-Induced Checkpointing Protocols with Rollback-Dependency Trackability, *IEEE Transactions on Parallel and Distributed Systems*, vol. 9, No.10, pp. (963 - 971).

R. Baldoni, J. M. Helway, A. Mosterfaoui, and M. Raynal, (1997). A Communication-Induced Checkpointing Protocol That Ensures Rollback Dependency Trackability, *Proc. IEEE Int'l Symp. Fault-Tolerant Computing*, pp. (68-77), 1997.

J. M. Helary, A. Mosterfaoui, R. H. B. Netzer, and M. Raynal, (2000). Communication-Based Prevention of Useless Checkpoints in Distributed Computations', *Distributed Computing*, vol. 13, No.1, pp. (29 - 43).

D. K. Pradhan and N. H. Vaidya, (1994). Roll-forward Check Pointing Scheme: A Novel Fault-Tolerant Architecture, *IEEE Transactions on Computers*, vol. 43, No. 10, pp. (1163 - 1174).

R. Baldoni, F. Quaglia, and P. Fornara, (1999). An Index-based Check Pointing Algorithm for Autonomous Distributed Systems, *IEEE Transactions on Parallel and Distributed Systems*, vol. 10, No. 2, pp. (181 - 192).

3

Advanced Energy Efficient Communication Techniques for Wireless Ad Hoc and Sensor Networks

Marios I. Poulakis, Athanasios D. Panagopoulos and Philip Constantinou
National Technical University of Athens
Greece

1. Introduction

Ad hoc and wireless sensor networks (WSNs) have recently attracted growing interest in the research and commercial community. Wireless devices are becoming smaller with lots of embedded computing capabilities. In addition, mobile computing, which is the ability to use computing capabilities even when being mobile, has also become the focus of very recent research efforts. The use of this ability has been greatly enhanced by wireless networking.

The key feature of mobile computing technologies is mobility/portability. However, as mobile devices are battery limited, energy efficient communication techniques have become of critical importance. Increased data transmission on the wireless interface results in more consumed energy, while local data storage and data processing might also incur significant energy costs. Consequently, it is very important for the modern wireless networks to reduce the energy consumption of the communication part in order to maintain high battery autonomy. The energy saving problem in wireless communication networks has attracted the interest of the researchers for many years now. Many approaches on various OSI layers have been proposed for energy efficiency, from the classical wakeup mode to energy efficient routing protocols and applications. Nevertheless, most of the research efforts are focused on the lower layers: Physical and MAC.

The objective of this chapter is to survey methods for the preservation of this limited resource - energy. Firstly, it presents a brief description of a simple energy consumption model for wireless communications in order to familiarize the reader with the major energy consumption causes. Afterwards, there are introduced two advanced energy efficient communication techniques: the opportunistic scheduling and the collaborative beamforming. Particularly, according to the first technique, channel fluctuations are exploited opportunistically (through time or multi-user diversity) in terms of minimizing energy consumption and transmitting in good channel conditions. On the other hand, the main idea of collaborative beamforming is grouping nodes to collaboratively send their shared data to the same destination in order to increase the cumulative transmission power and save energy. The basic principles of each technique are presented together with an analytical survey of literature's proposed schemes for the purposes energy consumption minimization. Finally, their advantages and disadvantages are also discussed.

2. Power consumption in wireless communications

This section makes a brief presentation of the basic energy consumption model for wireless communication devices and the typical power consumption values. A wireless device (e.g. ad hoc device, sensor node, etc) consumes energy for many operational functions (communication, processing, memory, etc). One of the most power expensive functions, which is of utmost importance and interest for a communications engineer, is data exchange, namely data communication. In order to focus on the wireless communication part, the total power consumption of a wireless module will be considered as the aggregation of the power consumed for communication (P_{com}) and the power consumed for other electronic functions (P_{electr}) and can be given by:

$$P_{tot}=P_{com}+P_{electr} \tag{1}$$

A realistic wireless communication module (Wang et al., 2006) can be shown in Fig. 1. This simplified module consists of a power supply (battery) that provides energy to device's circuits (radio circuits and other electronics' circuits). The radio or communication circuits are responsible for the communication of the device with the environment and thus for the data transmission or reception. They are consisted of the baseband digital circuits, the IF/RF circuits (responsible for the frequency conversion, modulation or demodulation, etc.), the RF amplifiers (power amplifier-PA for transmission and low noise amplifier-LNA for reception) and finally the switch that schedules when the module behaves as a transmitter and when as a receiver.

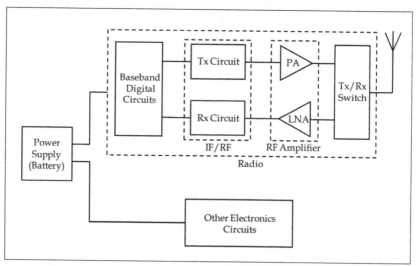

Fig. 1. A simple structure of wireless communication module

Since the focus of this chapter is on communication's energy consumption, the first term of (1) will be analyzed in the following. More specifically, the communication's power consumption consists of the power that is used for transmitting (P_T) and the power for receiving (P_R), as follows:

$$P_{com}= P_T + P_R \tag{2}$$

Based on the structure of communication module of Fig. 1 and assuming that the physical communication rate is constant, the total power consumption for transmitting and for receiving are given respectively by the following expressions:

$$P_T(g) = P_{TB} + P_{TRF} + P_A(g) = P_{T0} + P_A(g) \tag{3}$$

$$P_R = P_{RB} + P_{RRF} + P_L = P_{R0} \tag{4}$$

where P_{TB}/P_{RB}, P_{TRF}/P_{RRF} and $P_A(g)/P_L$ are the power consumption consumption in baseband circuits, in IF/RF circuits and in amplifiers during transmission and reception respectively and g is the channel gain of the wireless link (consists of path losses, shadowing and multipath phenomena/fading). The power consumption for receiving (P_{R0}) is considered constant since it is assumed that it does not depend on the transmission range and the link conditions. On the contrary, the power consumption for transmitting can be modeled in two parts, one constant that doesn't depend on the transmission range and the link conditions (P_{T0}) and the power consumed in the power amplifier ($P_A(g)$) that depends on the transmission requirements and the channel of the wireless link. It is interesting to refer some typical values of commercial RF modules (Wang et al., 2006). For ultra low power RF transceiver CC1000, we have P_{R0}=22.2mW and P_{T0}=15.9mW at 433MHz and for IEEE 802.15.4 compliant and ZigBee ready RF transceiver CC2420, we have P_{R0}=59.1mW and P_{T0}=26.5mW at 2.4GHz.

The RF output power of the transmitter's amplifier is given by:

$$P_{Tx}(g) = \eta \cdot P_A(g) \tag{5}$$

where η is the drain efficiency of the amplifier (Kazimierczuk, 2008), which depends on its' class (e.g. drain efficiency of Class B RF amplifier is ideally 78.5%). Consequently, the total power consumption for transmission can be given by:

$$P_T(g) = P_{T0} + P_{Tx}(g)/\eta \tag{6}$$

Moreover, in order to achieve the required signal level at the receiver (receiver's sensitivity) (P_{Rxmin}) for correct decoding, the transmission power consumption of the communication module for single-hop communication and for a given radio environment, is given by:

$$P_T(g) = P_{T0} + \frac{A \cdot P_{Rx\,min}}{\eta \cdot g} \tag{7}$$

where A can be determined by the characteristics of the transmitting and receiving antennas.

Finally, considering the inherit multi-hop functionality of wireless ad hoc and sensor networks, it is useful to evaluate the power consumption model for a multi-hop network. It is assumed that the nodes that participate at the multi-hop transmission can decode and forward data having no amplifying capability and in all the hops, nodes have the same antenna receiving and transmitting diagrams. Thus, we can obtain the total multi-hop power consumption (for n hops) adding up the transmission and reception power of individual hops, considering identical received requirements (P_{Rxmin}) for each node, as follows:

$$P(n) = n\left(P_{R0} + P_{T0}\right) + \frac{A \cdot P_{Rx\,min}}{\eta} \sum_{i=1}^{n} \frac{1}{g_i} \tag{8}$$

In rest of the chapter, we will focus on the contribution of the communication power consumption that was analyzed above and thus we can assume that this part is the dominant part comparing to the power consumption at the other electronics. In some specific applications that are using for example great processing power (e.g. video monitoring), the power consumption of the other electronics has major contribution but this is out of the scope of this chapter.

3. Energy efficient communication techniques

This section focuses on infrastructureless wireless ad hoc and sensor networks and it will extensively present some advanced energy efficient communication techniques. The concept of energy efficiency communications has been created by the attempts of engineers to optimize the communication's energy consumption. The general minimization problem (Cheng et al., 2011) that can be considered in energy efficient communications, is the following:

$$\min \left\{ Energy\ Consumption \right\}$$
$$\text{s.t. } Rate \text{ or } SNR_{receiver} \text{ constraint} \tag{9}$$
$$Delay\ constraint$$

where $SNR_{receiver}$ is the signal to noise ratio at the receiver. In most cases, energy consumption is translated in the energy consumed for the transmission of a single bit. Considering the Shannon's theorem, the transmitted power for a AWGN channel can be given by:

$$P_{Tx} = \frac{\left(2^{R/W} - 1\right)N}{g} \tag{10}$$

where R is the channel capacity, W is the channel bandwidth, g is the channel gain and N is the noise power. Thus, in order to derive the transmitted energy per bit (in J/bit), the transmitted power must be multiplied by the transmission time of one bit $(1/R)$ and it is expressed as follows:

$$E_C = E_{Tx} = \frac{P_{Tx}}{R} = \frac{\left(2^{R/W} - 1\right)N}{gR} \tag{11}$$

In the rest of this section, there will be discussed two energy efficient techniques highlighting their advantages and their critical issues. The first one is opportunistic scheduling communications, while the second one is the emerging collaborative beamforming technique. Both techniques can be employed for efficient energy usage of the battery-limited wireless devices with great results. The basic principles of these techniques will be analyzed and an analytical survey of the methods that have been proposed in the literature will be presented.

Finally, we note that in order to evaluate an energy efficient technique, a useful metric is the energy efficiency (ε) that can be described as the percentage of energy consumption gain, comparing the energy consumption with the presence $(E_{C,W\text{-}})$ of the corresponding technique and its absence $(E_{C,W/O})$ and can be expressed by:

$$\varepsilon = 1 - \frac{E_{C,W/-}}{E_{C,W/O}} \cdot 100\% \tag{12}$$

3.1 Opportunistic scheduling

In wireless networks, the random fading environment varies channel conditions with time and from user to user. Although, channel fluctuations are traditionally treated as a source of unreliability, according to recent researches they can be opportunistically exploited when and where the channel is strong, by scheduling data transmissions. Opportunistic scheduling (Zhang et al., 2007; Gulpinar et al., 2011) commonly referred to opportunistically transmitting (more) data when the channel between the sender (e.g. user) and receiver (e.g. base station - BS) is in a "good" state and no (or less) data when the channel is in a "bad" state. This technique increases system throughput and reduces the total energy consumption.

More specifically, there are two main categories of opportunistic transmission scheduling. The first one exploits the time diversity of an individual link by adapting the transmissions to the time-varying channel conditions. In other words the sender transmits at higher rates or just transmits when the channel conditions are better, while he transmits at lower rates or postpones transmission when the channel conditions are worse (see Fig. 2). The second one exploits the multi-user diversity, which jointly exploits the time and spatial inhomogeneity of channels to schedule transmissions. In a multi-user network, like the one depicted in Fig. 3, a BS may receives data originated from multiple users. Scheduling their transmissions and selecting instantaneously an "on-peak" user with the best channel condition improves system performance.

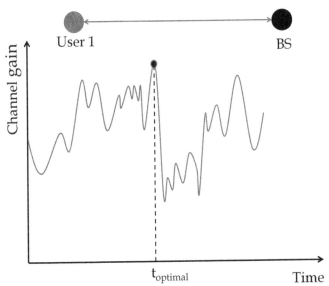

Fig. 2. Time diversity

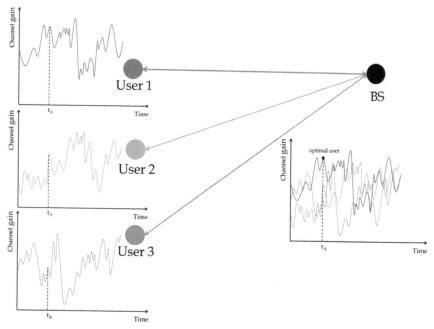

Fig. 3. Multi-user diversity

The basic assumption of opportunistic scheduling is the knowledge of channel state information (CSI). Through a feedback channel, the transmission scheduler learns perfectly the state of the channel between each sender and each receiver at the beginning of every time slot. Its' scheduling decisions are usually based on all past and current states of the channel, but none of the future channel conditions. This is commonly referred to as causal or full CSI. This can be also referred as online scheduling to differentiate from the technique where the scheduler learns all future channel states at the beginning of the time horizon and can be called offline or non-causal scheduling. Nevertheless, the full CSI is an ideal assumption and in many practical cases cannot be implemented. Thus, many researchers use the partial CSI, a more realistic assumption where the various imperfections on CSI acquisition are explicitly taken into account.

3.1.1 Time diversity scheduling

This subsection presents how the time diversity provides energy efficiency. In order to formulate the energy efficient time diversity scheduling, there are two main approaches. Based on the relation of energy consumption in (11) with the channel gain and the rate (channel capacity), which can be depicted in Fig. 4 through a set of curves, one can reduce energy consumption simply if he schedules data transmissions when the channel condition exceeds a specific channel gain threshold or if he adapts transmission rates depending on current channel condition. In the following, we briefly discuss research efforts on energy efficient time diversity scheduling.

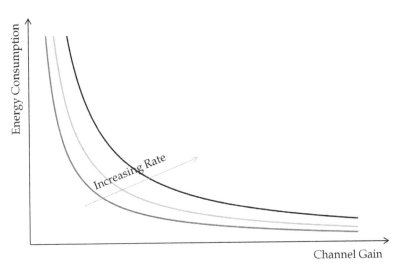

Fig. 4. Set of energy consumption-channel gain curves for different rates

A distributed cooperative rate adaptation scheme in order to achieve energy efficiency in wireless ad hoc networks by exploiting time diversity in opportunistic transmission, is proposed in (Zhang et al., 2007). Since it is hard to optimize the overall system performance without cooperation among nodes, the authors in (Zhang et al., 2007) prompt the "cooperative and opportunistic transmission" concept in fading environments. More specifically, the proposed scheme consists of information exchange and rate selection which can be fulfilled through node cooperation. Each node obtains relevant information on all the links in its maximum interference range by information exchange. This information includes the required channel time for satisfying the traffic requirements and the corresponding power consumption under all possible rates on the link. After that, all nodes calculate the most energy-efficient setting of rates for all the links in their interference range, using a rate selection algorithm. Then, each node consults the neighboring nodes about the feasibility (the probability that quality of service-QoS requirements can be fulfilled) of this new rate setting. The above procedure is repeated until it converges and the rate become feasible. Finally, the rate setting is changed and it can reduce energy consumption. This rate-adaptive power minimization problem is NP-complete and thus the authors decompose the problem into sub-problems for each node and seek a heuristic solution for the rate selection algorithm.

In (Phan & Kim, 2007), the authors propose an energy-efficient scheme for WSNs over fading wireless channels. The proposed scheme takes an opportunistic approach where transmissions are initiated whenever it is possible and only under good channel conditions. In particular, it uses the combination of two parts of MAC protocol, a binary decision based transmission and a channel-aware backoff adjustment. The binary decision based transmission scheme determines when to initiate transmission according to the current channel conditions. Particularly, transmission starts only when the channel quality exceeds a specified threshold. This technique avoids whenever possible the unsuccessful transmissions causing a waste of energy. The optimal threshold for successful transmission obtained using the Markov decision process formulation and computed with dynamic programming techniques. Furthermore, the channel-aware backoff adjustment algorithm favors the sensor nodes that have better channel conditions. A smaller contention window is assigned to those nodes in order to access the channel faster, while a relatively larger one is given for the opposite cases. For simulation purposes, these transmission algorithms are used in the IEEE 802.11 distributed coordination function standard with some necessary modifications and the results show that the proposed scheme improves the energy efficiency up to 70% compared with the plain IEEE 802.11, while the throughput results are comparable.

The authors in (Chakraborty et al., 2006) introduce an energy minimization scheme that schedules transmission by exploiting the movement history of wireless mobile nodes. According to this scheme, the communication may be postponed until a tolerable delay, so as to come across with smaller path loss values. Particularly, in order to save energy in wireless communication, they take advantage of the fact that the reduction in physical distance between two communicating nodes often leads to reduction in energy consumption. In the single hop communication case, this is obvious since transmission power is proportional to the square of the distance (under line of sight-LoS condition) between communicating nodes. Nevertheless, in the multi-hop case, the decrease in physical distance doesn't always imply decrease in network distance. There are some other important factors like the network's state and density of the nodes in the network. However, the lengths of the individual hops are expected to be smaller and in a not very sparse network, reduction in physical distance between two nodes it is likely to save energy.

More specifically, this work considers the problem of predicting when two nodes will move closer to each other. If it is predicted that a mobile node will move closer to the target, communication can be postponed until the future time subject to an application imposed deadline. Once a node decides to postpone the communication, the next problem is to decide when to communicate within an allowable delay. This problem is analogous to the well known *secretary problem* in common optimal stopping theory (Ferguson, 2006). Secretary problem is a selection problem in which one must make an irrevocable choice from a number of applicants, whose values are revealed only sequentially. The solution of that problem is called the "37% rule". According to this rule, the first 37% of the candidates are just evaluated, but not accepted. Then, the candidate whose relative rank is the first among the candidates seen so far is chosen. Based on that, the authors proposed an optimal policy that consists of a simple and efficient heuristic, the least distance (LD). They assume that have already seen the first 37% or more of the candidates as the location history and so the node communicates at the first chance when its distance of the target is less than or equal to the least seen so far. Therefore, in each timeslot the node checks if current distance is less than the minimum so far until the delay threshold in order to schedule transmissions.

Low-complexity and near-optimal policies for delay-constrained scheduling problem for point to point communication is considered in (Lee & Jindal, 2009). This work studies the considers the problem of transmitting B bits over T time slots, where the channel fades independently from slot to slot. The transmission scheduler determines how many bits to transmit depending on the current channel quality and the number of unserved bits remaining. The proposed scheme gives insight into the optimal balance between opportunism (channel-awareness) and deadline-awareness in a delay-limited setting and it can be used to model deterministic traffic in multimedia transmission when there are hard deadlines.

Especially, the proposed scheduler determines the number of bits to serve at each time slot, so as to minimize the expected energy and serve all the bits until the deadline T. It takes into account a combination of parameters: the remaining bits, the number of remaining slots, the current channel state, and a threshold channel level. If the current channel quality is equal to the threshold, then a fraction of the remaining bits are transmitted. If the channel quality is better or worse than the threshold then additional or fewer bits are transmitted. Consequently, the scheduler behaves very opportunistically when the current time slot is far away from the deadline and less opportunistically as the deadline approaches. The optimization problem can be formulated sequentially via dynamic programming. Due to the difficulty to obtain an analytical form of the optimal scheduler the authors make some relaxations and propose suboptimal algorithms. Additionally, the authors consider the case when the number of bits to transmit is small. In that case, the transmission of the entire packet at once may be wanted due to the potential overhead of multiple slot transmission.

Finally, considering that opportunistic scheduling asks for channel awareness, another important issue that must not be ignored is the cost of channel state acquisition. The authors in (Li & Neely, 2010) consider scheduling algorithms for energy and throughput optimality. They take into account a more realistic assumption that channel acquisition incurs power overhead and they propose a channel acquisition algorithm that dynamically acquires channel states to stabilize a wireless downlink. Due to the fact that it may be adequate and more energy efficient to transmit data with no CSI in low traffic rate cases, the authors propose a dynamic scheduling algorithm, which accomplishes data transmission with or without CSI, using queue backlog and channel statistics. Simulations verify that the algorithm efficiently adapts between channel-aware and channel-blind modes for various system parameters, including different values of channel probing power, different transmission power and different data rates.

3.1.2 Multi-user diversity scheduling

Due to the presence of many users, with independent fades, in wireless communication networks, there is a high probability that one (or some) of the users will have good channel(s) at any one time. By allowing only that user(s) to transmit, the shared channel is used most efficiently and the total system efficiency is maximized. The greater the number of users, the better tends to be the good channel(s), and the multi-user diversity gain is greater. Similarly with the observations about time diversity scheduling presented above, the main approaches that can formulate energy efficient multi-user diversity are inspired from the nature of energy consumption's function in (11). Fig. 5 shows the set of energy consumption-rate curves for different instantaneous channel gain representing the channel conditions of different users that aims at communication with the same node. Consequently, one approach in order to reduce energy consumption falls to the selection of the best user or the group of best users that will become active users (representatives), in terms of channel condition and they will be scheduled to data transmission considering some specified constraints (e.g. rate constraints). The critical issue here is the strategy that specifies the active users, which may be for example a threshold policy as in time diversity scheduling. Moreover, a multi-user diversity scheduler should guarantee fairness among the users' communication and not sacrifice it in order to result more system efficiency. The rest of this subsection presents research publications and proposed approaches on this energy efficient technique.

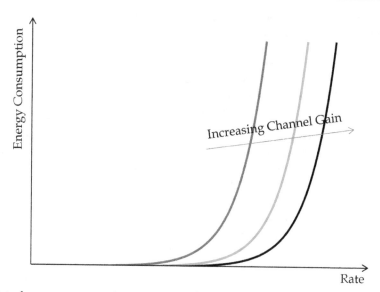

Fig. 5. Set of energy consumption-rate curves for different users (channel gains)

In (Bhorkar et al., 2006), the authors discuss energy optimal opportunistic control strategies for a multi-user TDMA (time division multiple access) network subject to minimum rate constraints. Particularly, they consider a multi-user TDMA system where base station has the role of centralized scheduler. It is assumed that time is divided into slots of equal duration, the channel is suffering from slow fading and the scheduler has perfect CSI for all wireless links. Moreover, the scheduler determines at any given timeslot the unique user who can transmit and its transmission power considering a specific rate constraint. Their method is to opportunistically schedule the user with the best channel condition such that rate is guaranteed and temporal fairness are achieved and average transmission power is minimized.

The authors propose a joint minimization problem of average transmission power subject to average rate constraints. Using Lagrangian method and a stochastic approximation based online algorithm to estimate the necessary parameters, they obtain the optimal policy that selects which user to transmit and with what power. Despite the energy efficiency that can be achieved through multi-diversity opportunistic scheduling, an issue that must always be taken under consideration is fairness among users. Thus, an additional long term fairness constraint with time average fraction of slots allocated to each user is considered. This constraint guarantees average proportional time share and specifically that each user has average access to certain number of time slots. Since considering only long term fairness has problems in some case, the authors also discuss a short term fair scheduler and devise a heuristic based algorithm. Their results show that as expected due to multi-user diversity when the number of users increases, the gain obtained from the proposed power scheme increases.

The work in (Hwang et al., 2009) proposes a method that reduces transmission power consumption of carrier-sense multiple-access (CSMA) based wireless local area networks (WLANs) by utilizing multi-user diversity and power control. According to this scheme, a terminal sends a packet at a slot if the terminal's SNR is above a specified threshold associated with the slot. Multi-user diversity is attained by using the opportunistic p-persistent CSMA (OpCSMA) scheme. In a simple pCSMA system, each user accesses the wireless medium with probability p, independently from the value of the corresponding SNR. On the contrary, in the OpCSMA system, each user maintains the same access probability by using a specific random variable defined by the corresponding SNR, exploiting the multi-user diversity. In particular, a user accesses the channel only if its SNR exceeds a predetermined threshold given by a specific formula (related with the inverse cdf of SNR) during the specific slot. This threshold's values decrease as time advances and thus this method makes the user with the largest SNR access the shared medium earlier than the others and transmit with less power.

In order to evaluate power efficiency, the authors use the expected sum-power metric, which is the expectation of the sum of transmitted power per packet of all users and represents the aggregate power consumption of an entire random-access network. Thus, the expected sum-power depends on the power control policy and the number of transmitting users per transmission opportunity. So as to reduce the expected sum power, this work combines the truncated channel inversion power control method with OpCSMA, applying the described threshold policy. The authors consider the infinite-user model and the simulation results show that the proposed scheme saves substantial energy compared to the conventional pCSMA, while maintaining the same throughput. Also, the proposed scheme was tested in an IEEE 802.11 WLAN and the results shown significant power saving as well as long-term fairness. Finally, the authors discuss some possible problems of the proposed scheme, like short-term fairness problems that may cause a large delay jitter (something undesirable for real-time applications). Additionally, they note that the transmission power control may hamper the operation of CSMA because it can deteriorate the hidden-node problem. After these problems are solved, the OpCSMA should be a highly effective protocol for wireless networks.

An opportunistic transmission scheme for the type-based multiple access system, which selects a set of sensors to transmit in order to provide energy efficiency is proposed in (Jeon et al., 2010). The discussed problem considers an unknown target to be detected and sensors that have statistically and temporally independent and identically distributed observations on this target and transmit them to a fusion center. The authors' goal is to minimize average power consumed by the sensors in order to achieve a detection error performance constraint. Thus, they propose a channel-aware opportunistic type-based multiple access scheme over a fading channel, exploiting the multi-user diversity for large WSNs for better energy efficiency, where all sensors do not need to be activated. Due to the multi-user diversity in WSNs, the authors allow the sensors experiencing higher channel gains than a given threshold (broadcasted by the fusion center) to participate in type-based multiple access and transmit data at their controlled power levels in a time-division duplexing manner. This set of sensor nodes (activated sensors) requires smaller amount of total energy consumed for reporting their observations reliably to the fusion center, and thus the lifetime of WSNs can be prolonged.

In particular, the authors formulate an optimization problem to minimize the average power consumed by the activated sensors while satisfying a given detection error performance. To solve this problem they first determine a power control policy to maximize an error exponent of the detection error performance and find a threshold to minimize the average power consumed by the activated sensors. The evaluations of the proposed scheme show that smaller number of sensors and reduced total energy are required, for the same detection performance in the low SNR regime, comparing with a random selection scheme, where nodes are activated regardless of their communication channel qualities.

Finally, the work in (Yoon et al., 2011) discusses another very important issue that arises when a scheme exploits multi-user diversity, the fundamental tradeoff between energy saving and throughput. Specifically, the performance gain from the multi-user diversity and the energy consumption for the channel feedback should be balanced. Thus, the authors propose an energy-efficient opportunistic scheduling scheme that goals to improve energy efficiency under the constraint of fair resource allocation by controlling the number of users that feedback their channel conditions to a BS. This can be achieved by combining opportunistic scheduling with energy-efficient sleep/awake scheduling.

In particular, this work considers a time-slotted system with a single frequency downlink channel that is consisted of N low mobile users and a single BS. At each time slot, the BS broadcasts a pilot signal and then n out of N users respond of their received SNRs to the BS. The users that report their channel statuses are referred as non-sleeping, and the others as sleeping. Then the BS chooses a single user (active user), to transmit/receive at this time slot. The other non-sleeping users are idle and deactivate their transceivers so as to save energy, similar with the sleeping users. In order to formulate the optimization problem, the authors consider the energy efficiency in bits per energy unit, given by the ratio of the expected throughput to expected energy consumption for a given set of non-sleeping users. Their objective is to maximize the average efficiency under the constraint of fair resource allocation which expressed as the time average of active users.

The authors first consider a network where each user has an identical mean SNR. Then, they express the energy efficiency in relation with the non-sleeping users and the initial problem simply becomes finding an optimal number of non-sleeping users that maximizes average efficiency. This is a quasi-convex integer problem that can be solved through the method of integer constraint relaxation on non-sleeping users. After that, they consider a more general network where users could have different channel statistics (different mean SNRs). Since it is hard to obtain an optimal solution due to complexity, there are proposed two heuristic approximations of the considered problem: one that uses the average mean SNR and another that classifies users into several groups according to similar mean SNRs. The performance of energy-efficient opportunistic scheduling scheme shows that it enables the network lifetime to be prolonged significantly at the cost of a slight degradation in the system throughput.

3.2 Collaborative beamforming

This subsection discusses the concept of collaborative beamforming in order to improve the energy efficiency and the transmission range of wireless networks. Specifically, the basic principles of collaborative beamforming are presented in the following, together with a brief analysis on the research efforts and the energy performance of this technique. Moreover, the critical issues of this technique are considered.

3.2.1 Principles of collaborative beamforming

Beamforming is a technique that can handle the problem of signal fluctuations at the receiver caused by several phenomena such as path loss, shadowing, and multipath fading. It is used for directional signal transmission or reception and it relies on the artificially creation of multipath fading by equipping the transmitter with multiple antennas and by sending the same signal from each antenna. Nevertheless, battery-limited devices in wireless ad hoc and sensor networks are likely to be equipped with a single antenna and so they cannot use beamforming. A solution to this problem is nearby users to cooperate with each other such that by sharing their transmission data and then synchronously transmit the compound data to the destination receiver. In essence, a set of distributed wireless nodes organize themselves as a virtual antenna array (see Fig. 6) and produce a desired beam pattern. Such beamforming is often referred to as a collaborative (or distributed) beamforming, because all the nodes that are grouped together collaboratively send their shared messages to the same destination (Ochiai et al., 2005; Ochiai & Imai, 2009). The term distributed beamforming is frequently used in the general case of wireless networks and the term collaborative beamforming is more usually used in WSNs. Nevertheless, there are some main technical challenges when implementing collaborative beamforming. The most important are the feasibility of precise phase synchronization between the collaborative nodes in order to produce the optimal output, the accurate channel estimation and the efficient sharing of messages among the nodes.

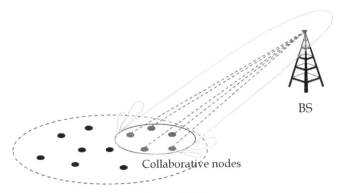

Fig. 6. Collaborative beamforming example in a WSN

Collaborative beamforming may be adopted in modern wireless ad hoc and sensor networks for the reasons below (Feng et al., 2009):

1. The black-out spots in the networks are minimized, which means that the transmission energy of the individual nodes is balanced and saved over multiple transmitters. This prevents some of the nodes from draining of energy much faster than the others (for example near sink nodes in WSNs).
2. It allows the signals to travel farther and reach a receiver too far for an individual transmitter (beyond its' range).
3. Data security is substantially improved. Beamforming reduces or completely eliminates signals to undesired directions.

Collaborative beamforming can be achieved by manipulating the initial phase of synchronized transmitting signals with identical message. Thus, all the nodes must be phase synchronized. This can be achieved by appropriately setting the initial phase of the transmitting signal of each user. Two possible scenarios can be used (Ochiai et al., 2005): closed-loop and open-loop scenario. In the first one, each node independently synchronizes itself to a beacon sent from the destination node adjusting its initial phase. Hence, the beam is formed in the direction of arrival of the beacon. In contrast, the open-loop scenario considers that all nodes within a group or a cluster acquire their relative locations from a beacon of a nearby reference point, the master node or the cluster head. In this case, the beam is steered toward an arbitrary direction.

In most of the literature's schemes that consider collaborative beamforming, there are made some identical assumptions. At first, each sensor node is equipped with an ideal isotropic antenna. Moreover, all nodes transmit with identical energies, and the path losses of all nodes are also identical with the absence of signal reflection and scattering. Also, all nodes are sufficiently separated such that mutual coupling effects are negligible and they are perfectly synchronized. The above are some general assumptions that are not always strictly followed.

Furthermore, a very important issue is the effects of the locations of distributed collaborative nodes in the derived beam pattern, which is discussed in (Ochiai et al., 2005; Ochiai & Imai, 2009). The authors consider many location distributions, but the most reasonable when someone deal with wireless ad hoc sensor networks, is that distributed antenna nodes are located randomly by nature. Therefore, the beam patterns of these random arrays are determined by particular realizations of randomly chosen node locations. As it is shown, if the sensors are randomly distributed and fully synchronized, the resulting beam pattern formed by these sensors has a nice sharp mainlobe and low sidelobes, with high probability.

3.2.2 Energy efficiency through collaborative beamforming

Collaborative beamforming is a signal transmission technique that can prolong the lifetime of a wireless network. Improving directivity of transmitted signals in order to be stronger at the receiver, it can save transmission energy. Each transmitter can individually save energy using lower power, since the energy consumption is spread over multiple transmitters. Particularly, if N distributed nodes are considered that transmit the same signal, each at power P, all transmissions add up coherently at the destination. As a result, the power of the received signal at the destination is proportional to N^2P. Thus, this technique leads to a N^2 gain at the received SNR, with only a N factor increment in total transmit power. Alternatively, we can say that the transmission range can be increased by N times farther and each node can reduce its transmit power to P/N, gaining a factor of N in power efficiency. Consequently, collaborative beamforming can achieve high energy efficiency.

Specifically, consider N distributed nodes, let E_{single} be the energy that a single node needs to transmit one bit to the destination and D be the amount of the data to be transmitted. In order to achieve efficiency, the transmitters have to coordinate their phases with high accuracy. Since, this is not always absolutely possible (allowing some tolerance in phase differences), collaborative beamforming is characterized of an efficiency (e) factor that is defined as the ratio of achieved signal strength and the highest possible signal strength. Consequently, using collaborative beamforming, each transmitter needs to only use $E_{single}/(N \cdot e)$ energy for sending one bit and that leads to the energy saving E_{saving} for each transmitter.

Moreover, collaborative beamforming can be divided into two stages: preparation and operation. At the pre-beamforming preparation stage all the necessary functionalities of synchronization and data sharing are taking place. During the operation stage all the collaborative nodes transmit their data simultaneously to the same destination. In order to formulate the total energy profit of collaborative beamforming, one must take into account the additional energy consumed by the data sharing and synchronization procedures that is referred as energy overhead $E_{overhead}$. Considering the above, the total energy profit for each node using collaborative beamforming is given by:

$$E_{total} = E_{saving} - E_{overhead} = E_{single} \cdot D \cdot \left(1 - \frac{1}{N \cdot e}\right) - E_{overhead} \tag{13}$$

Fig. 7 represents how the number of collaborative nodes affects energy saving of each node. Regarding the $E_{overhead}$, it depends on many technological constraints and cannot be simply represented.

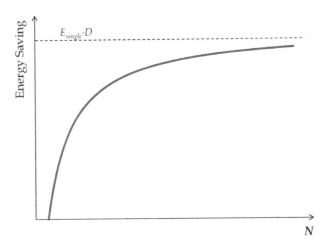

Fig. 7. Energy saving of each node using collaborative beamforming.

Several studies can be found in the literature that tackle the problem of collaborative beamforming and particularly the utilization of this technique in terms of reducing the energy consumption in a wireless networks. This technique is widely considered for WSNs, but the principles are the same for all the wireless network technologies. The rest of this subsection aims at quoting the most representative proposed techniques that deal with this problem.

The authors in (Feng et al., 2009) investigate the energy gain attained by using collaborative beamforming based on two critical factors, the number of collaborative nodes and the total size of data needed to transmit. In particular, in order to achieve beamforming's efficiency, all phases among the participating nodes must be proper coordinated with high accuracy. This requires communication among the nodes and consumes energy. Accuracy is measured by the wireless carrier's frequency and for example a π/6 accuracy of a 900 MHz carrier implies that the transmitters' clocks must be synchronized within 0.1 ns with a maximum location error of 2.8 cm. This phase synchronization can be achieved using an iterative algorithm for communication among nodes. Ideally, the phase difference must be zero for waves arriving at the destination to achieve *100%* efficiency (e) and the algorithm converges in several iterations something that increases the energy consumption for synchronization.

A tradeoff among efficiency and maximum phase difference is proposed in this work. Particularly, if the transmitters are allowed to have phase differences, the efficiency may be lower but convergence will be faster. For example, at a maximum phase difference π/6 the efficiency is *95%*, while at π/3 is almost *70%*. Consequently, by relaxing the convergence requirement, the transmitters can determine their phases faster and save energy in pre-beamforming preparation. Even for phase differences greater than zero, collaborative beamforming can still increase the received signal strength.

Moreover, in order the beamforming technique to save energy, the total profit of (13) must be greater than zero. These leads the authors to determine the minimum size of data D_{min} to be transmitted in order to balance the preparation overhead when the total number of nodes is given, as follows:

$$D > D_{\min} = \frac{E_{overhead}}{E_{single} \cdot \left(1 - \dfrac{1}{N \cdot e}\right)} \tag{14}$$

The simulation results verify that for a fixed number of transmitters, higher efficiency requires more iteration in pre-beamforming preparation and a larger minimum size of data to compensate this energy overhead.

Considering that for better performance, the nodes with small phase differences are always used, these nodes will exhaust their energy much faster than the others. This may cause coverage holes in WSNs, which referred to areas that are not monitored because the corresponding sensors run out of energy. To avoid this, a scheduling scheme that selects the transmitters in each round is necessary in order to balance the remaining energy over the entire network. A scheduling algorithm for nodes participating in collaborative beamforming is proposed in (Feng et al., 2010a). This algorithm is called energy and phase (EP) and selects the transmitters in each round in order to prolong network lifetime. Three rules are used in order to implement this selection: the remaining energy in all nodes need to be balanced, the signal gain at the receiver need to exceed a minimum level and the amount of data transmitted need to be maximized.

Especially, to prevent the nodes with low remaining energy from being energy-exhausted, the nodes with higher remaining energy should be selected first. Also, since smaller phase differences provide larger beamforming gain, the proposed scheduler selects nodes by giving higher priorities to smaller phase differences relative to a reference phase at the receiver. Thus, for each round, the authors sort and select nodes one by one based on their priorities (a specific product considering remaining energy and phase difference), to minimize wasted energy. After one node is selected, the signal gain at the receiver is computed. If it is greater or equal than the minimum required, the currently selected nodes are assigned to transmit for this round. This transmission schedule can be computed offline and broadcasted to all nodes. Finally, it can achieve 60% more beamforming transmissions than a phase partition algorithm, which divides transmitters into several groups based on their phases without considering the remaining energy in each node and the signal strength at the receiver.

In (Feng et al., 2010b), the authors discuss how data sharing affects the network lifetime and collaborative beamforming's energy performance. Data sharing is necessary, since the information collected by nodes at different locations may not be the same. It requires communication among collaborative nodes, which consumes energy and shortens the lifetime of the network. Consequently, this energy abates the energy saved by beamforming. This work proposes a procedure for data sharing and examines the energy that consumes. Specifically, the considered nodes are divides into groups and each collaborative beamforming transmission is assigned to one group at a time. The groups transmit to the base station in turns using TDMA. Also, nodes are assumed to be synchronized. There are four types of nodes in each round of sensing and transmission: beamforming transmitters, a master node, sensing nodes, and the other nodes that don't belong to the previous categories. Among all transmitters in each group, the one with the highest remaining energy considered as the master node. He gathers the data from all sensing nodes, aggregates and compresses them and finally multicasts the result data to the other transmitters. The simulation results show that collaborative beamforming is energy-efficient, when the sensor nodes are deployed far away (d=50 km) from the base station comparing with the deployment area (ρ=0.1 km) and the energy consumption of data sharing negligibly affects the network's lifetime. Thus, the energy consumed on long distance transmissions dominates compared with the energy consumed on data sharing.

In addition, the authors in (Luskey et al., 2006) also discuss the energy saving of utilizing collaborative beamforming over the transmission of a single sensor node accounting the additional total overhead that comes for its implementation. According to this work, the total network's overhead is related with the number of nodes that participate in procedure and it can be further analyzed in the following terms:

- E_{synch}: the energy consumed in synchronizing,
- E_{pos}: the energy consumed in calculating of each node's precise position,
- E_{distr}: the energy consumed in distributing of the data to all nodes,
- E_{pre}: the energy consumed in communication operations prior to collaborative transmission such as modulation, mixing, filtering and
- E_{digit}: the energy consumed in performing all calculations associated with synchronization and beamforming (except the position estimation).

Consequently, the overall energy balance depends on how the energy saving and energy overhead scale with network size. This implies that the overhead energy is a critical issue due to the demand of positive energy profit that is still open and depends on the considered implementation scheme of collaborative beamforming.

Furthermore, a modern mathematical formulation of the problem under consideration can be presented using game theory in order to control the power consumption of wireless devices (Betz & Poor, 2008). According to this work, cooperating nodes form clusters to retransmit local data to faraway destinations. Multiple clusters are transmitting at the same frequency and at the same time. A non-cooperative game is considered, where the clusters are considered as players and each cluster chooses its average transmit power in order to selfishly optimize its utility function that is expressed as the ratio of the throughput to transmit power. Thus, this work combines the cooperative technique of collaborative beamforming with a non-cooperative game. In general, cooperative approaches can achieve better results, but they usually introduce great cost for centralized control in large networks. The proposed game has a Nash equilibrium, which is unique. Moreover, the utility at the Nash equilibrium has been shown numerically to be significantly higher than if all nodes transmit at maximal average transmit power.

Finally, the authors in (Pun et al., 2009) propose an energy-efficient opportunistic collaborative beamforming scheme for ad hoc sensor networks that suffer from Rayleigh fading. This scheme is a fusion of collaborative beamforming and opportunistic node selection. In contrast to conventional collaborative beamforming schemes where each relay node uses accurate CSI to compensate its channel phase and carrier offset, in the proposed scheme the collaborative nodes are selected by the destination and do not perform any phase compensation. The authors note that the proposed scheme differs from opportunistic beamforming schemes, which consider the data transmission scheduling from a given source to the optimum destination exploiting multi-user diversity.

Considering the opportunistic collaborative beamforming model, the destination node broadcasts a node selection vector to the available nodes in order to opportunistically select a subset of them. Since the selection vector only indicates which relay nodes will participate in the collaborative beamforming and does not convey any CSI, only 1-bit of feedback is required per node. Thus, the total transmitted feedback from the destination is a single K-bit vector. Also, the nodes do not need to adjust their phases prior to or during transmission. The important issue in this scheme is the computation of the selection vector. In particular, this vector is calculated by the destination, aiming at maximizing the power gain of the collaborative beamformer. However, these calculations are exponentially complex in the number of available nodes and the authors propose three low-complexity sub-optimal node selection rules (the sector-based, the iterative greedy, and the iterative pruning) that provide near-optimum beamforming. Theoretical analysis shows that the received signal power at the destination scales linearly with the number of available nodes under a fixed total power constraint, similar with the ideal collaborative beamforming.

4. Conclusion

This chapter studied the state of the art techniques employing energy efficiency in wireless ad hoc and sensor networks. Due to the battery powered nodes of these networks, the efficient use of the limited energy resources is necessary in order to prolong networks' lifetime. In the first section, there was a short description of the basic principles of communications' power consumption in wireless systems and afterwards a survey of two advanced techniques that provides energy efficiency was presented. The first technique was opportunistic scheduling, which exploits the random channel fluctuations of wireless networks that are traditionally viewed as a source of unreliability. Due to these channel variations, there is provided the opportunity to schedule data transmissions by choosing the best time (time diversity) or the best user (multi-user diversity) in terms of channel conditions. Data transmission in good channel conditions can save energy. Moreover, the second technique was collaborative beamforming, which uses a set of collaborative nodes that act as a virtual antenna array and form a beam to cooperatively transmit a common signal. Each node can use lower transmission power and save energy, since the energy consumption is spread over multiple transmitters.

The opportunistic and collaborative techniques, which are mostly designed in Physical and MAC layer, can be seen as the basis of the generalized framework of opportunistic (and collaborative) computing (Conti et al., 2010) that mainly refers in upper layers. This concept considers the opportunistic and collaborative use of any resource available in the network, exploiting the functionality of the other available devices in the environment and maybe changing node roles during runtime (Avvenuti et al., 2007).

5. Acknowledgment

This work has been financed by NTUA Basic Research funding program "PEVE 2010".

6. References

Avvenuti, M.; Corsini, P.; Masci, P. & Vecchio A. (2007). Opportunistic computing for wireless sensor networks, *Proceedings of IEEE Internatonal Conference on Mobile Adhoc and Sensor Systems 2007*, pp.1-6, ISBN 978-1-4244-1455-0, Pisa, Italy, Oct. 8-11, 2007

Betz, S.M. & Poor, H.V. (2008). Energy efficient communication using cooperative beamforming: A game theoretic analysis, *Proceedings of IEEE 19th International Symposium on Personal, Indoor and Mobile Radio Communications (PIMRC) 2008*, pp.1-5, ISBN 978-1-4244-2643-0, Cannes, France, Sept. 15-18, 2008

Bhorkar A., Karandikar A. & Borkar V.S. (2006). WLC39-3: Power Optimal Opportunistic Scheduling, *IEEE Global Telecommunications Conference (GLOBECOM) 2006*, pp.1-5, ISBN 1-4244-0356-1, San Francisco, CA, Nov. 27 -Dec. 1, 2006

Chakraborty, S.; Dong, Y.; Yau D. K. Y. & Lui, J. C. S. (2006). On the Effectiveness of Movement Prediction to Reduce Energy Consumption in Wireless Communication, *IEEE Trans. Mobile Computing*, Vol.5, No.2, pp.157 – 169, ISSN 1536-1233

Cheng, W.; Zhang, X.; Zhang, H. & Wang, Q. (2011). On-Demand based wireless resources trading for Green Communications, *Proceedings of IEEE Conference on Computer Communications Workshops (INFOCOM WKSHPS) 2011*, pp.283-288, ISBN 978-1-4577-0249-5, Shanghai, China, April 10-15, 2011

Conti, M.; Giordano, S.; May, M. & Passarella, A. (2010). From opportunistic networks to opportunistic computing, *IEEE Communications Magazine*, Vol.48, No.9, pp.126-139, ISSN 0163-6804

Feng, J.; Lu, Y.-H.; Jung, B. & Peroulis, D. (2009). Energy efficient collaborative beamforming in wireless sensor networks, *Proceedings of IEEE International Symposium on Circuits and Systems (ISCAS) 2009*, pp.2161-2164, ISBN 978-1-4244-3827-3, Taipei, Taiwan, May 24-27, 2009

Feng, J.; Chang, C.-W.; Sayilir, S.; Lu, Y.-H.; Jung, B.; Peroulis, D. & Hu, Y.C. (2010). Energy-Efficient Transmission for Beamforming in Wireless Sensor Networks, *Proceedings of 7th Annual IEEE Communications Society Conference on Sensor Mesh and Ad Hoc Communications and Networks (SECON) 2010*, pp.1-9, ISBN 978-1-4244-7150-8, Boston, Massachusetts, June 21-25, 2010

Feng, J.; Nimmagadda, Y.; Lu, Y.-H.; Jung, B.; Peroulis, D. & Hu, Y.C. (2010). Analysis of Energy Consumption on Data Sharing in Beamforming for Wireless Sensor Networks, *Proceedings of 19th International Conference on Computer Communications and Networks (ICCCN) 2010*, pp.1-6, ISBN 978-1-4244-7114-0, Zurich, Switzerland, Aug. 2-5, 2010

Ferguson, T. (2006). *Optimal Stopping and Applications.* Available from: http://www.math.ucla.edu/~tom/Stopping/Contents.html

Gulpinar, N.; Harrison, P. & Rustem, B. (2011). *Performance Models and Risk Management in Communication Systems*, Springer, ISBN 978-1-4419-0533-8, New York

Han, Z. & Poor, H.V. (2007). Lifetime improvement in wireless sensor networks via collaborative beamforming and cooperative transmission, *IET Microwaves, Antennas & Propagation*, Vol.1, No.6, pp.1103-1110, ISSN 1751-8725

Hwang, C.-S.; Seong, K. & Cioffi, J.M. (2009). Improving power efficiency of CSMA wireless networks using multi-user diversity - [transaction letters], *IEEE Transactions on Wireless Communications*, Vol.8, No.7, pp.3313-3319, ISSN 1536-1276

Jeon, H.; Choi, J.; Lee, H. & Ha, J. (2010). Channel-Aware Energy Efficient Transmission Strategies for Large Wireless Sensor Networks, *IEEE Signal Processing Letters*, Vol.17, No.7, pp.643-646, ISSN 1070-9908

Kazimierczuk, M. K. (2008). *RF Power Amplifiers*, Wiley, ISBN 978-0-470-77946-0, New York

Lee, J. & Jindal, N. (2009). Energy-efficient scheduling of delay constrained traffic over fading channels, *IEEE Transaction on Wireless Communications*, Vol.8, No.4, pp. 1866-1875, ISSN 1536-1276

Li, C.-P. & Neely, M. J. (2010). Energy-optimal scheduling with dynamic channel acquisition in wireless downlinks, *IEEE Transaction on Mobile Computing*, Vol. 9, No. 4, pp. 527 539, ISSN 1536-1233

Luskey, S.; Jin, C. & Schaik, A. V. (2006) Energy Savings from Implementing Collaborative Beamforming for a Remote Low Power Wireless Sensor Network, *Proceedings of Conference the first Australian Conference on Wireless Broadband and Ultra Wideband Communications (AusWireless '06)*, Sydney, Australia, March, 2006.

Ochiai, H.; Mitran, P.; Poor, H. V. & Tarokh V. (2005). Collaborative beamforming for distributed wireless ad hoc sensor networks, *IEEE Transaction on Signal Processing*, Vol. 53, No. 11, pp. 4110– 4124, ISSN 1053-587X

Ochiai, H. & Imai, H. (2009). Collaborative Beamforming, In: *New Directions in Wireless Communications Research*, V. Tarokh (Ed.), pp. 175-197, Springer, ISBN 978-1-4419-0672-4, New York

Phan, C. V. & Kim, J. G. (2007). An Energy-Efficient Transmission Strategy for Wireless Sensor Networks, *Proceedings of IEEE Wireless Communications and Networking Conference (WCNC) 2007*, pp. 3406-3411, ISBN 1-4244-0658-7, Hong Kong, March 11-15, 2007

Pun, M.-O.; Brown, D. & Poor, H. (2009). Opportunistic collaborative beamforming with one-bit feedback, *IEEE Transactions on Wireless Communications*, Vol.8, No.5, pp.2629-2641, ISSN 1536-1276

Wang, Q.; Hempstead, M. & Yang, W. (2006). A realistic power consumption model for wireless sensor network devices, *Proceedings of IEEE Sensor, Mesh and Ad Hoc Communications and Networks (SECON) 2006*, pp. 286–295, ISBN 1-4244-0626-9, Reston, VA, USA, September 2006

Yoon, S.G.; Joo, C. & Bahk, S. (2011). Energy-efficient opportunistic scheduling schemes in wireless networks, *Computer Networks*, Vol.55, No.9, pp. 2168-2175, ISSN 1389-1286

Zhang, Q.; Chen, Q.; Yang, F.; Shen, X. & Niu, Z. (2007) Cooperative and opportunistic transmission for wireless ad hoc networks, *IEEE Network*, Vol.21, No.1, pp.14-20, ISSN 0890-8044

Part 2

Mobile Software Life Cycle

4

Software Testing Strategy for Mobile Phone

Guitao Cao, Jie Yang, Qing Zhou and Weiting Chen

Software Engineering Institute, East China Normal University, Shanghai, China

1. Introduction

With the rapid development of embedded systems and extension of embedded application domain, the scale and complexity of requirements for embedded software have continuously improved. And the product quality and marketing time depend upon its software quality and development cycle. As a result, embedded software testing becomes a hot issue of the research.

Embedded system usually adopts hierarchy as their software architecture based on real-time kernel, as shown in Fig.1 [1]. From this figure we can see that the system software is separated into the following layers:

Application Layer
Middleware Layer
Operating System Layer
Driven Layer
Hardware

Fig. 1. Software structure of embedded system

1. Driven Layer (also called Hardware Abstraction Layer, HAL), as the bottom of software, is closest to hardware. This layer directly makes contact with hardware, providing hardware interfaces for operating system and applications, in other words, gives drivers support. The manufacturers generally supply complete software of driven layer during the process of selling hardware so that developers can use them directly.

2. Operating System Layer (known as System Software Layer). It is responsible for cooperating with application layer to improve their scheduling, management and exception handling. Thanks to the support of this layer, especially the real-time kernel, the difficulty of developing embedded software has been eased greatly and the development cycle has been shortened.

3. Middleware Layer refers to Software Realization Supporting Layer. The realization of embedded application software requires the support of programming languages, such as procedure-oriented C, and object-oriented C++ and Java. When using these languages to develop application programs running in embedded systems, relevant compiler and interpreter are required to convert the programs into machine code in order to realize the corresponding functions.

4. Application Layer (called Application Software Layer). Application layer lies in the top of the embedded system hierarchical architecture, mainly comprising multiple relatively independent application tasks to accomplish specific work, such as I/O, computing and communicating. Operating system is in charge of scheduling these tasks.

Embedded software testing is more complex than general business-oriented software because of its characteristics such as real-timing, insufficient memory, shortage of I/O channels, expensive development tools, close relationship with hardware dependency, and various CPUs. Meanwhile on account of the high reliability demands of embedded system, safety invalidation will probably bring out catastrophic results. So it is of great importance to perform strict test, validation and verification on increasingly complicated embedded software[2].

Embedded software testing shares the same objectives and principles with other general software testing to verify and reach the reliability requirements. However, as a special kind of software testing, embedded software testing owns its unique characteristics as follows:

1. Specific hardware dependency. Embedded software can only run in specific hardware environment. Thus, the most important purpose for testing is to ensure the embedded software could run more reliably in this particular environment.
2. Real-time characteristics. Besides high reliability, the testing also needs to guarantee the real-time characteristics.
3. Memory test. In order to meet the demands of high reliability, memory leak is not allowed in embedded system. Therefore, embedded software testing not only consists of performance test, GUI test and coverage analysis test but also memory test.
4. Product testing. The ultimate purpose of embedded software testing is to make embedded products satisfy safety and reliability while fulfilling other functions. Hence, we need to perform product testing after the first embedded product has been produced.

By now, the majority work of embedded software testing emphasizes on debugging phase instead of studying comprehensive techniques. Along with the widespread popularization of embedded software application and increase requirements of quality assurance, testing needs more systematic and engineered technical supports apart from debugging.

This paper takes mobile phone testing as an example to introduce the implementation process of embedded software testing and analyze the methods after presenting testing techniques and tools, attempting to form a kind of engineered solution for testing.

2. Software testing

Software testing is a process of choosing appropriate test cases and executing the program to be tested for the purpose of detecting program defects according to the IEEE 1983 standard. In IEEE Std 829-1998, which is the revision of IEEE (1983), testing is defined as software analysis procedure of (A) testing one or more sets of test cases, or (B) testing one or more sets of test processes, or (C) testing one or more sets of both test cases and test processes, aiming to find the place where the realization of software function does not accord with the requirements and also to evaluate the software[3].

2.1 Software testing techniques

Software testing technology provides specific support method for each stage of software test. It can be divided into static testing and moment testing from the perspective of whether tested software needs to be executed.

2.1.1 Static testing and moment testing

Static testing is the process of searching for defects that probably exist in program and assessing program code, rather than executing the program. Static testing mainly consists of code reviews, code walkthrough, desktop check, technology check and static analysis. Among them, the first four processes are all conducted manually while the static analysis proceeds automatically by software tools[4].

Moment testing, also called dynamic testing, executes test cases via software to obtain the real operation situation. It chiefly includes black box and white box testing. Every engineering product can choose one of the following ways to test:

1. Suppose the function specification of the product has been generated, whether each function complies with the requirements can be proved by testing.
2. Suppose the internal working process of the product has been determined, we can verify that each internal operation is in accordance with the designed requirements and guarantee all internal components have been inspected.

These two kinds of methods from different angels are both commonly used in testing. The former is black box testing and the latter is white box testing.

2.1.2 Black and white box testing

Black box testing is also known as functional and data-driven testing, considering system as a dark box. We only need to check whether the program functions meet the specification requirements while ignoring internal logic of the program. Testers are forbidden to use their knowledge of system internal structure or experience. The typical black box testing methods are equivalence partitioning, boundary value analysis and cause-and-effect diagram.

Black box testing mainly contributes to find a few kinds of mistakes[5]:

1. Incorrect functions or omitted functions;
2. Improper input and output;
3. Data structure error or access failure to external information (such as data files);
4. Poor performance compared with requirements;
5. Initialization or termination error.

White box testing, referred to structure testing and logic-driven test, regards test object as a transparent box, allowing testers designing and choosing test cases in the view of internal logical structure of the program and relevant information, and testing program logical paths. Through inspection of the program status at different states, testers can determine whether the real state is consistent with expected[6].

We can follow these steps to examine the program:

1. Test all independent execution paths in program modules at least one time;
2. For all logical judgments, test them at least one time in true and false conditions, respectively;
3. Execute the loop in the boundary of circulation and body;
4. Test the effectiveness of internal data structures, etc.

White box testing is an exhaustive path testing. In fact, the number of independent path running through the program is probably fabulous in amount, and it is difficult to traverse all paths. Even though we think each path has been tested and the coverage has reached 100%, the program still might be wrong.

White box testing methods comprise logical coverage, circulation coverage and basic path coverage test. Among them, logical coverage can be distributed into statement, decision, condition, decision/condition, condition combination and path coverage.

Besides white box and black box testing, there is another kind of test method-gray box testing. Just like black box testing, gray box testing is executed through the user interface. Moreover, testers must understand the design of the source code or relevant software functions, and even have already read part of the source code. Owning in-depth insight into the product internal design and thorough knowledge about it, testers can perform certain purposive condition/function tests and test its performance from the user interface more effectively.

2.2 Software testing type

The process of software system testing includes conducting unit test of software modules, assembling them for integration testing, combining the subsystems into software, and finally validating and verifying the system functions in the real environment according to the specification[7].

2.2.1 Unit testing

Unit testing inspects the correctness of program modules, aiming to find the errors possibly exist in each module by testing cases designed according to the program internal structure, which is the reason why we choose white box testing technology. For embedded software, it runs usually on host machine[8].

2.2.2 Integration testing

Integration testing is a system testing technology to detect errors associated with software interfaces after each module is integrated into subsystem or system according to the design requirements (e.g. structure diagram). Both white box testing and black box testing are used in this technology, and test cases are mostly built by black box testing. Integration testing usually executes in host environment similarly[9].

2.2.3 System testing

System testing contributes to discover the inconformity and contradictory between software and system definition by comparing with the system specification. The test object is the entire software system, including not only the software itself, but also the hardware/software environment it relies on. System testing needs to be performed on the target machine.

2.2.4 Acceptance testing

Acceptance testing is also known as validation testing. It is responsible for verifying the validity of the software, which means to verify whether the software function, performance and other properties are consistent with the user requirements. This testing usually adopts black box testing and commonly implements on the target machine[10].

3. Embedded software testing technology

Due to the characteristics of embedded system differing from the desktop system, the development and testing of embedded software is pretty different from commercial software. Developers still develop their own testing platform because of lack of available general tools. The following factors will influence the software testing:

a. Platform of application and development separation from operating;
b. Complexity and diversity of development platform;
c. Strict limit of hardware resource and development time;
d. Software and hardware developing concurrency, and modularization and hierarchy combination alternatively;
e. Lack of visual programming mode;
f. Ceaselessly upgrading of software quality requirements and certification standards because of business change.

3.1 Testing environment

Simulation is commonly used to test external devices in embedded software testing, which makes use of specific software or hardware simulation tools so as to simplify the testing environment. Simulation classifies into hardware simulation and software simulation. In embedded software testing, hardware simulation attempts to replace hardware and software by means of external equipments, which are identical to the target device in software interaction functions and fairly close performance. Software simulation is developing corresponding software to substitute for peripherals. The alternative software has the same software interaction function as target hardware, but their performance differs a lot[11].

3.1.1 Emulator

According to the difference between testing environment and real environment, embedded software simulation testing environment (ESSTE) can be distributed into full physical, semi physical and full digital simulation testing environment[12].

3.1.1.1 Full physical environment

The software is tested in the real physical simulation testing environment. The entire system (including hardware platform and embedded software) directly cross links with other physical equipments, forming a closed loop. It focuses on examining the interface between testing system and other interactive equipments. The requirements of testing environment are relatively low.

3.1.1.2 Semi-physical environment

Semi-physical simulation testing utilizes simulation model to emulate the linking equipments, and the testing system is actual. The linking environment of the system consists of hardware and software formed by input/output devices and their I/O interfaces, fulfilling closed-loop testing automatically, real-timely and non-intrusively. The emulator is required to simulate input and output of the real physical environment, and can drive the tested software to run preventing any other input and acquire the output results.

3.1.1.3 Full digital environment

Full digital simulation testing environment is a set of software system including simulated hardware and peripheral. It is established on the host machine with the combination of CPU control chip, I/O, terminal and clock simulation, providing a precise digital hardware environment model. Full digital simulation testing has the most complex requirements among these three kinds of test environment.

3.1.2 Cross-debug

Embedded software debugging has a great difference with general software. In common desktop operating system, the debugger and programs to be debugged are located at the same computer with the same operating system. For example, when we develop applications using Visual C++ in Windows platform, the debugger is an independent process, running and controlling the tested process via interfaces provided by the operating system. However, in embedded operating system, developing host and target locate at different machines. So we could adopt cross-testing to debug and test the program on target machine, and capture whether it receives test data normally.

Cross debug, also regarded as remote debug, means that the debugger runs on the desktop operating system of the host, and the tested program is executing on the embedded operating system of the target machine, respectively. Cross-debug allows debuggers control the operation mode of the process, examine and modify all kinds of variable values in memory unit, register and process on the target machine.

The communication between host and target machine can be realized through serial port or Ethernet port basis on TCP/IP protocol.

3.2 Testing tools

We can adopt general software testing techniques and tools for embedded software system testing, such as static and dynamic test techniques, and requirement analysis and static analysis tools. According to the research on embedded software testing, technical challenges still exist:

1. The poor commonality or even lack of testing tool that fits some certain area.
2. Inability to visualize the software execution procedure because of instruction pipeline, dynamic reset, cache, etc.

3. Waste of time to correct problems that can be prevented formerly, such as memory allocation error.

4. Failure to confirm the testing validity. The testing accuracy is sensory evaluated, so we do not know which tests are valid and which are not[13].

Nevertheless, the use of test tools is necessary. At present time, software plays an important role in embedded system. The testing stress occurs because of the rapid development of software itself and great pressure in transaction cost, the complexity of software functions and the shortage of development time. Moreover, systematized testing becomes inaptitude for meeting the requirements independently in a short period of time. Therefore, we must use test tools such as CodeTest so as to ensure the progress and quality of testing.

Currently, the testing tools of embedded software can be divided into software testing tools, hardware testing tools, and combination tools of software and hardware[14]. The principle, advantages and disadvantages of these kinds of testing tools are described as follows.

3.2.1 Software testing tools

Software testing mostly adopts software simulation, which is to simulate the target machine in the host, making the majority of the test can be done in the simulated host. Most of the embedded testing tools use this technology, including LogiScope by Telelogic and Coverage Scope from Wind River.

Host/Target software testing tools use instrumentation technology[15], inserting some functions or statements in the test code to generate data and send them to the shared memory of target system. In the meantime, a task is running in target system to preprocess data and convert them to the host platform through the debug port by target processor. In this way, testers are able to learn the current running state of the program.

However, instrumentation functions and preprocessing tasks inevitably exist and will increase the system code and reduce the efficiency of the system by more than 50%. Preprocessing occupies the resource of CPU time, shared memory, and communication channels of the target system to complete data processing and transmission. Besides, large amounts of instrumentations will affect system operation during coverage analysis. Therefore, software testing tools based on Host/Target lack of performance analysis because they are unable to analysis functions in the target system and run time of the tasks accurately. They also fail to observe memory allocation dynamically.

3.2.2 Hardware testing tools

Multimeter, oscilloscope and logic analyzer are used not only in hardware design and testing, but also in software testing. Among these tools, the logic analyzer is the most commonly-used. It can be acquainted with the working status of the system and the current condition of the program by the means of monitoring system instruction cycle on bus, capturing these signals in certain frequency and analyzing these data. Whereas some important signals will be inevitably lost because of the way it works by sampling, and it can merely analyze limited functions. So it is really difficult to come to satisfactory results.

Meanwhile, hardware tool has no ability of analyzing and checking memory allocation[16] because hardware tools capture data from system bus when doing coverage analysis. For example, when Cache opens, the system will adopt the instruction prefetch technology to read a section of code from the auxiliary storage into L1 Cache. Once the logic analyzer has monitored signals that the codes have been read on bus, it will report that the code has been executed. However, the codes sent to the Cache may not be hit actually. To avoid this error, Cache must be closed out which means the system is not in real environment. More seriously, Cache off can lead to the system working disability.

3.2.3 Combination tools of software and hardware

The combination testing tools of software and hardware have inherited the respective advantages of software and hardware testing tools, abandoning their shortcomings at the same time. For instance, CodeTest, designed by Applied Microsystems Corporation (AMC) is a kind of high performance testing tool for embedded developers using instrumentation technology, applying for both native and in-circuit testing.

CodeTest inserts an assignment rather than instrumentation function as in software testing tools. It runs extremely rapidly while avoiding interrupted by other interrupts, so it has little effects on the target system and instrumentation processes. Meanwhile, it captures data on bus only when the program runs into an inserted special point by monitoring the system bus instead of fixed sampling. So it ensures precise data observation.

CodeTest provides the following functions:

1. Performance analysis;
2. Coverage analysis;
3. Dynamic memory allocation analysis;
4. Execution traces analysis.

Although the software instrumentation and bus data-capturing techniques have improved, the drawback that CodeTest depends on hardware is exposed. CodeTest must be customized for different signal acquisition probe and related data acquisition mechanism on different hardware platforms, which makes CodeTest poor in flexibility and portability. At the same time, this mechanism also greatly restricts the product adaptability to the market, increasing the cost and the development cycle for new products[17].

From the above analysis, we can find that one or more following technologies are used in various testing tools:

1. Part of the program has been pushed forward by inserting lots of "printf".
2. Software testing tool is a kind of simulation that it doesn't work in real system.
3. Target software testing tool runs on the same hardware platform with tested software at the same time, taking up resources of the testing system, such as CPU time and communication port.
4. Hardware testing tools, such as logic analyzer and simulator, cannot run in the Cache open mode.
5. Hardware-aided software tool, like CodeTest, is a real-time online testing system, available in the cache open mode and not occupying any resources on the target board.

Although some test tools have already led to a certain good results in some applications, these tools still fail to meet the requirements in specific applications because of the diversity of the embedded system. So it is difficult to form test solutions that fit all specific test cases.

4. Mobile phone software testing

This paper takes the testing of mobile phone contact module that locates in software system MMI (Man Machine Interface) layer as an example to research testing technology of embedded software.

The development of mobile phone software system uses sequential life cycle model, named V model[18], as shown in Fig.2.Correspondingly, testing must accompany with the development process of the project, as shown in Fig. 3. Therefore, test plan ought to be set down when development plan is being formulated; test case should also be prepared when the software requirements have been determined; moreover, when the project development is completed, it must be followed by the reports on test execution, progress and summary.

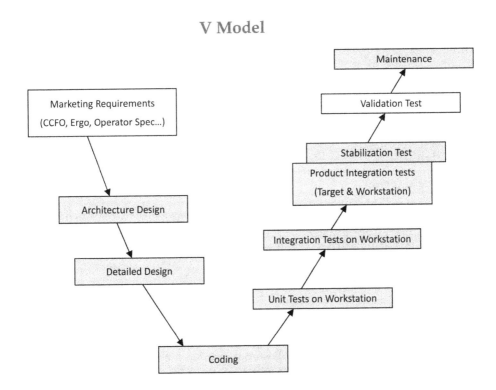

Fig. 2. V model

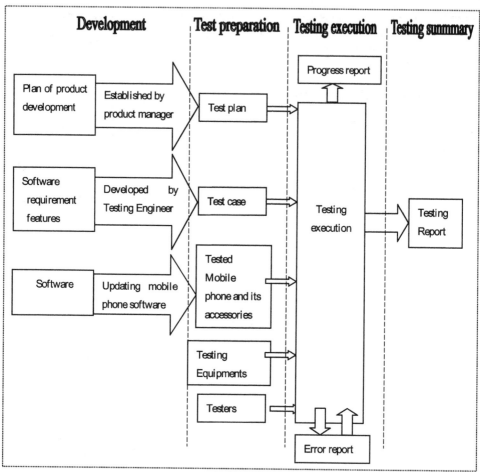

Fig. 3. Testing flow chart

Testing process must base on the overall project requirements to define, restrict and manage all the processes, activities and changes in the whole testing life cycle. Its critical function includes testing requirements extraction, test strategy and planning, test design, test execution and test result analysis.

This research uses TestLink[19] and Bugzilla[20] as management tools in the testing process.

4.1 Introduction to mobile phone operating system

Different from the general operating system and its variety functions, the purpose of embedded operating system is so definite and direct that it only works to resolve one or several functions. Mobile phones are required to satisfy the specific requirement of fast response time as communication tools, which is a typical real-time operating system. For instance, phone call should be answered in 90 seconds; otherwise it will be hung up.

Mobile phone operating system can be divided into two parts: one is the kernel, named Real-Time Executive (RTX); another is I/O. Since there is less demand for I/O in embedded system, the mobile phone operating system is essentially a real-time executive program to manage increasingly complex system resources and map hardware effectively, especially the growing embedded processors. Whatever embedded Micro Controller Unit (MCU), Embedded Micro Processor Unit (EMPU), Embedded Digital Signal Processor (EDSP) or highly-integrated System on Chip (SOC), the operating system can provide identical API interfaces, making developers get rid of busy with driver transplantation and maintenance. Moreover, it can also supply library functions, drivers, tool sets and applications, etc.

Compared with the common desktop operating systems, mobile phone operating system has distinctive features in storage space, tailorability and reliability[21]. Popular mobile phone platforms are Symbian, Windows Mobile, Linux, Palm, Apple, Google Android, and so on. In this research, we choose Google Android as our testing platform.

Android is an open source operating system based on Linux developed by Google, including all required software for mobile phone, such as operating system, user interface and applications, and without any proprietary obstacles that will hinder mobile phone innovation. The system uses WebKit browser engine, with the functions of touch screen, senior graphic display and Internet. Users can check emails, web search and watch video programs on the mobile phones.

Android system architecture as shown in Fig. 4 is separated into four layers, Linux kernel, system runtime libraries, application framework, and applications[22].

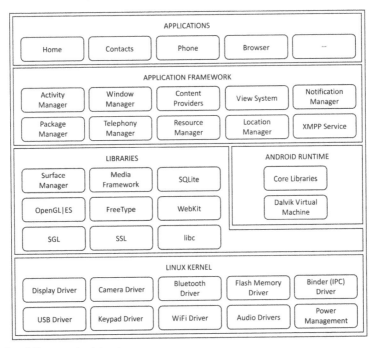

Fig. 4. Android System Architecture

4.1.1 Linux kernel

Android depends on Linux kernel 2.6 to provide core services, such as security, memory and process management, network protocol stack, and driver model. At the same time, the kernel can be served as the abstract layer between hardware and software stack.

4.1.2 System runtime libraries

Android contains a number of C/C++ libraries, which can be used in different components in Android system. They serve for developers via Android application framework. Besides, it includes a core library, called runtime library, providing most functions in programming language JAVA.

Each Android application program runs in its own process with an independent Dalvik virtual machine instance. Dalvik is designed to be a device that can run multiple virtual systems efficiently at the same time, relying on some Linux kernel functions, such as threading and memory management mechanism.

4.1.3 Application framework

Developers can access the API in the core application framework. This architecture simplifies the reuse of components, with each application can publish its functional blocks and others can use them under the security restriction. Similarly, the application reuse mechanism also allows users to replace the program components easily.

A series of services and systems are concealed in each application, they are:

1. Rich and expandable views, building applications including lists, grids, text boxes, buttons, and even embeddable web browser.
2. Content providers, allowing the application to access or share data with another application (such as contact database).
3. Resource manager, providing access to non-code resources, such as local strings, graphics, and layout files.
4. Notification manager, displaying custom message in status bar.
5. Activity manager, managing the life cycle of the application and navigation regression function.

4.1.4 Applications

Android can release a series of core application packages at one time, including Email clients, SMS short message program, calendar, maps, browser, and contact management programs. They are all written in language JAVA.

4.2 Test process management tools

4.2.1 TestLink

TestLink[19] works for managing testing process by managing test requirement, test design, and test execution. In the meantime, this tool also provides many kinds of statistics and analysis of test results, making them clearly.

TestLink, as one of the open source projects of Sourceforge, is a Web based management system. Its main functions include:

- Test requirement management;
- Test case management;
- Coverage management of test cases for test requirement;
- Test plan formulation;
- Test case execution;
- Measurements and statistics of large amounts of test data.

TestLink has following features:

- Supporting Web access, including Mozilla, Firefox, and IE browser;
- Product test in the test plan according to testing process;
- User can customize characters, such as test leader, tester etc.;
- Keywords are used to support profound test organization;
- Assigning testing to testers according to the priority and defining milestones;
- Providing test report;
- Exporting documents to HTML, WORD or Excel format;
- Sending out test report message directly;
- Localization and internationalization;
- Combining with general bug tracking system, such as Bugzilla, mantis and Jira etc.;
- Requirements management based on testing.

Use this tool to implement complete management of testing process, combining defect management tool—Bugzilla, can guarantee testing accomplish successfully.

4.2.2 Bugzilla

Bugzilla establishes a perfect defects recording and tracking architecture, including Bug report and solution, record query, and report forms generation automatically. The characteristics of the Bugzilla are shown as follows:

1. It is a tool based on Web with simple installation, convenient operation and safety management.
2. Bugzilla is propitious to explain bugs clearly. The system provides comprehensive and detailed report entry and generates standard bug report with the help of database management. There are also a large number of options and powerful query matching ability for bug statistic according to various condition combinations. When the error changes in its life cycle, developers, testers, and managers will receive dynamic information timely, allowing them to obtain and refer to its history during checking error state.
3. The Bugzilla system is flexible and occupies powerful configurable capacity. The tool can set different modules for software product and designate developers and testers, so it can send reports to assigned responsible person automatically. Besides, different groups and authorities can be set and divided to make users with different authorities can deal with bugs effectively. Distinguishing severity and priority can manage errors

from the initial report to the final solution, to ensure that the error will not be ignored while focusing on the errors with high priority and severity.

4. The tool can also notify relevant personnel by sending emails automatically. The latest dynamic information will be sent to the different person according to their responsibilities, promoting communications between testers and developers effectively.

So, the test process can start with the help of these two test tools.

4.3 Mobile phone software testing process

Testing process must systematically define, restrict, and manage all the processes, activities and changes in the testing life cycle, following a series of principles, methods, theories and demand of the project. The critical activities include test requirement extraction, test strategy and planning, test design, test execution, test result analysis, and so on. The test process mainly establish the main test plan, directive testing strategies and methods, partition priority, restrict milestone, effective organize test resources (test team, hardware and software environment, for instance), etc. based on project goals. And then, make certain test requirements, test object, test objectives and performance index. According to the test plan and test design, testers can work effectively, such as developing and designing test cases, selecting test tools, designing automatic test framework, writing automated test code, executing test, and finding and reporting defects, etc.

4.3.1 Test requirement

To evaluate software project success or not, we need to judge whether it has solved users' problem which is embodied as user requirements in software engineering. The carelessness in requirement phase may lead to large amounts of rework in software implementation. Statistics show that more than 50% of the system errors are due to wrong requirement or lack of requirement, more than 80% expense is spent in the tracking requirement error because of the intertwined and duplicated work in the tracking error process.

Test requirement analysis is the most important work in requirement analysis in V model, coping with users' original demands and software functional demands, and then decomposing the results reasonably. It targets at the entire product, concerning the whole product system level.

Product testing requirement analysis activities are divided into original requirement extraction and product testing analysis. First is to extract the original demand and analyze each of them using certain engineering method, then to generate the product test specification. There may be repetition and redundancy in the specification via different engineering methods, which could be regarded as initial test specification. Afterwards, it can be integrated according to the testing type and functional interaction.

There are two main requirements for testing phone book module in the phone software, one is SIM card and the other is mobile phone. And the SIM card phone book can be separated into AND (Abbreviated Dialing Numbers) and FAN (Fixed Dialing Numbers). All these phone records must comply with the international standards.

Now, we need to decompose and organize the product testing requirement on TestLink because a product can contain multiple test requirement specifications and a specification can contain multiple test requirements.

1. Create test specification. To simply describe the test requirement, including name and scope.
2. Create requirement. Test requirement includes requirement ID, name, scope, state, and the cases for requirement coverage. TestLink provides two kinds of state to manage requirements: valid and not testable.
3. Import test requirements from file. TestLink makes the possibility of importing requirements from files whose types are CSV and CSV (door).

So, the test requirements can be formed and created.

4.3.2 Test plan analysis and design

Professional testing must be on the basis of a good test plan. Although each step in the test is independent, a test plan is of necessity which is the initiative step and the architecture to link the whole testing process.

Preparing test plan can add opportunities of discussion and communication in the project team. After collecting sufficient information of project, function, state, and performance by group chat, we can confirm the goal of the test plan in the review meeting, including function, performance and schedule goals and so on. So, we can carry the work forward toward a common goal. Otherwise, the team often puts a premium on details in the later phase of testing which will even deviate from the original target finally.

Test plan consists of many contents, from test methods to all individual test cases (referred to test set or test package) which will be used in real testing. In this project, we can distribute test plan into two parts: one is test plan mainly about the plan content; the other is a specific test case document, namely test package.

A detailed test plan needs to elucidate the testing scope, software and hardware resources, staffing, entry and exit criteria, test method, scheduling, major milestone, bug tracking, and version management, etc. In TestLink, it comprises:

1. Name of the testing stage, such as integration test stage and system test stage.
2. Milestone identifies the beginning and end time of each test stage, and implements the ratio of three priorities which are A, B, and C.
3. Build version defines the version to be tested in this test plan, generally named as "product name + time".
4. Test participants arrange test participants through selecting personnel from users list, shown as Fig.5.
5. Test case set.

Establish rules of priority. The system will determine the priority grade in the light of the combination of custom importance and risk levels which refer to Low, Medium, High and 1, 2, 3, respectively.

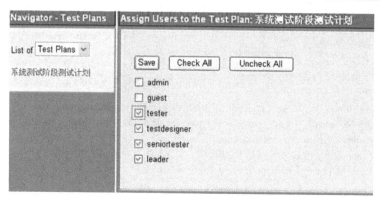

Fig. 5. Selecting test participants in TestLink

- Select test case sets of this test plan from test cases.
- Define the importance level and risk level of each test case Category.
- Assign the ownership of each test case Category. The owner is selected from the list of responsible tester and the tester will complete the test cases execution.

So test plan is required to write at length for later reference. Along with the refinement of the test requirements, we could clarify the test plan and pay more attention on the following contents, as shown in Fig.6.

```
⊞ 2.3.1  PBK_SIM_INIT Tests Family
⊞ 2.3.2  PBK_ADN_DIR Tests Family
⊞ 2.3.3  PBK_FDN_DIR Tests Family
⊞ 2.3.4  PBK_ME_DIR Tests Family
⊞ 2.3.5  PBK_ALL_DIR Tests Family
⊞ 2.3.6  PBK_RESTRIC_DIR Tests Family
⊞ 2.3.7  PBK_PERSO_DIR Tests Family
⊞ 2.3.8  PBK_THUMBNAILS_DIR Tests Family
⊞ 2.3.9  PBK_NEWCASE_TST Tests Family
⊞ 2.3.10 PBK_FAVORITE_NEWCASE_TST test family
⊞ 2.3.11 PBK_MOSTCALLED _NEWCASE_TST
⊞ 2.3.12 CR & Critical Cases from PR test family
⊞ 2.3.13 PBK_ROBUST_CASES _FAMILY
⊞ 2.3.14 PBK_MAXIMUM_CASES _FAMILY
```

Fig. 6. Test plan in TestLink

4.3.3 Test case design and implementation

We can design detailed test case after test plan has accomplished and passed the review. If there is no test case or only a simple test function description, testing will become difficult to control and test results will be poor in reliability. In addition, simple test cases with poor reliability and reusability may produce ambiguity and errors in the test execution stage, which is extremely adverse to the test result. Hence only detailed test cases can guarantee high reliability, the convenience to estimate the execution time, and the ease of control.

Designing test cases should account for a basis, a purpose and a basic idea. The fundamental base is the requirement specification. For system test cases, testers should design the cases strictly according to the user requirement specification to ensure that they are in line with the requirements. For integration test cases, both software or user requirement specification can be applied as bases to design. The main purpose of designing test case is to make the case simple to be understood. That is to say test case should be in detail enough for any person, including the fresh man, to start testing quickly. The basic idea—one point more cases, means tester could build multiple test cases corresponding to one test or functional point. All test cases design run through these three factors.

Test case management supported by TestLink consists of three layers: Component, Category, and Test case. Component corresponds to the project function modules and each module is linked with Category where Test cases are written. We could use search function to find the required test cases from different projects and thousands of test cases, and even copy test cases directly from other projects. These would help us solve the problem of test case management and reusability.

In test management, testers are deeply concerned about the test case coverage to the test requirements. However, the correspondence between them keeps still unsolved. TestLink provides function of managing their corresponding relationship after test requirements are extracted from specification.

1. Create component: component consists of name, introduction, scope, relevant content, and constraint.
2. Create category: category contains name, test scope and goal, configuration information, test data, and test tools.
3. Create test case: case elements include test case name, brief description, steps, expected results, and keywords.

Fig.7 presents a test case tree in TestLink. For one test case, select the corresponding requirement to assign, their coverage relationship establishes. The ultimate test case spanning tree is shown in Fig. 8.

4.3.4 Testing process

After testing preparation has been well done and the first version of the software has been published, test group could begin testing according to the test plan and schedule. In addition, due to time pressure, we usually appropriately optimize and select the testing content during the test execution process in order to reduce the workload, achieving test purpose as well. Then we execute test cases and record the execution situation of each build edition using one of the following four kinds of test results:

1. Not Run: unexecuted;
2. Pass: execution successes;
3. Failed: execution fails;
4. Blocked: the test case cannot perform due to other failed cases.

TestLink provides abundant measuring statistical functions according to the recorded data in testing process, allowing testers acquire the data to be analyzed and summarized directly during the test management process:

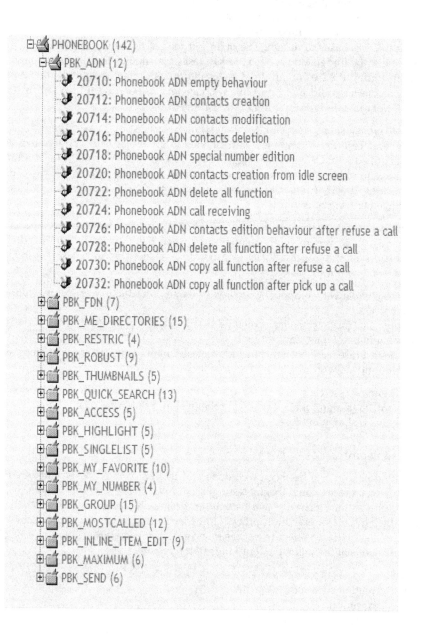

Fig. 7. Test case tree

```
⊟2.3 Test case
  ⊟2.3.1 PBK_SIM_INIT Tests Family
      2.3.1.1 PBK_SIM_INIT_ 01 (RFG_prio_3)
      2.3.1.2 PBK_SIM_INIT_ 02 (RFG_prio_3)
      2.3.1.3 PBK_SIM_INIT_ 03 (RFG_prio_2)
      2.3.1.4 PBK_SIM_INIT_ 04 (RFG_prio_2)
  ⊟2.3.2 PBK_ADN_DIR Tests Family
      2.3.2.1 PBK_ADN_DIR_01 (RFG_prio_3)
      2.3.2.2 PBK_ADN_DIR_02 (RFG_prio_1)
      2.3.2.3 PBK_ADN_DIR_03 (RFG_prio_2)
      2.3.2.4 PBK_ADN_DIR_04 (RFG_prio_2)
      2.3.2.5 PBK_ADN_DIR_05 (RFG_prio_2)
      2.3.2.6 PBK_ADN_DIR_06 (RFG_prio_2)
      2.3.2.7 PBK_ADN_DIR_07 (RFG_prio_2)
      2.3.2.8 PBK_ADN_DIR_08 (RFG_prio_2)
      2.3.2.9 PBK_ADN_DIR_09 (RFG_prio_2)
      2.3.2.10 PBK_ADN_DIR_10 (RFG_prio_2)
      2.3.2.11 PBK_ADN_DIR_11 (RFG_prio_2)
      2.3.2.12 PBK_ADN_DIR_12 (RFG_prio_2)
  ⊟2.3.3 PBK_FDN_DIR Tests Family
      2.3.3.1 PBK_FDN_DIR_01 (RFG_prio_2)
      2.3.3.2 PBK_FDN_DIR_02 (RFG_prio_2)
      2.3.3.3 PBK_FDN_DIR_03 (RFG_prio_2)
      2.3.3.4 PBK_FDN_DIR_04 (RFG_prio_2)
      2.3.3.5 PBK_FDN_DIR_05 (RFG_prio_2)
      2.3.3.6 PBK_FDN_DIR_06 (RFG_prio_2)
  ⊟2.3.4 PBK_ME_DIR Tests Family
      2.3.4.1 PBK_ME_DIR_01 (RFG_prio_2)
      2.3.4.2 PBK_ME_DIR_02 (RFG_prio_2)
      2.3.4.3 PBK_ME_DIR_03 (RFG_prio_2)
      2.3.4.4 PBK_ME_DIR_04 (RFG_prio_2)
      2.3.4.5 PBK_ME_DIR_05 (RFG_prio_2)
      2.3.4.6 PBK_ME_DIR_06 (RFG_prio_2)
      2.3.4.7 PBK_ME_DIR_07 (RFG_prio_2)
      2.3.4.8 PBK_ME_DIR_08 (RFG_prio_2)
      2.3.4.9 PBK_ME_DIR_09 (RFG_prio_2)
      2.3.4.10 PBK_ME_DIR_10 (RFG_prio_2)
      2.3.4.11 PBK_ME_DIR_11 (RFG_prio_2)
      2.3.4.12 PBK_ME_DIR_12 (RFG_prio_2)
```

Fig. 8. Ultimate test case spanning tree

1. The requirement coverage: including which requirements have passed the test and which have not, which are in blocked state, and which testing has not yet begun.
2. The test case execution results of each version:
   - The ratio of test case execution with various priorities;
   - The ratio of test case execution for each module;
   - The ratio of test case execution for each tester.
3. The execution result of each version.
4. The execution situation of all test cases in different versions.
5. The list of blocked test cases.
6. The list of failed test cases.
7. The bug report in testing. If combined with bug tracking system, the tool can also statistic the number of bugs in each test case.

When there are blocked and failed tests, we need software patches and new software version to achieve the final effect on mobile phone.

4.3.5 Software defect management

During test process, testers will find a lot of bugs (also called problem, defect, or error), fault and other content that hard to record on paper. It is unrealistic and extremely unfavorable to attempt to use human brains or a document to remember or record all the mistakes, because this would hinder effective contact between the test team, programmers, other developers and the project management team, which is very negative for improving product quality and working efficiency. Therefore, there is a need for an effective method to track a series of state of each error from beginning to end. The seamless combination between TestLink and Bugzilla (shown in Fig. 9) will make bug easier to manage.

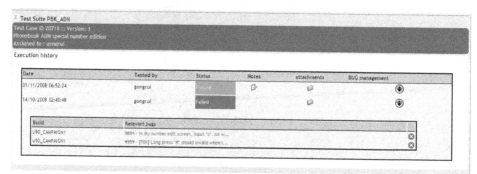

Fig. 9. The combination of TestLink and Bugzilla

a. Once testers or developers find bug, they will judge which module does the error belong to, then they will fill in the bug report, notifying the project leader or developers by emails.
b. The project leader reassigns the task to the developer who is responsible for the bug.
c. After the developer receives Email information and determine whether the bug should be revised by him. If not, he will reassign it to the project leader or the one ought to fulfill it; if yes, then he is required to resolve it and get the solution by creating patch attachment and supplementary specification.
d. After bugs have been modified by developers, testers will perform test again, creating test case attachment. If the tester verifies the test case to be correct, the state will be set to "VERIFIED". When the entire product has been released, the state should be updated to "CLOSED". If there are still problems existing, the tester needs to change the state back to "REOPENED" and email for notification.
e. If the bug keeps unprocessed in one week, Bugzilla will use email to harass its owner until he take actions[23].

Nice error tracking system requires misattributions and stakeholders record history log of the error report in order to capture those important events in the wrong life cycle process, which means testers, developers, project managers and other relevant person need add their logs to the error report, especially the changes. For instance, when developer has modified a bug and he or she needs to set the state to 'review the test case', and add log to explain the revision content. It can facilitate technical experts' review and supply technical clues for acceptance testing. When developers and project manager consider a certain error report as invalid and need to change the case state into invalid, there is a must to add log demonstrating the reason as much detail as possible, making testers understand and agree the modification easily. Otherwise, testers will still resubmit the error, leading to unnecessary circulation. When the project manager or developers think that a certain bug report needs delay processing, the reason for the delay should be explained in logs so that others can re-examine this error report clearly later, etc. Obviously, the log information is of great importance not only to the project manager, but also to the developer and tester. However, in many projects, part of the team members are not accustomed to writing logs, instead, they just click the button and change the case state. They do not recognize that a few more operations on log can benefit a lot.

In our project, we suggest choose good tool which is complete in functions to work as our bug tracking system. The more comprehensive functions and higher automation degree the tool has, the better it will support the work flow. To take ClearQuest as an example, when changes of the error state occur, the tool can be set to automatically send an email to the stakeholders, notifying the relevant personnel to timely cope with the mistakes or abstracting their attention.

Of course, process automation is only half of the process. Each member of the project team, project manager and test manager must conscientiously carry out their duties, ensuring that each error report go through the life cycle and reached the final state quickly. This is the key of guaranteeing the project progress and quality.

4.3.6 Test case maintenance

No matter how well the test case design and review performs, there are always loopholes in test system. Budget and time pressure, along with human error, will result in incomplete test. Some test cases miss the conditions they ought to cover, some test packages do not contain important test case, or some procedure faults of test case can lead to the wrong purpose of testing. Therefore, test case maintenance, or so-called incremental improvement, is an indispensable step in testing process. If the requirement changes, such as increasing or modifying certain demand, there is also need for upgrading test cases.

The maintenance and upgrading of test case is a necessary long-term work. It can not only deal with errors in the test case, reducing the occurrence of incomplete tests, but also learn from test omission and summarize, providing an experience for next test case design, which will definitely turns to less incomplete test or case error. Its critical part lies in when to be modified and which to be increased. Case upgrading is simple that as long as there is a notification of changing requirement, the test manager could arrange relevant personnel to modify corresponding test cases. The maintenance is relatively elastic for two reasons. The first is that it depends on the tester's consciousness which is associated with their self-quality. Once tester discovers that the test result differs from expected and confirms the inconformity does not arise from bug, or he finds incomplete, error, or uncovered case, he needs to timely inform the case author and test manager. Secondly, the maintenance also relies on test manager's supervision. The manager has the responsibility to check whether the problems occurred in test execution are all covered by test cases, if not, he needs to arrange new test cases.

We recommend a method usually used in project development, named derived case method, for test mangers. Test manager can inspect error tracking database weekly or daily and check the existing test package to ensure that each problem has a test case to cover. If it is found that some problems have no corresponding test cases, the test manager needs to arrange related personnel to add cases and certain derivation, which means to consider other related cases according to the new case.

Some questions found by developers instead of testers in bug tracking database will result in lack of test cases with the testing steps designed by testers. On the other hand, sometimes problems are found when testers are performing random testing that the testing itself is very casual and without strict steps. In this case, we could draw out these problems as a new test case to design, write and verify.

Using above method to improve and maintain test cases absolutely leads to more and more abundant contents of test package. The coverage goes wider and the quantity of test cases will correspondingly become larger, which makes setting priorities for these cases extremely important. Derivation cases also need to specify the priority and pass the review. Otherwise, it will probably bring about the waste of labor force or testing omission due to too high or too low priority.

5. Testing results analysis and suggestions

The research mainly targets on mobile phone software testing on account of its characteristics. In terms of the software testing theory and methods, we divide test plan and execution into six phases: test requirement analysis, test plan analysis and design, test case design and implementation, test execution and results, test software defect management, and test case maintenance analysis. In the meantime, multiple testing strategies are applied to guarantee the correctness and feasibility of these test processes. The experience in each stage of the test is summarized as follows.

5.1 Test requirement analysis

Requirement analysts must keep in mind that users cannot give complete, clear, and standardized demands at a draught. Instead, they will continue coordinating and regulating the requirements. The analysts need to constantly dig and regulate the demands to acquire user desired requirements. So, we recommend the following ways to collect and coordinate requirements.

5.1.1 Data

Data is static information related to the requirements and described from the user perspective. In the system design process, they are managed and standardized using object-oriented method, forming Class Diagram.

5.1.2 Activity

Activity is the business logic and rules the project has to meet. It comprises at least two levels:

- Basic goal: briefly describing the business logic and rules.
- Function description: representing the execution process, as well as the relevant resources, association, dependencies, and constraints. On account of the consistency of the requirements analysis and system design, activities in system design phase can be expressed by use cases and refined by sequence diagram, activity diagram and state diagram.

5.1.3 Personnel organization

Personnel organization describes the structure of personnel, such as enterprise leaders, departments, department personnel, related customer information, and so on.

In addition, there are some popular requirement analysis software, such as IBM's RequisitePro, Telelogic's DOORS, and Borland's CaliberRM. They occupy different characteristics which can meet the demands of functional requirement analysis.

To summarize, requirement analysis is a team work, and relevant commercial products can be adopted under the guidance of requirement analysis theory.

5.2 Analysis and design of test plan

Good software test plan takes various factors into account. The following is what we need to pay attention to in this process.

Firstly, clarify the test purpose. The test goal must be clear, measurable and quantifiable rather than an ambiguous macroscopical description. In addition, the goal should be relatively concentrated and a series of targets should be avoided. Because it will probably make us emphasize on trivial goals while ignoring those of great importance. Besides, making efforts to fulfill every target will cost a waste. According to the analysis of user requirement document and design specification, we could determine the software quality requirements and the goal need to achieve. Moreover, there are also other demands in test plan, including high coverage of functional requirements, effective test methods, testing tools that are easy to use, intuitionistic and accurate test results, etc.

Secondly, the real-timing of test plan. Test plan comprises many contents and may be restricted by testers' experience and degree of understanding software requirements. Software development is an incremental process, so it is possible that the initial test plan is not perfect and still needs to be improved. When a new requirement generates or omission has been found in test execution process, testers should timely update the test plan.

Finally, explicate the test process and content. Test plan, as the architecture and guide of the test, should give a detailed description about the test content and process, highlighting the critical points in tested content by listing the key and risk content, attributes, scene, and testing technology. Besides, practical methods should be applied in partition of testing process stages, document, bug, and schedule management.

Only meet the three above-mentioned characteristics of the test plan can we satisfy the basic needs of the project. In establishing mobile phone testing plans, we are also required specialized document for detailed test plan due to the limitation of TestLink.

5.3 Test case design

There are three layers of test case management supported by TestLink in the project: Component, Category, and Test case. The Component corresponds to the project function module, with its functions corresponding to Category where Test cases are written. In addition, TestLink can also provide the assignment between requirements and test cases. This guarantees the integrity and reusability of test case design in essence.

With the excellent test case management of TestLink, we need to pay attention to the following aspects:

5.3.1 Cross test case

Cross test is of great significance in mobile phone as a multi-task system with different priority levels because of their various functional orientations. For example, making phone calls and sending short messages occupy higher priority than any other applications. As a result, the priority order and division of different tasks appears to be particularly critical in mobile phone design. Meanwhile, the phone, as a communication device, can receive messages from the outside world at any moment, such as calls, short messages, third-party Bluetooth connection requests, and so on. These events undoubtedly will affect the running tasks, i.e. games and media playback. When a new event approaches, the system needs to make correct response. Therefore, cross test between different applications plays a primly important role in mobile phone software system testing.

5.3.2 Robust test

Compared with general application software, embedded software requires higher on reliability, which makes robust test essential. For instance, keyboard keys, memory fill, and read and write test of phone book are all in need of repeatability extreme test to ensure their stability.

5.4 Analysis of test results and version management

TestLink, providing abundant measuring statistical functions according to the recorded data in the testing process, can directly acquire the data to be analyzed and summarized in the test management process as long as each build version is guaranteed, and cases could be completely executed and verified constantly in the new version.

It is necessary to analyze the ultimate execution results of the test cases. If failed or blocked cases exist, we need to use software patches or new software version to execute the cases over and over again. Mobile phone software usually needs a dozen of versions to ensure its stable. During this process, bugs are required to timely submit to Bugzilla for management.

5.5 Defect management

Software defect is a by-product in the process of software development, even leading to software products failure to fulfill the needs of customers to some extent. Whether software testers can express the severity and priority of the bug accurately not only has an effect on the quality of software defect management, but also possibly influences the time of treating bugs. Especially in the later testing period, it will affect if the software can release on time. The standard of classification should refer to the customers' demand, which means to classify the severity in terms of whether the users can accept this defect or not.

Bugzilla is utilized in managing defects, identifying the defect severity and priority by P0, P1, and P2. Among them, the partition of the three priorities relies on three indicators the probability of defect reproduction × the extent to influence customers × customer satisfaction. Only strictly divided priority in accordance with such criteria can we guarantee the rationality of defect severity classification.

The generation of bugs will definitely be accompanied by software patch release. However, it is often seen that old patch causes new defects in projects. To avoid this situation, validating the software patch carefully and considering its influence synthetically seems to be particularly significant. And developers could also mutually supervise each other, establishing good mechanism to prevent this kind of bug.

Automation tools and history logs of the error report are very important for a good error tracking system.

5.6 Maintenance and analysis of test cases

During test execution phase, the test manager is often on the wing executing tests and bug tracking so that he possibly ignores the case maintenance. In this project, we recommend derived case method for test manager examine bug tracking database every week or every day. If some problems are found not corresponded to test case, the manager should ask concerned personnel to add cases and do certain derivation, that is, to think over other related cases on account of the new case. For the problems submitted by developers or random testing which result in lack of test cases, the manager could draw out them as a new function test case to deal with.

6. Conclusion

Along with the acceleration of information society, personal mobile communication has increasingly become so popular that the number of mobile phone users grows rapidly, with diversified requirement and high quality. However, the research on mobile phone software testing and testing tools are quite rare in view of the particularity of its testing platform.

This chapter has made a systematic and detailed study on the mobile phone software testing process. In addition, using software engineering theories combined with actual projects, we have assessed experience and lessons, and put forward some improved practical methods. The contribution includes making requirement analysis methods, test plans and test scheme, designing and executing test cases, analyzing test results, selecting and using test tools, and so on.

Our later work will primarily focus on studying test tools as well as white box testing methods. We hope that, with the increasingly maturity of science and technology, we could become capable of doing further in-depth research on testing tools, especially in automation testing tools, accomplishing more effective automation rather than simple button simulation. Only with an efficient testing tool can testers guarantee the software quality. Moreover, studying on white box testing methods and tools are recommended in order to increase test coverage and expand test range.

7. Acknowledgment

This work was supported by Natural Science Foundation of China (61021004, 81101119), and the National High Technology Research and Development Program of China (2011AA010101863).

8. References

[1] Kang Y.; Zhang Y.; Li Z.; Hu .; Hu W. (2008). *Testing Embedded Software*, China Machine Press , Beijing

[2] Hawkins J.; Howard R. B.; Nguyen. H. V (2002). *Automated real-time testing for embedded control system*, IEEE 2002: 647-652.

[3] IEEE, *IEEE Standard for Software Test Documentation*. IEEE Std 829-1998.

[4] Park C.Y.(1997). Predicting Program Execution Times by Analyzing Static and Dynamic Program Paths. Real Time Systems. 1997, 13(1): 67-91.

[5] Gu L.; Shi J.L. (2004). *An introduction to software testing technology*, Qinghua University Press, Beijing

[6] Myers C.J., Revised and Updated by Tom Badgett and Todd M.Thomas with Corey Sandler(2004). *The Art of Software Testing(Second Edition)*, John Wiley&Sons Inc, Hoboken, NewJersey: 14-20.

[7] Lin N.; Meng Q.(2005). *Practical guide to software testing*Qinghua University Press, Beijing

[8] Hatton L.(2004). *Embedded System Paranoia:a tool for testing embedded system arithmetic.* Information and Software Technology, 47(2005)555-563, 2004.10.

[9] School of Computer and Information Science, University of South Australia. *Software Testing*, Available from: http://www.sweforum.net/test/softwaretesting.pdf. 2002.2.

[10] Pressman R. S.(2007). *Software Engineering: A Practitioner's Approach*. China Machine Press, Beijing

[11] Chen Y.; Li M.; Yang Y.(2004). *Open source embedded system software analysis and practice - based on SkyEye and ARM development platform*, Beihang University Press, Beijing

[12] Zhang H.; Ruan L. (2002). *A study on the Simulation Modeling for Embedded Software Testing*, Measurement and control technology

[13] Zhang L. (2005). Structural Testing Technology for Embedded Computer System Software. *Ship Electronic Engineering*, 2005, (3): 63-64.

[14] Wan K.; Lu Q. L.; Peng Y. L.(2001). Study and Realization of the Chain Method for Testing Examples Automatic Building. *Journal of Armored Force Engineering Institute*, 2001,Vol.15, No.3: 55-58.

[15] Sun C.; Jin M. (2001). Program Instrumentation Approach to Implementing Software Dynamic Testing. *Journal of Chinese Computer Systems*, 2001, 22(12): 1475-1479.

[16] Sun C.; Le L.; Liu C.; Jin M. (2000). Test technology of real-time and embedded software. *Journal of Chinese Computer Systems*, 2000.9, 21(9), 920-924.

[17] Zhang X. (2006). Chinese embedded software industry development report. *Software World*. 2006.5.

[18] Brian Marick. Analysis of V model problem. Available from http://tech.ccidnet.com/art/1086/20030225/38813_1.html. 2003.2.

[19] TestLink User Manual.version1.8. Available from http://testlink.sourceforge.net/docs/testLink.php.2009.4.

[20] The Bugzilla Team. The Bugzilla Guide - 3.3.4 Development Release. Available from http://www.bugzilla.org/docs/3.4/en/pdf/Bugzilla-Guide.pdf. 2009.

[21] Lin X. (2006). Research on mobile phone software testing. Master degree thesis. Tonji University. 2006.

[22] Developers.What is Android. Available from http://developer.android.com/guide/basics/what-is-android.html.

[23] Meng Y.; Liu Z. F. (2005). The experience and practice of bug management (2rd) how to set up the bug management system. *Programmer*. 2005(2)

5

Supporting Inclusive Design of Mobile Devices with a Context Model

Pierre T. Kirisci et al.*

Universität Bremen (BIK, TZI),
Germany

1. Introduction

The aim of inclusive product design is to successfully integrate a broad range of diverse human factors in the product development process with the intention of making products accessible to and usable by the largest possible group of users (Kirisci, Thoben et al. 2011). However, the main barriers for adopting inclusive product design include technical complexity, lack of time, lack of knowledge and techniques, and lack of guidelines (Goodman, Dong et al. 2006), (Kirisci, Klein et al. 2011). Although manufacturers of consumer products are nowadays more likely to invest efforts in user studies, consumer products in general only nominally fulfill, if at all, the accessibility requirements of as many users as they potentially could. The main reason is that any user-centered design prototyping or testing aiming to incorporate real user input, is often done at a rather late stage of the product development process. Thus, the more progressed a product design has evolved - the more time-consuming and costly it will be to alter the design (Zitkus, Langdon et al. 2011). This is increasingly the case for contemporary mobile devices such as mobile phones or remote controls.

The number of functions and features on these products requiring user attention and interaction has increased significantly as illustrated in **Fig. 1**. Thus, the impact on end users with mild-to-moderate physical or sensory impairments is that they often have difficulties when interacting with such kind of products. These difficulties could be anticipated and avoided if acknowledged earlier in the development process.

Additionally, typical use-cases for interacting with mobile devices include a wide range of environments which they may be used in. The mobile phone in order to cope with these

*Klaus-Dieter Thoben[1], Patrick Klein[1], Martin Hilbig[1], Markus Modzelewski[1], Michael Lawo[1], Antoinette Fennell[2], Joshue O'Connor[2], Thomas Fiddian[3], Yehya Mohamad[4], Markus Klann[4], Thomas Bergdahl[5], Haluk Gökmen[6] and Edmilson Klen[7]

[1]*Universität Bremen (BIK, TZI), Germany*
[2]*National Council for the Blind of Ireland (NCBI), Ireland*
[3]*RNID, UK*
[4]*Fraunhofer FIT, Germany*
[5]*DORO AB, Sweden*
[6]*Arcelik A.S., Turkey*
[7]*Universidade Federal de Santa Catarina, Brazil*

use cases, must be 'dynamic' or responsive. Dynamic means the device will have the ability to cope with a changing environment and user requirements during the completion of any given activity: e.g. writing a text message on a mobile phone while walking from an indoor into an outdoor environment, or dealing with changes in noise, light, glare, etc. The impact of factors such as location, mobility, and social and physical environments, further increases the level of comprehension and attention needed to operate the device. Accordingly, the features and capabilities of the mobile device should take the context of use into account, and appropriately support and facilitate ease-of-use. With this wide range of possible situations, the features and capabilities of the mobile device should be in line with the needs of the user, in order to support device interaction in a responsive way.

Fig. 1. Some examples of mobile devices (mobile phone from 1998 vs. modern smart phone) highlighting the difference in the amount of user interface elements.

Often it is difficult for the product manufacturers and designers to easily implement such contextual support into existing functions of mobile devices, even if they have awareness of the varieties of context of use as well as an understanding of the requirements of user groups with impairments (e.g. physical, vision, hearing or dexterity). And even though a wide variety of tools and methods exist to support e.g. user-centered design in general, they often fail to implement those needs into the user interfaces of the products. As such, a majority of existing consumer products only partially fulfil the accessibility requirements of impaired users. The reason for this situation is relatively easy to explain: as there is a lack of supportive functions in design tools such as Computer Aided Design applications, which would promote context-related design of products by default and enable the designer to understand where there is an error in their design and how to fix it.

2. Challenge

A major challenge lies in defining an appropriate technique which can secure inclusive design of consumer products while integrating with existing design tools and frameworks. If this technique is based upon the use of an "inclusive model", then there is a need for a well-defined context model which incorporates all aspects related to the user, the environment and her/his intended interactions. From the research perspective the challenge may be seen as elaborating an advanced context model which is valid for settings where mobile devices are typically used, and can be consulted for specifying, analysing and evaluating mobile devices such as mobile phones as well as other mobile devices with similar interaction paradigms. Addressing these challenges, this chapter explores the potential of model-based semantic reasoning support for achieving inclusive design of user interfaces of mobile consumer products. A sophisticated context model which is considered and called "Virtual User Model" has been developed for this purpose, and represents the main contextual aspects of potential user groups – namely their profiles, tasks and environments. It shall be demonstrated, that through the usage of logical rules and constraints (which are based upon expert knowledge gained from an observational study), and semantic reasoning techniques (i.e. semantic reasoning engine), the conceptual design of a mobile phone (as representing mobile consumer products) can qualitatively and quantitatively be supported by providing easy to use add-on modules to common design/development applications.

3. Related work

This section provides an overview of related work regarding methods and tools, which are from the view of the authors suitable for inclusive product development and especially applied in the conceptual phases of product development: sketch, design, and evaluation. Most tools and methods introduced in this section are based upon the usage of some kind of conceptual models. Due to the near affinity to model-based approaches, an overview of related work regarding the usage of Virtual User Models along the product development process is initially presented here.

3.1 Virtual user models

One promising practice for realizing inclusive product design is to employ virtual user models (VUM) (Kirisci, Thoben et al. 2011). Virtual user models have the potential of complementing real tests with real users in the early design stages, while a VUM can be seen as an abstract representation of a human's behaviour (Kirisci, Klein et al. 2011). Virtual User Models are three-dimensional, model-like images or avatars and usually contain the following functions: (1) Human body modelling and analysis (2) Animation of virtual users (3) Interaction of virtual users with virtual objects (VICON-Consortium 2010). Nowadays virtual user models are widely used for ergonomic analysis in vehicle and workplace design within the automotive or aerospace industry. They are used to validate the design in a simulation environment, check in an iterative loop if the design is suitable, refine it considering recommendations and best practices and finally, when found suitable produce a prototype to be checked by end users as shown in **Fig. 2**. For the sketch phase static models of the user are plied, while during the design phase virtual user models of humans can have the notion of three-dimensional human models. The usage of virtual user models for a continuous support of sketch, design and evaluation phases can be considered as unique (Kirisci, Klein et al. 2011). Thus, contemporary approaches where virtual user models are utilized are only partially suitable for inclusive design. With respect to this background it is of particular interest to explore how virtual user models are capable of complementing the involvement of real users within the early product development phases.

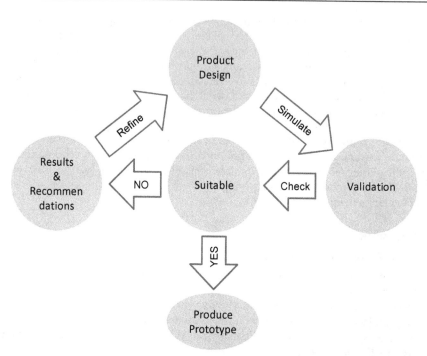

Fig. 2. The process of validating and refining designs with Virtual User Models (VICON-Consortium 2010)

3.2 Methods and tools supporting the sketch phase

For the sketch phase a mixture of qualitative and quantitative methods are common such as user studies, field and user trials, market studies or interviews. Since the initial product development steps are often characterized by loose creativity, innovation and a need to react flexibly to changing requirements, software tools that provide inclusive design support in the sketch phase are rarely in use (Kirisci, Thoben et al. 2011). Moreover, information technology is limited to a more indirect role, such as providing structures for a quick idea exchange as in Mind-Maps or the preparation of sketches and initial drawings like in graphic design software such as ADOBE Illustrator. On the other hand, for idea generation creative techniques like brainstorming or 635 method are well known and used in product development. Next to creative techniques, guidelines and checklists are also well-established supportive tools for the early product development phases such as within the sketch phase, and are nowadays in use in industry. Some of the most notorious guidelines are the ISO guidelines such as ISO 13407 (Human-centred design processes for interactive systems) or ISO 9241 (Ergonomics of human-system interaction). The drawback of guidelines is however that they fail to consider all product possibilities and features (Zitkus, Langdon et al. 2011). These kinds of guidelines are usually very general and rarely of quantitative nature. Moreover, they are often described in descriptive texts and tables which is not very much in line with preferences of product developers for the presentation or visualisation of design recommendations. Furthermore, the input to the sketch and design phases may come from several internal and external sources like customers, competitors, marketing and research and production (Pahl, Beitz et. al. 2005), (Westkämper 2005). Methods where the integration of end users within the development process is envisaged are often referred to as "user-centered design techniques". In this respect, user trials and observations are the more well-established techniques which are applied by some product manufacturers in the early product development phases. Although the benefit of these techniques is evident up to a certain extent, the time involved to organise the trials or observations, as well as the time to recruit and select a representative sample, negatively impact the design process. An alternative technique which has less impact upon time and budget constraints of the product developers is "self observation". Self observation is a frequently used technique by product designers in order to test the usability and accessibility through product mock-ups (Zitkus, Langdon et al. 2011). A disadvantage of this technique is evident when the product tests are done by the same persons who are involved in the development of the product. This means when the testers are too acquainted with the product, their judgement about the usability and accessibility might become subjective. It should also be noted that when the designers involved in the testing process do not have physical impairments, it is impossible to experience the same capability and interaction demand that an impaired user group would experience. In order to compensate this drawback, wearable suits such as the 'Third-Age Suit', 'Age Explorer' and 'Simulation Toolkit' have been applied by designers in order to experience certain physical limitations while interacting with products. Due to the substantial physical effort and amount of time involved in wearing these solutions, product developers tend not to wear the suits continuously during the design process (Zitkus, Langdon et al. 2011).

From the academic domain, especially in HCI-Human Computer Interaction, a variety of methods and tools exist for designing software user interfaces, under the consideration of specific end user needs. These tools are often referred to as tools for "user-centered design". In spite of the vast amount of research conducted in this area, only limited efforts have been spent so far in advancing methods and tools for designing physical or mechanical interaction components of consumer products in an inclusive manner (Kirisci and Thoben 2009). An approach with special focus on inclusive design is the "Inclusive Design Toolkit", which was developed by the Engineering Design Centre of the University of Cambridge (Clarkson 2007). The toolkit can be considered as an online repository of inclusive design knowledge and interactive resources, proposing inclusive design procedures and inclusive design tools which designers may consult to accompany them through their product development process. For supporting the sketch phase the tool provides general design guidance recommendations. In order to explore the capability loss related to some impairments and their severity, the toolkit offers a tool called "Exclusion Calculator". The tool calculated an estimate of the overall exclusion or the exclusion based on each capability demand. Although the Inclusive Design Toolkit raises the designers understanding about the way different disabilities affect the user perception and thus, their interaction with a product, the methodology is strongly dependent upon comprehensive input from the product developer. As emphasized in (Zitkus, Langdon et al. 2011), the exclusion calculation is based on designers' selections of specific tasks, thus the designer's assumptions have a risk of not being accurate, which can drive to incorrect assessments.

When focusing strictly upon the design of specific physical interaction elements of products (e.g. dials, switches, keys, displays, etc.), only two model-based design methods could be identified by the authors, which are capable of supporting the sketch phase of a product, and accommodating the accessibility needs of users. These two methods are based upon the configuration of pre-defined user models which have synergies with the context used for existing virtual user models. Although the methods apply to the design of wearable computing systems, some of the mechanical components are also up to a certain extent relevant to technically more advanced consumer products (e.g. mobile phones, etc.).

In the first approach, a "mobile and wearable computer aided engineering system" (m/w CAE System) was proposed by Bürgy (Bürgy and Garett 2002). By defining a constraint model, typical usage scenarios are described where support for a primary task is needed. Based on this model, existing comparable solutions are identified or new adapted systems are drafted. The description of an exemplary scenario is realized by using elements of four sub models: (a) the user model, (b) device model, (c) environment model, and (d) application model.

The other approach for a design support regarding mobile hardware components was published by Klug in 2007 (Klug and Mühlhäuser 2007). The approach focuses on the documentation and communication of specific use cases. Shortcomings in these fields lead to misunderstandings and false assumptions which will produce many subsequent errors during the design process. This challenge is met by the definition of models allowing a correct representation of typical scenarios where wearable computers are applied to enable systematic documentation of use cases. These models consist of: a work situation model, a user model, and a computer system model. The goal is to make the representation comprehensible for the whole design team and thus enabling the interdisciplinary communication between the members from different backgrounds. The author points this characteristic out to be of outstanding importance on the way to the design of an optimal wearable device for a given scenario. Due to the intense and specific design to a certain type of use case, the approach does not easily adapt to other scenarios. The work aims to describe use cases in a very fine granularity, which makes it suitable for well-defined, recurring tasks in a fixed, well-known environment. Use cases with changing environments and slightly unpredictable tasks cannot be described on such a high level of detail without limiting the flexibility, necessary to cope with dynamic change.

3.3 Methods and tools supporting the design phase (CAD phase)

Regarding the design phase of products, the authors refer explicitly to the phase of conceptualizing the product model, where most of the development tasks and sub-tasks are typically supported by so called Computer Aided Technologies (CAx), while "x" stands for a bunch of applications (Mühlstedt, Kaußler et al. 2008). Since commonly Computer-Aided-Design (CAD) tools are used for this purpose, the related design phase can be called "CAD phase". Originally CAD focused on the preparation of technical drawings, nowadays nearly all systems provide 3D models of parts and assembled products based on true to life parameters. In order to cope with the needs to achieve inclusive design of a product, several CAx applications provide virtual user models within their portfolio. The most widely used applications in companies include Pro/Engineer, CATIA, and Solidworks (VICON-Consortium 2010). High-End CAD systems, such as those mentioned, are extensible through digital human model plugins, such as Manekin, Ramsis, Jack, or Human Builder, to name just a few. However, the purpose of these plugins usually addresses ergonomic aspects such as validating the usability of user interface components in products (operating a machine, interacting with an aircraft cockpit, or space analysis in a car). In the scope of providing a design support for the inclusive product design, it should be noted that contemporary virtual user models often only have a limited ability to represent specific user groups such as users with certain physical impairments (Mühlstedt, Kaußler et al. 2008). This means that physical impairments are not sufficiently incorporated. In this respect the simulation of human fine motor skills such as movement of single fingers and joints (e.g. for interacting with the keys of a mobile phone) exceeds the capabilities of most virtual user models available today. It should also be noted that simulation is performed according to the designers' assumptions, which are dependent upon their design experience and knowledge about the end user groups to be included.

3.4 Methods and tools supporting testing and evaluation phase

For ergonomic analysis, testing and evaluation of product designs, tools incorporating virtual user models are available mainly in the area of product lifecycle management e.g. Tecnomatix (Siemens/ UGS) or Siemens NX, some of which were already mentioned above (Demirel and Duffy 2007). These tools are used for testing via simulation by building Virtual Reality (VR) environments to illustrate novel technology, and let user representatives evaluate the concepts by watching the VR simulation and interacting with it. Up to a certain degree this helps to get early user feedback, long before real prototypes are available. This approach is used to let user representatives have an immersive VR-based 3D experience of a future system. One example for this kind of approach using an Immersive Simulation Platform was conducted in the European Co-funded project VAALID. In this solution a user immerses in a virtual environment, allowing the user to experience some situational aspects of the virtual environment (Schäfer, Machate et al. 2010). A shortcoming of this approach from the point of view of the authors of this paper is that the evaluation of a product is dependent upon the participation of real users. From a technical point of view the system cannot be integrated with e.g. existing CAx applications, and needs a very powerful computing environment in order to take advantage of the full simulation capabilities of the system. A similar VR approach was used as a way to collect user feedback throughout the design of wearable computing IT to support fire-fighters (Klann, Ramirez et al. 2006), (Klann 2007). Here virtual and pervasive prototyping was used to test and design supportive technologies (ubiquitous and wearable technology) for the very specific domain of fire-fighting. Instead of elaborate user models, simple ones were used in conjunction with strong user participation in simulation sessions.

In the military domain, there exists Virtual User Model called SANTOS, which was developed in the frame of the Virtual Soldier Research Program of the University of Iowa (Zheng, Xue et al. 2010). It uses accurate biomechanics with models of muscles, deformable skin and the simulation of vital signs. With this system analyses of fatigue, discomfort, force or strength can be done. Furthermore modules for clothing simulation, artificial intelligence and virtual reality integration are available for real-time systems. However, a smooth integration into product development software is not possible. Some other models like the Boeing Human Modelling System (BHMS) or the System for Aiding Man-Machine Interaction Evaluation (SAMMIE) complete this listing (Sundin and Örtengren 2006).

Beside simulation, VUMs can be used to detect accessibility and usability problems of human interface designs. In the area of accessibility only one case study was identified, which is HADRIAN. HADRIAN provides an extension of the CAD Software SAMMIE CAD. HADRIAN was especially developed to study tasks for elderly and disabled people. The system includes a database drawing from an anthropometric survey with 100 individuals with a wide range of abilities (Marshall, Case et al. 2004). The aim pursued in this approach is to detect accessibility issues during the interaction between users and ATM (automatic teller machines) machines (Summerskill, Marshall et al. 2009). One of the disadvantages is that the digital human models in HADRIAN are based on a series of movements and forces that are not the maximum, but, instead the comfortable range for each specific task under analysis (Porter, Case et al. 2004). Another disadvantage of this system is similar to the ones encountered with other Virtual User Models as described above, namely regarding the limits of simulation of human fine motor skills (VICON-Consortium 2010). It is also worth mentioning that several European Union co-funded projects such as VICON, VERITAS, GUIDE, and MyUI are currently working on defining a common Virtual User Model which incorporates a wide range of disabilities and physical impairments of users, addressing the most frequent accessibility issues when interacting with products.

4. The design approach

Context represents on a universal scale, the relevant aspects of the situations of the user groups (Hull 1997). Hence, a context model describes the characteristics, features, and behaviour of a specific user group. Complementarily it also includes the aspects related to the tasks, interactions, user interface, and the environment, where she or he interacts with consumer products (Kirisci, Klein et al. 2011). Accordingly, the context model as proposed in this paper possesses different facets for supporting the development process. Likewise, a virtual user model is an abstract representation of an envisaged user group which complementarily involves a description of the underlying context. Therefore it is legitimate to consider the envisaged context model a "virtual user model". Fig. 3 provides an overview of the underlying concept - at first introduced in (Kirisci, Klein et al. 2011) and (Mohamad, Velasco et al. 2011) - emphasizing the interplay between the virtual and real world.

The data for the context model (referred to as virtual user model in Fig. 3) is based upon (1) accessibility needs of the envisaged end user groups, (2) the user profile, (3) the tasks of the users, and (4) the environment in which the users are interacting. The context model interacts with the sketch, design and evaluation phase of a product in providing qualitative and quantitative design recommendations and constraints. From the point of view of a designer, in the initial sketch phase, a support appears in form of text-based recommendations with respect to potential user interface elements. Up to this point, the recommending character of the context model can be compared to an expert system as defined in (Castillo, Gutiérrez et al. 1997). However, expert systems are usually highly domain specific, thus are not easily adaptable to other domains. Next to the feature that the context model should be easily adaptable to other contexts by the designer, the design concept goes beyond the provision of recommendations. In the design phase the context model will guide the designer with templates and design patterns for interaction components of consumer products. For the evaluation phase, a 3D virtual character in a virtual environment will be established in order to evaluate a developed product design against predefined usage scenarios. After several iterative development cycles, the results are then used for realization of a physical prototype and ultimately a final product. Results that have an impact upon the context model are fed back into the model. This way it is ensured that the context model is extendable and continuously kept updated with contemporary design knowledge.

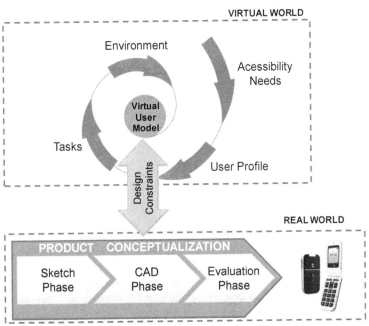

Fig. 3. Approach of the context model-based design support

5. Prerequisites for creating the context model

One of the prerequisites for creating an appropriate context model is to identify and record key usability issues. Those should then be presented to the designers in a usable and easily adaptable manner, rather than overburdening them with lengthy guidelines (Kirisci, Thoben et al. 2011). Moreover, it should be the aim to provide filtered knowledge with respect to a specific context of use. In order to support the above objective, an observational user study has been conducted with the aim of identifying and describing key usability issues for users with mild-to-moderate impairments. The procedure and results of the study have been published comprehensively in (Fiddian, Bowden et al. 2011). The observational study was not only meant to record the impairments per user, but moreover to understand the relevance regarding the performance of certain tasks in a specific environment. For instance, the impact of a mild to moderate vision impairment of a user will be strongly affected by e.g. light conditions in the environment. Keeping this in mind, it should indirectly impact the functionalities, design and capabilities of a mobile device.

To identify and describe key usability issues that people encounter when using specific consumer product types focus was upon people with one of three common impairments and people showing combinations of these impairments. One group was of users with one minor developed impairment such as vision impairment, hearing impairment, and manual dexterity impairment. Another one was of elderly users with age related impairments – usually a combination of mild to medium of the previously mentioned impairments. These can also be referred to as multiple sensory impairments. The levels of impairment severity covered by this research were mild to medium (as opposed to severe or profound) and these were determined for each participant during the research process. The mentioned impairments were chosen because of the commonality of the afflictions, the effect it has on using consumer products (touch, sight and hearing, are the primary senses used when interacting with an object). Besides mobile phones, the consumer products that were investigated in this study in detail were white goods such as washing machines. The research involved carrying out detailed observational studies of the participants in their own home. The most important aspect of this research was identifying key problem areas with existing product designs, looking for commonality within and between impairment groups and differing products, and presenting this information accurately and in an accessible and usable format.

5.1 Methodology

A detailed ethnographic research was carried out on a group of 58 elderly people from the UK, Ireland and Germany who had a range of mild to medium impairments. Three types of WHO classified impairments were focused upon; hearing loss (B230), sight loss (B210) and manual dexterity (B710/730). The research comprised of a combination of interview and observational techniques and investigated the main usability problems which these specific users encountered when using their washing machine and mobile phone in a typical use environment. The main research methodology employed was detailed observational studies carried out in the participant's own home environment. This methodology was used in the first phase of user testing as the participants have already had sufficient time to use their own products.

The research methodology involved detailed questioning and observation of a relatively small number of participants, 58 in total. The reason for this is that in order to identify the key usability issues a researcher will not only need to ask the opinion of the participant but also to observe where problems occur, record events and encourage greater feedback from the user.

It was considered important that the research should be carried out in suitable environments. When using a mobile phone the environment can have a considerable impact on the usability of a product. For practical reasons it was decided that users should carry out tasks using their own mobile phone in their normal domestic environment. However, whenever possible it was suggested that the user was observed using the phone in both low and high lighting conditions. Additionally the users were observed using the product in both static and mobile environments, so the users were encouraged to use their mobile phone both indoors and outside.

The researcher directed the participant to carry out specific tasks related to the everyday use of the products, made objective observations and asked relevant questions. This procedure followed a standard questionnaire/methodology formulated before and during the pilot research. Furthermore users were asked how easy/difficult they found the task. This had to be explored in detail, including talking through the process, if there were particular problems or if it was deemed relevant. The observer needed to investigate how much each usability issue was down to the specific impairment/s of that user as opposed to being more specific to product design or environmental factors. Observations were recorded in written, abbreviated form.

In the second phase of user testing, the participants had been asked to evaluate a set of unfamiliar products, which helped the researchers to identify issues relating to first time use, for example, how intuitive the product is and how useful the instructions are.

5.2 Results of the study

With the mobile phone, many users (n = 15) reported having difficulties using the On/Off control. One issue was related to the force required to press the button. Many users (n = 10) had difficulty with this task either as a result of having to use too much force or because they experienced pain or discomfort. 1 user reported leaving the phone on continuously, to avoid the difficulty of turning it on and off, as she had arthritis. In the observations 12 people reported that the button required force to operate, so this was obviously a significant problem.

Eight participants had problems when making a voice call and all of these problems were related to the operation of the number keys and other controls. Three users had problems due to the number keys being too close together, so they often pushed more than one button at the same time.

Other individual problems included buttons being too small and fiddly, buttons being difficult to operate if the user has long finger nails, problems deleting incorrect numbers, the numbers on the keys being hard to read and force being required to operate the keys. No users reported having problems when receiving a voice call. Observations recorded few negatives but in 3 cases the ring was too quiet and 1 user had problems with the keypad lock.

There were many positive observations made including; loud ring, strong vibration, easy to know when I am receiving a call and screen lights up. Over half (n =25) of the users used the 'Ring and Vibrate' setting to alert them to incoming calls, but almost as many (n=19) used ring only. 2 users were alerted to calls by ring and light but none chose to be alerted by vibration alone. When asked why they chose a particular alert, 10 users said that that was the way the phone was set up for them - the phone was either already on this setting, or a family member had selected it for them. Other replies generally explained and justified most users chosen method of being alerted to a call.

Of the 49 participants who took part in this research, only 26 (59%) send SMS text messages and answered questions on these tasks. This indicates that although many elderly people now have mobile phones, their primary use is likely to be for occasional voice calls instead of text messaging. 28 participants attempted this task. Similar to the results for receiving a voice call, 50% (n =14) used the 'Ring and Vibrate' setting to alert them to an incoming message and 43% (n=12) used Ring/Tone only.

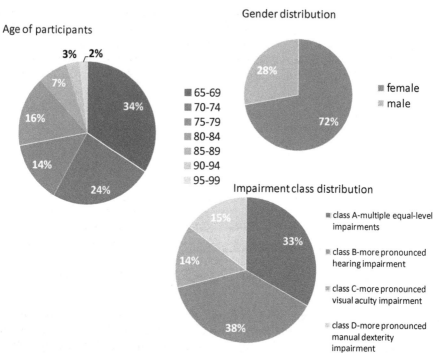

Fig. 4. Composition of the user group according to age, gender, impairments (Fiddian, Bowden et al. 2011).

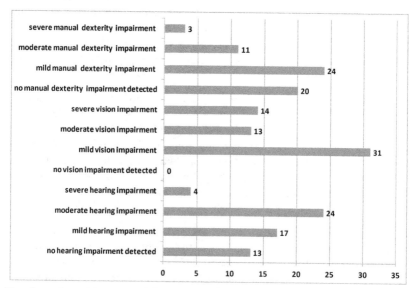

Fig. 5. Number of participants with hearing, vision, and manual dexterity impairments (Fiddian, Bowden et al. 2011).

Many users (n=17) had problems when they were asked if the number keys were large enough for them. 10 users specified that the keys were too small; 7 said that they found the keys too small and fiddly, 2 stated that they tended to push two keys at once and 2 obviously found the keys too small. Other problems recorded include the number keys not being arranged in a straight line, the buttons not protruding enough, having to use fingernails to operate the small controls and a rounded button shape making it too easy for the finger to slip off and press the neighbouring button by mistake.

Some users (n = 10) reported not finding the display easy to read or having problems with it. 3 users (2 from group B and 1 from C) found the displays on their phones too small and 1 of these also disliked having dark grey figures on an orange background. 2 users (from group A and B) found that their phone had an energy saving function which darkened the screen, this happened too quickly for them making the display difficult to read. A single user (group A) commented that the calendar and menu functions looked quite faint. For mobile phones, this was the usability issue which had the most problems associated with it. 21 participants reported having problems when they were asked 'do you understand the icons or descriptions'. 12 users said they were not sure about some of the words or icons used and 3 people did not understand the menu functions and so don't use them. 2 users thought the descriptions were not intuitive and another 2 thought the instructions and language were too complicated. 2 users commented that they liked the clear diagrams (icons) and words. Less than half of the users (n=23) attempted to add contact details to the phonebook, as they had previously tried and were unable to complete the task.

The results of the observational user study were completely exploited for the creation of the user profiles, tasks, environment, and design recommendations used in the context model. As such it was more easily possible to create user model, environment and task instances and variables, including rules and constraints for user profiling and recommendation instances.

6. The Context model – Description and implementation

This section describes the proposed context model in detail and illustrates how the context model has been implemented.

6.1 Description of the context model

The context model should possess the capability to determine recommendations for appropriate interaction components for a consumer product. Therefore, it incorporates well-defined partial models which are logically interrelated with one another in order to determine appropriate recommendations for the designer. Using the results of the observational study introduced in the preceding section, a suitable taxonomy for the context model has been rudimentarily described in (Kirisci, Klein et al. 2011), which consists of the following partial models:

User Model, where all information about the potential users of the product is stored. Focus is upon exemplary users with mild to moderate physical impairments. The respective user models are divided into several subgroups (profiles), which are divided into different levels of impairments. Additionally there are mixed profiles describing the group of elderly people who are subject to a mixture of hearing, sight and dexterity impairments.

Component Model describes specific user interface components and adds functionalities to specific instances. E.g. a button can be pressed, so the button consists of the functional attribute of a switch with two states. This model is also used to connect recommendations with components - especially in the CAD phase, where the designer's input is related to a component.

Model for Recommendations, where guidelines and experience of the designer are stored. These consist of the predicates "Name", "Text", "Summary", Rules, Phases and an Attachment, where e.g. Sketch Phase Template Layers can be stored. A component attribute defines rule sets for the design phase, if a recommendation is related to a specific component or component functionality like "Audio Output".

Environment Model, where all data of the environment is stored. That includes the physical conditions of the environment of the real world, objects and characteristics of the environment etc.

Task Model describes how to perform activities to reach a pre-defined goal. This model may be based e.g. on Hierarchical Task Analysis (HTA) providing an interface, where the designer can define actions of the user for the evaluation in the virtual environment envisaged in the evaluation phase.

6.2 Overall architecture

In relation to functional requirements, such as gaining component recommendations as an output, the context model needs to be able to parse the sub-models using logical constraints. This is necessary in order to build an inference model with all relevant data. For the implementation, an architecture is proposed which includes the context model as a knowledge base. **Fig. 6** shows the system architecture of the overall system for implementing the context model. It is divided into the parts: the backend, where all data of the context model is stored, the frontend, where company-specific design and testing applications, as well as all client-specific features to obtain recommendations (recommendation module) are integrated. The middleware layer provides a seamlessly accessible connection between the front end applications and the reasoning engine with a socket connection handler and socket server.

In this respect a software framework has been specified upon a reasoning engine, as drafted in **Fig. 6**.

The proposed architecture provides, the frontend services, where the user can conduct the required functionalities. The recommendation system can be accessed in the sketch phase as well as in the detailed CAD phase. Thus three different types of front-end modules are provided to the user. The middleware services deal with all in- and outgoing connections and provide all relevant data to front-end modules. All recommendations are marked with a phase attribute, which defines at which phase a recommendation will be presented. Additionally every recommendation instance consists of a user model-, environment-, task- or component rule. The backend services provide the access to the ontology-schemes, algorithms and data in order to control and manage the framework.

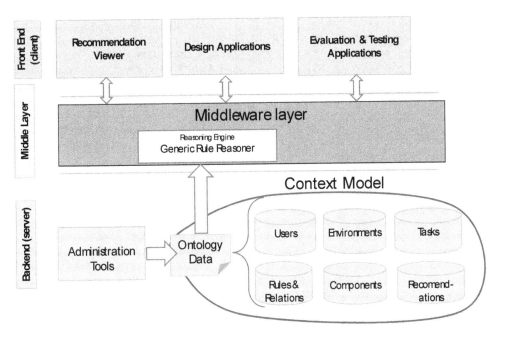

Fig. 6. Architecture of the proposed software framework

6.3 Setting up the context model in the sketch phase

The sketch phase is signed by providing qualitative design recommendations to the designer. These recommendations can be used for drafting the user interfaces of the envisaged product. In order to offer the designer flexibility within the creativity process, only qualitative (high level) design recommendations are offered to the designer in this phase. An idealized work-flow could mean to have corresponding recommendations (such as "use a maximum of 5 buttons in total") directly on screen while drafting the product-shape on paper or a digitizer tablet. The designer can save all settings among the given recommendations by saving a status file called "VSF". The VSF is not only to save and reload corresponding information but also to "import" all information into the subsequent modules (e.g. CAD Module).

The idea is that the context model is sequentially established through four main steps, which apply specified rule sets by every step as illustrated in Fig. 7 (Kirisci, Klein et al. 2011):

1. **Applying of user model Rules**
   The General Rule Reasoner uses the user model rules to define all instances of the user model class as members of specified WHO ICF profiles (e.g. a specific profile for moderate hearing impaired people).
2. **Generation of initial Recommendations**
   This step is the same as the first step, with the difference to use the recommendation rules and instances based upon user model profiles.

3. **Creation of environment recommendations**

    This step creates classes which are based on the id names (IDs) of every environment, and adds all textual and component recommendations, which were reasoned by the environment rules, as members of these new recommendation classes (e.g. a recommendation class for an instance of the environment). These rules can also use the previous defined recommendation classes.

4. **Creation of task recommendations**

    The last step creates all task related recommendations based on task rules and all previously defined recommendations. This procedure is the same as the creation of environment recommendations, all tasks id names define dynamically created classes, which contain recommendations for specific tasks.

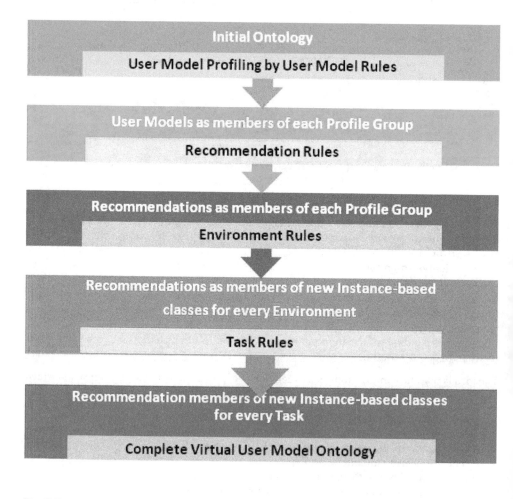

Fig. 7. Iterative creation of recommendations

6.4 The context model in the CAD phase

The user data, which is used in the CAD phase, contains in addition to the user model, environment and task selection of the first phase an annotation for components. The annotation option for each component part is obtained from the component model of the context model as seen in **Fig. 6**.

Fig. 8 shows the so called "annotation view" of the context model, which is directly loaded in the CAD software (Siemens NX), including the annotation option for each component part. In this step each name of the annotated object is set to the component id as defined in the component model. Each recommendation instance contains a component variable, which defines tags of component names that are addressed within a specific recommendation.

After, the annotation, the module presents recommendations dedicated to the annotated user interface component. Although it is likely that some recommendations may overlap, the majority of recommendations will be added to those recommendations of the first phase (sketch phase), providing more detailed insights.

As already defined, the inference of the CAD design recommendations is created by using component tags for each recommendation instance. Additionally the instances can also define component rules, which limit minimum parameter values for the annotated objects. The corresponding parameter values must have already been defined in the CAD product to establish a linkage to the recommendations (e.g. a "button_height" parameter must be defined within a CAD model to be manipulable by a corresponding rule).

If a component rule and a corresponding value are defined for the current selected recommendation, an "Apply" button becomes visible in the recommendation view of the CAD module as shown in Fig. 9. The designer can accordingly use the button to check and change minimum parameter values directly within the CAD model.

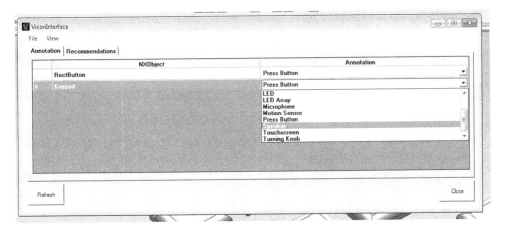

Fig. 8. CAD Module Annotation View

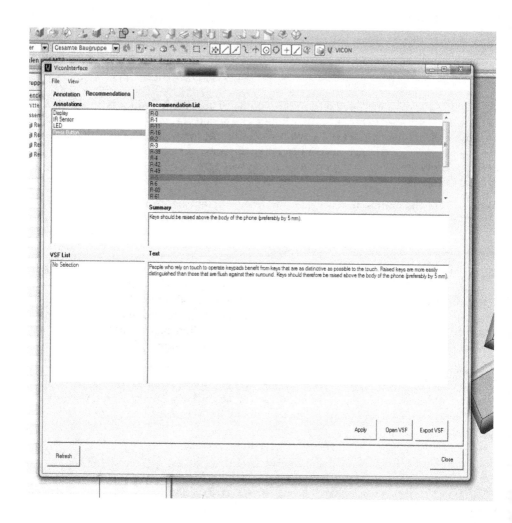

Fig. 9. CAD Module Recommendation View

7. The evaluation of the context model

In order to highlight the advantages (but also the limits) of the proposed context model for inclusive product development, a real use case of a European mobile phone manufacturer serves as a reference scenario. Technically spoken, this section describes how the context model can be used along the development process of mobile phones by product developers and design teams. Hence the underlying idea is to secure inclusive design aspects - starting as early as in the sketch phase, via the design phase - up to an initial product evaluation. In order to make this approach more comprehensive a typical design scenario is introduced.

7.1 Scenario – Development of a mobile phone

A designer is developing a new mobile phone which will be made available on the mainstream mobile phone market. He wants the product to be as accessible and usable as possible to as many people as possible, while at the same time looking attractive and appealing to customers. He sketches a new design idea and uploads it onto the computer. As the designer marks up the sketch he assigns the appropriate labels to the various user interface components. As he does so, design recommendations are provided by the system to warn him well in advance about potential usability issues with each component and to ensure that he addresses these issues at the earliest possible stage. The cost of making changes increases exponentially as the design reaches the later development stages, so Designer B wants to identify and address as many usability issues as possible at this earliest stage.

Once the designer gets into the next phase of the design project, he further develops the design and starts to conduct virtual user tests of the user interface. Since he wants this new mobile phone to be as universally designed as possible, he tests the design with all of the preset virtual user profiles and in a range of virtual environments. He has decided to design a touch screen phone, so most of the buttons and controls are onscreen.

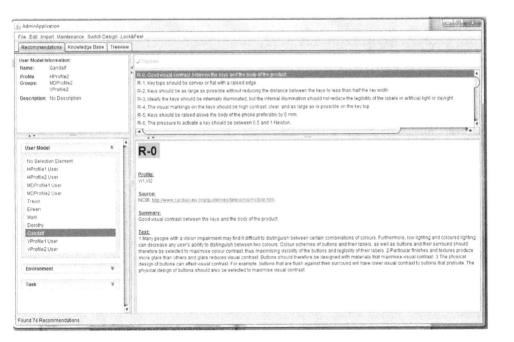

Fig. 10. Sketch design application of the framework

7.2 Technical view on the scenario

The designer wants the product to be as accessible and usable as possible to as many people as possible, which means that he must be aware of possible impairments, which will have an impact on the product design. To accomplish this, he first starts with the sketch phase and also the sketch design application of the framework.

The User Model "Gandalf" is the most impaired user model of the framework. As seen in Fig. 10 in the user model information field, the model is a member of the WHO ICF based groups of moderate hearing, manual dexterity and visual impaired profiles. As a result of this selection, the designer receives a list of appropriate recommendations, which all describe problems with impairments of the user model.

After the selection of the user model, the designer can select different environments analogously, so he can get additional recommendations in relation to each selection. Accordingly, if the designer has made all different selections of user model, environment and tasks, he can export the current results of recommendations into the status file (VSF).

In the next phase the designer creates his product in a virtual environment. Fig. 11 shows a product development view of Siemens NX in the design phase, including the annotation module, where the designer defines his components.

After the annotation he can import the VSF into the CAD Module in order to receive the recommendations in line with the previous selections. In the recommendation view of the module he can select his annotated component and the imported VSF and receives all recommendations for his component as highlighted in Fig. 9.

7.3 Discussion

The authors of this chapter are convinced that the adoption of tools for inclusive design by product designers is more likely to happen, the less their impact is upon the design process. In other words, the earlier a product meets the user's requirements, the lesser the changes impact the design process, which includes the effect in the project budget, the project plan and the design activity. It is therefore of crucial importance to understand the product development process in detail, in order to know in which phases to integrate with tools that support inclusive design. To establish tools that are able to integrate into the existing design process is therefore one of the key issues to foster acceptance of inclusive design tools in industry. This justifies that the proposed design approach focuses upon the integration of a widely used CAD application such as Siemens NX, thus offers at the same time an effective and undisruptive way to present design recommendations to the product developer. Since the presented findings are based upon ongoing research, it is too early to draw final conclusions about the willingness of product manufacturers to adopt this approach into their existing design processes. Although, a European mobile phone manufacturer who has already vast experience with adopting more traditional user-centered design approaches, is testing the solution within their product design department. Additionally the solution is being evaluated by a major manufacturer of white and brown goods with the development of washing machines and remote controls for TV sets. Throughout these tests, the validity and the limits of the proposed context model shall be identified, with the aim of improving the overall solution to the benefit of the product designers.

Fig. 11. CAD prototype of a mobile phone and annotation module

8. Conclusions

The presented design approach based on the described context model is capable of supporting the product development process in the early stage before the realization of prototypes. It should however, not be understood as a total substitution of real users, but moreover as complementing the involvement of real users, thus an opportunity to minimize the effort of applying more costly and time-consuming techniques in the early design phase. The benefit for mainstream manufacturers of mobile products such as mobile phones, gadgets, and remote controls is obvious as they would be able to develop their products in an inclusive manner, making them accessible for users with mild to moderate impairments. At the same time, it is vital that the product remains attractive for non-impaired users as well. A main challenge was to seamlessly integrate the context model into the existing product development processes of manufacturing companies by integration into mainstream CAD applications. This challenge was tackled by integrating the context model in Siemens NX 7.5 (as representing a widely used CAD application), and presenting the designer with qualitative and quantitative recommendations based on the specified values in the CAD software. The next development phase of the proposed system will focus upon the evaluation phase, where the designers will have the possibility to test their recommendation-based product design in a virtual environment through a digital human model, which corresponds to the data of the context model as configured by the designer in the sketch phase. It is foreseen that this shall be done while remaining within the same CAD application Siemens NX. As a digital human model, "JACK" shall be used and adapted according to the collection of profiles of impaired end user in the context model. The proposed design approach envisages that the output of the evaluation phase should flow back into the preceding phases such as CAD phase and sketch phase. In this way a continuous update of the context model shall be realized. The demonstration of this mechanism shall also be considered in the next iteration. Finally, it should be noted that focus of the present research is mainly upon the feasibility of the approach than to guarantee the validity of the data in the context model. Even though a comprehensive field study has been conducted within this research, for the future the quality of the data (recommendations, design constraints, user interface components, etc.) in the context model is highly dependent upon the availability of quantitative, accurate data. At the same time the authors are confident that through the developed design framework, research findings of quantitative user studies can be integrated more easily and cost-efficiently into the early product development.

9. Acknowledgements

This work has been done under the research project VICON (project No. 248294) funded by the European Commission under the ICT Framework (ICT-2009-7.2). We wish to acknowledge our gratitude and appreciation to all the project partners for their contribution during the development of various ideas and concepts presented in this chapter.

10. References

Bürgy, C. and J. Garett (2002). *Situation Aware Interface Design: An Interaction Constraints Model for Finding the Right Interaction for Mobile and Wearable Computer Systems.* 19th International Symposium on Automation and Robotics in Construction Gaithersburg, Maryland: 563-568.

Castillo, E., J. M. Gutiérrez, et al. (1997). *Expert systems and probabilistic network models,* Springer LNCS.

Clarkson, J., Coleman, R., Hosking, I., Waller, S. (2007). *Inclusive Design Toolkit,* Cambridge Engineering Design Centre.

Demirel, H. and V. Duffy (2007). "*Applications of digital human modeling in industry.*" Digital Human Modeling: 824-832.

Fiddian, T., C. Bowden, et al. (2011). "*An End User and Environment Field Study for an Inclusive Design of Consumer Products.*" Human-Computer Interaction. Users and Applications: 443-452.

Goodman, J., H. Dong, et al. (2006). "*Factors involved in industry's response to inclusive design.*" Designing accessible technology: 31-39.

Hull, R., Neaves, P., Bedford-Roberts, J. (1997). "*Towards Situated Computing*". 1st International Symposium on Wearable Computers. Digest of Papers: 146-153. ISBN 0-8186-8192-6

Kirisci, P., P. Klein, et al. (2011). *Supporting Inclusive Design of User Interfaces with a Virtual User Model*. Universal Access in Human-Computer Interaction. Users Diversity. C. Stephanidis, Springer Berlin / Heidelberg. 6766: 69-78.

Kirisci, P. and K.-D. Thoben (2009). "*Vergleich von Methoden für die Gestaltung Mobiler Endgeräte.*" icom - Zeitschrift für interaktive und kooperative Medien 8(1): 52-59.

Kirisci, P. T., K. D. Thoben, et al. (2011). "*Supporting Inclusive Product Design with Virtual User Models at the Early Stages of Product Development*". 18th International Conference on Engineering Design (ICED11), Vol. 09: Design Methods and Tools, Part 1; Copenhagen, The Design Society, 80-90, ISBN 978-1-904670-29-2

Klann, M. (2007). "*Playing with fire: user-centered design of wearable computing for emergency response*". Proceedings of the 1st international conference on Mobile information technology for emergency response, Springer Verlag Berlin, Heidelberg: 116-125. ISBN:3-540-75667-1 978-3-540-75667-5

Klann, M., L. Ramirez, et al. (2006). "*Playing with Fire: towards virtual prototyping of wearable computing for highly situated contexts of use*". Proceedings of 3rd Int. Forum on Applied Wearable Computing (IFWC), Bremen, Germany, 1-10, ISBN: 978-3-8007-2954-8

Klug, T. and M. Mühlhäuser (2007). „*Modeling human interaction resources to support the design of wearable multimodal systems*". Proceedings of the ninth international conference on Multimodal interfaces ICMI 07, ACM Press: 299-306. ISBN 9781595938176

Marshall, R., K. Case, et al. (2004). "*Using Hadrian for eliciting virtual user feedback in'Design For All'.*" Proceedings of the Institution of Mechanical Engineers, Part B: Journal of Engineering Manufacture 218(9): 1203-1210.

Mohamad, Y., C. Velasco, et al. (2011). "*Virtual User Concept for Inclusive Design of Consumer Products and User Interfaces.*" Universal Access in Human-Computer Interaction. Users Diversity: 79-87.

Mühlstedt, J., H. Kaußler, et al. (2008). "*Programme in Menschengestalt: digitale Menschmodelle für CAx-und PLM-Systeme.*" Zeitschrift für Arbeitswissenschaft, Vol.02/2008: 79-86. ISSN: 0340-2444.

Pahl, G., W. Beitz, et al. (2005). "*Konstruktionslehre: Grundlagen erfolgreicher Produktentwicklung. Methoden und Anwendung.*" Springer Verlag Berlin Heidelberg, Vol.06. ISBN 3-540-22048-8

Porter, J. M., K. Case, et al. (2004). "*[] Beyond Jack and Jill': designing for individuals using HADRIAN.*" International Journal of Industrial Ergonomics 33(3): 249-264.

Schäfer, J., J. Machate, et al. (2010). "*VAALID: Eine Entwicklungs-und Simulationsumgebung für AAL-Projekte.*" Proceedings of 3rd German AAL Congress. VDE-Verlag ISBN 978-3-8007-3209-8

Summerskill, S., R. Marshall, et al. (2009). "*Validation of the HADRIAN System Using an ATM Evaluation Case Study.*" Digital Human Modeling: 727-736.

Sundin, A. and R. Örtengren (2006). "*Digital human modeling for CAE applications.*" Handbook of human factors and ergonomics third edition. Chapter 39. John Wiley and Sons Inc.:1053–1078. DOI: 10.1002/0470048204

VICON-Consortium (2010). *D1.3 Virtual Users in a Human-Centred Design Process.* www.vicon-project.eu

Westkämper, E. (2005). „*Einführung in die Organisation der Produktion*". Springer Berlin Heidelberg, Vol. 01. ISBN-10: 3540260390

Zheng, C., Q. Xue, et al. (2010). "*Research of virtual dismounted mechanized infantry squad combat modeling and simulation based on DI-Guy*", Proceedings of Int. Conference on Computer Application and System Modeling (ICCASM 2010). IEEE: 388-391. E-ISBN: 978-1-4244-7237-6

Zitkus, E., P. Langdon, et al. (2011). Accessibility Evaluation: "*Assistive Tools for Design Activity in Product Development*". Proceedings of the 1st International Conference on Sustainable Intelligent Manufacturing Leira, Portugal, IST Press: 659-670.

6

MSpace: An Emergent Approach, Modelling and Exploring Mutable Business-Entities

Mohamed Dbouk[1*], Hamid Mcheick[2] and Ihab Sbeity[1]

[1]Lebanese University, Faculty of Sciences (I), Beirut
[2]Université du Québec à Chicoutimi, Québec,
[1]Lebanon
[2]Canada

1. Introduction

Things evolve and change states, e.g. a human being may have *Single* as social state, and may become *married*, *divorced*, etc., an employee may become *manager*, *president*, etc. software, databases, etc., may evolve as well, everything evolve.

Roughly speaking, in the literature object's or agent's evolutions are usually handled using objects/agents moving models and multi-dimensional representation. Most of traditional and powerful analytical systems prefer using multi-dimensional data structure that facilitating data/object representation and tracking. Those systems became popular in companies and industries that store and interpret historical information for decision-making purposes, e.g. data warehousing.

Dealing with unconventional and evolutive space is hard to undertake and reveal great challenges. Day by day, reactive and dynamic data are more and more pointed and solicited. This data may incorporate and stimulate huge amount of knowledge. In this context, the advance in technology, multidimensional analysis and business intelligent analysis are solicited more and more.

Traditional multidimensional approaches are almost concerned with historical cumulative data that constructed from the heap of *ETLed (Extracted, Transformed and Loaded)* data. The popular related technologies such as, data warehousing , data mining and On-Line Analytic Processing (OLAP) are key factors in the interactive analysis of large amounts of data-sets. These technologies are datasets-oriented and seem not enough flexible to deal with evolutive and mutable space, and not to consider a single record (entity) and exploring it along dimensions. Furthermore, existing approaches usually use offline copies of data, and sometimes this data may conflict and may give unexpected and inaccurate results. All of these feedbacks were the reason behind thinking about new approach.

Practically, concepts of evolutive space may reside in several kinds of real world business activities; the following examples meet our early approach [Dbouk & Sbeity 2009]:

*Corresponding author

Typical cases -Environmental related issues: risk management; flooding, forest (trees, etc.) evolutions, administering and monitoring agricultural practices, etc.

Educational monitoring and tracking: here we talk, for example, about the educational policies within a private university or within the entire country (ministry of education). Students and their activities are subject of investigation and analysis.

Site /City histories: modern city, archaeological site, construction site, volcanic site, etc., may have continuous stories and histories (images, video, maps, etc.); they evolve continually against key-features such as time and civilizations. Such information could be recorded and archived; it may become critical and useful for a certain application domains, e.g. Tourism.

Enterprise productivity inspection and tracking: in order to improve productivity, enterprises elaborate strategies and executive plans; they apply some kind of business intelligent human resource tracking. People (employees) within the enterprise could evolve by years and become more experimented and productive. Employees indeed could follow some policies and elaborated schemes.

Marine navigation tracking: merchant ships are for example considered as moving entities following pre-elaborated/evolutive trajectories. Ships may be equipped with dedicated materials and tools. Consequently, trajectories may be correlated / adjusted according to instantaneous and punctual analysis.

Biomedical treatments and experiments, etc...

The ultimate goal of the approach called "MSpace", that we propose, is to enable entity (individual space's element) evolution tracking and monitoring. We are going in this approach to elaborate a tool with OLTP and OLAP double roles and responsibilities, leading to analyse business entities' histories, managing entities' transitions and interactions between each other, observe and track current and up-to-date business entities' states in a multi-aspect/dimensional space, etc. The duty is to predict, direct and ultimately correlate entities' behaviours and any new and future activities.

To conclude, the approach, which we work on, represents a long research project, related models and tools are under elaboration and validation by referring to BI-like technologies and using Microsoft and Java platforms.

The rest of the chapter is organized as follows: in section 2 an overview of related works is discussed, and then the *ancestor approach* of MSpace is highlighted in section 3. In section 4, MSpace foundations and basis as well as software solution are established and deeply considered. Also, prototyping and validation issues are presented in this section. Finally, the outlines of future directions and conclusion are drawn in section 5.

2. Background and related works

The coming years will witness an important mass of on-line technologies, that use internet and satellite to find locations on Earth, example GPS (Global Position system), which depends on moving objects, location and time based multi-dimensional database to analysis and interpret geographical data. Here is the importance of dealing with moving objects dedicated databases that store the object attributes in addition to its location and time dimensions. There are many researches in this domain, for example: FuMMO [Praing & Schneider, 2007a] model that working with geo-features, Balloon [Praing & Schneider, 2007b] model for keep of tracking both historical and future moving-objects. In their work Praing & Schneider "are especially interested in the design of data models for continuously changing geometric objects over time, typically known as moving objects". Other geo-spatial model are reported, e.g. the land use model [Hammam et al., 2004], and the dynamic three-dimensional marine data model based on time series multi-surfaces [Zhang et al., 2007].

The moving objects data model "Balloon" deals with spatiotemporal changes; it provides an integrated support for both historical and future movements of moving objects. In contrast to basic "FuMMO" model [Praing & Schneider, 2007a] that working with low level object geo-features, "Balloon" [Praing & Schneider, 2007b] states for emerging both historical and future moving-objects' movements. It seems well made and may influence future efforts in the area. "Hermes" [Pelekis et al. 2006] deals with dynamic objects that change locations, shape and size, either discretely or continuously over time. Whereas [Erwig et al., 1999] rather than dealing with geometries changing over time and traditional dimensions, it invests in higher-dimensional entities where structures and behaviours are captured and considered as abstract data types. Besides, the emerging multidimensional spatiotemporal approach presented in [Pestana & da Silva, 2005] promotes spatial analysis, and applies narrowly the key concept of evolution specifications.

Otherwise, a land use model is presented in [Hammam et al., 2004], the author presents a new technique called "vector agent based simulation", which uses discrete irregular objects as an autonomous spatial entity beneath an agent modelling structure. Through computer simulation, this new technique has been applied to von Thunen's theory of agricultural land use as a hypothetical environment for model verification. The findings demonstrate that this proposal can be considered as a new paradigm for urban simulation. The model will be strengthened and examined using the basic elements of Cellular Automata: space, neighbourhood, and transition rules, state, and time. Here the author considers *the world as a serious of entities located in space*. Entities are usually an abstraction of the real world. An autonomous active object or agent is a digital representation of all part of an entity. In this model, the transition rules specify the behaviour of cells between time-step evolutions, deciding the future conditions of cells based on a set of fixed rules. However, the state of the object changes is based on the adaptation of an entity to its environment by the process of differentiation and increasing shape structure complexity. Also the time variant is considered as an element in this approach, in each entity lifespan, changes occur describing the evolution of its inner existence, or a mutation of its location in space. The model implements two time modes: synchronous and asynchronous.

Also, a marine navigation tracking mode is reported in [Zhang et al., 2007]. Here, the Ocean is multidimensional and dynamic in spatial-temporal structure, and effective marine data modelling and representing of marine multidimensional geographic information system is a new hot topic and challenge. Zhang proposes a new dynamic real three-dimensional marine data model based on time series multi-surfaces. It utilizes various surfaces to model different marine water bodies and creates three-dimensional topologic relations of objects in marine environments, then uses time series snapshots to delineate dynamic changes. The model is tested in safety estimation of navigation and motion of marine objects, and proved to be effective for the ship navigation.

GOLD model [Trujillo et al., 1999] was the base in pattern based multi-dimensional analysis. This model is an object oriented multi-dimensional data model, aims to identify of patterns based on the relationships between the dimensions attributes included in cube classes. These patterns will associate data together with OLAP operations and will allow us to have a concise execution model that maps every pattern of modelling into its corresponding implementation making users able to accomplish OLAP operations on cube classes.

As a result, based on "MSpace is an emergent approach" and in contrast with its intended goals, the above survey leads to conclude that each of these approaches and models shares basic concepts and foundations with MSpace; dynamic and or moving objects that change locations, multidimensional and spatial-temporal modelling, and pattern based multi-dimensional analysis, etc.

Strictly speaking, MSpace inherits basic ideas from our early GeoSEMA [Dbouk & Sbeity 2009], it indeed differs from this old approach (next section) by introducing the concept of multi-state business entities, and second, by applying a multidimensional modeling and analysis. Entities in MSpace, rather than temporal and the mobile (location-based) characteristics, they evolve in well organized behaviours. MSpace deals with contextual patterns (business profiles), in which dimensions are combined.

Finally, MSpace discusses and investigates research issues and advance solutions for modelling and exploring mutable and evolutive entities.

3. "GeoSEMA" the early approach

Our previous and early approach GeoSEMA [Dbouk & Sbeity 2009] is a conceptual platform dedicated to model a geospatial and evolutive space; it tends to emerge multidimensional and unconventional *geospatial* data.

Basically, GeoSEMA is interested in three principles: Space-environment characteristics, a classified set of geospatial evolutive mobile agents and a set of rules that governing and materializing the inter-agent interactions (extra-events). The considered geospatial space is seen as an unusual agent that grouping, collecting, associating, and coordinating a huge amount of unconventional geospatial agents.

Agents are expected to move, navigate, interact, etc. agents' behaviors reflect and/or materialize external events.

GeoSEMA initiative is intended to deal with evolutive agents; reported concepts are basic and seem to be a firm foundation, they are considered as starting point for the MSpace approach. GeoSEMA tries indeed to be generic; it doesn't specialized in how moving-mobile objects should be handled, it pleads for predicted trajectories and deals with evolved objects/agents and emerges fundamental concepts issued by [Pestana & da Silva, 2005].

Due to the key-concepts issued in this work: multi-aspect/dimensional, multi-state and transitional entities, MSpace rather than emerging the GeoSEMA key- features, it also incorporates both mutability (state-based dimensions) and mobility (location related dimensions or aspect) foundations.

4. "MSpace" a smart approach

The approach consists of an integrated tool tending to model and explore an evolutive and mutable well organized space. MSpace should answer the following questions:

- Mutable or evolutive space; what does this mean?
- Why dealing with so-called evolutive/mutable business entities?
- Mutable/evolutive business entities; what does mean?
- How the evolutivity concept could be outlined, achieved, etc.?
- Aspects / dimensions, entity states; what does this mean?
- And finally, how entity's transitions could be directed and how "pattern-based analysis" could help?

4.1 Basis and foundations

The space that we consider deals with unconventional schemes; it emerges multidimensional and unconventional data, it mainly consists of:

- a collection of mutable entities (business entities),
- a set of structural features (aspects/dimensions),
- set of behavioral features (transitions, business rules).

Business Entity (BE) – we introduce, in this approach, the concept of dynamic and mutable Business Entities. Entities are evolutive, multi-aspect (multidimensional), and multi-state; entities are reactive, move and transit constantly from one state to another state.

Business Entities are, basically, named one by one and should have two kinds of information (figure 1):

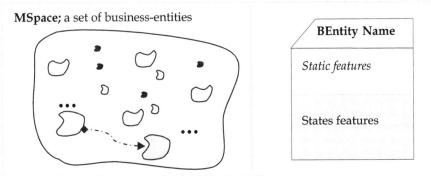

Business Entity: **Named Employee "Mark Rid";**
Static features: *he's called Mark, he is born on 15-03-1985, etc., he has a job-position and he still student, etc.*
States Features: "Mark" has *now (25-10-2008)* an MBA, *and* he become married, etc.

Fig. 1. MSpace basis

- Typical *static features,* e.g. name, date, etc. Those descriptive features usually have no direct effects on the entity state itself.
- A multiple *state-oriented key-features* recapitalize the entity reactions and behaviors, e.g. *"Mark got, by 10/07/2007, a degree in Computer-Science".* Those features should constantly be typified and well measured reflecting and characterizing entity related aspects (multidimensional concept).

Business Aspect – also called business dimension (practical vocabulary), it reflects and materializes our theory of evolutive and mutable space and entities. An aspect characterizes the space itself, it represents one face (entity-state) of the considered entities (figure 1; States Features); it consists of a collection of typified valuable indicators (sequences and or dispersed **values/intervals**). E.g. in the human resource management context, *"Education; in terms of degrees"* as well as *"Civil State; in terms of single, married, etc"*, etc., may act as business aspects.

Briefly, identifying/specifying aspects represent a major job during the space modelling phase. Entities should be assigned multiple aspects. Entity by entity should from time to time picks indicators/values related to the considered aspects; towards the concept of "multi-state entity".

Business Transitions, Entity States – entities are intended to evolve and change valued-characteristics over time, they transit with respect to the pre-designated dimensions (above aspects). Business transitions are timed and dated. We depict two main types *locale* (aspect-based, figure 2,3) and *global* (profile-based, figure 4) that materializing some external event and or entity-state re-evaluation, e.g. "Mark gets married", "Mark gets new job position, he may became *manager,* etc."

- **Local Transition** occurs (by some way) when a business entity is incited to get a new position/value from those of the considered dimension (aspect-based; $\tau_{aspect,time}$). E.g. "Mark gets a PhD in 14-09-2011"; the event/transition is made by an external institute at a specific time/date (figure 2, 3).
- **Primary-Sate**; as a result of a local transition, the entity gets a new business state called, also, "Primary-Sate". The Sequence of those primary-states (combining local-transitions, figure 2, 3) forms the true evolution scenario and story for the considered entity.

  Formally: $BE_{ij} = \tau_{ij}(BE_{ij-1})$

      BE_{ij}: ***primary-state*** *on "i", result of transition τ_j on the previous entity-state "$BEij_{-1}$".*

      τ_{ij} : *a **local transition** on aspect i and time j; allocating a new value to the adequate entity's feature.*

      "i" represents a specific aspect (dimension; "Dim-I").

  BE *evolution-scenario:* $\pi_{i,k}(\mathbf{BE}) = \tau_{ik}\, \mathbf{o}\tau_{ik-1}\mathbf{o}... \, \mathbf{o}\tau_{ij-1}\, \mathbf{o}\tau_{ij}\, \tau_{ij+1}\, \mathbf{o}... \, \mathbf{o}\tau_{i1}(\mathbf{BE}_{i0})$
- **Total-states and Business-Profiles;** A Total-Sate is formed by putting together primary-states one by one and one by aspect, e.g. <BE_{1i}, BE_{22}... BE_{ni}> (figure 4). Theoretically, huge amount of states could be generated; only some of them may form a useful and coherent collection. Those collections should be appointed and gave business names, useful states will represent that we call "Business-Profiles"; toward business pattern-based prediction and analysis.

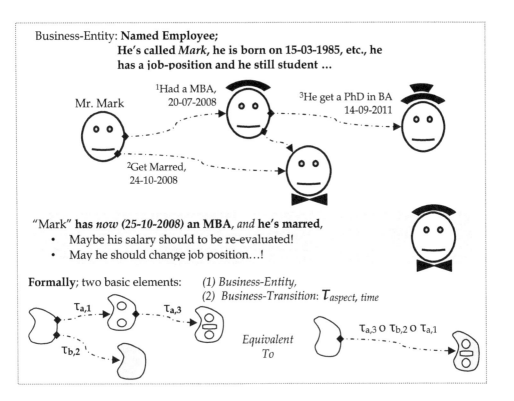

Fig. 2. Business-Transition basis

BE Total-State is "n-pstates" (**primary states**), it is a combination of type <BE_{11}, BE_{2j}, ...,BE_{ij} ..., BE_{nk}>, where:

"1, 2, ..., i, ..., n" indicate the space dimensions (aspects). BE_{ij}: represents a BE primary-state (pstate) over "i" (figure 3).

BE Business-Profile is a named BE Total-State or more general, it looks like: <SA_1, SA_2, ..., SA_i, ..., SA_n>, where SA_i represents an arrangement (a set) of designated positions (valuable as primary-states) on aspect "i". e.g. <BE_{13}, {BE_{22}, BE_{23}, BE_{28}}, ..., [BE_{ik}, BE_{ik+4}], ..., BE_{nm}>.

A Business-Profile may incorporate a set of useful Totat-Stales. E.g.   <BE_{12}, BE_{2j}, ..., {BE_{ij}, BE_{i2}}, ..., BE_{n2}> incorporates both <BE_{12}, BE_{2j}, ..., BE_{ij}, ..., BE_{n2}> and <BE_{12}, BE_{2j}, ..., BE_{i2}, ..., BE_{n2}> Total-states (figure 4).

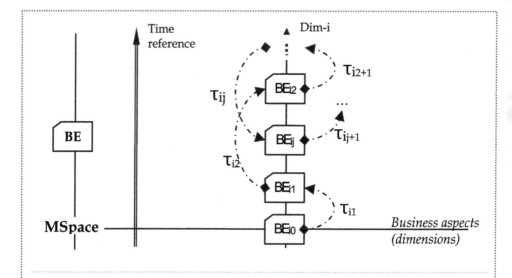

$$BE_{ij} = \tau_{ji} (BE_{ij-1})$$

- "i" represents a specific dimension "Dim-i".

- τ_{ij} : transition on *time* j; allocating a new value to the adequate entity's feature (primary-state on "i")

BE's primary-states, on "i", BE_{i0}, BE_{i1},... , BE_{ij} represent a time based sorted sequence called "**Evolution scenario**".

Fig. 3. Entity-States and Business-Profile basis and foundations

- **Global Transition and Business-Profiles**; named entities should have assigned at least one business-profile, e.g. "Mark get a new computer-science job position, **he is programmer**, and he *may became analyst* (predictable profile), etc." Moving from one business-profile "programmer" to another profile "analyst" is qualified as Global-Transition; profile-based:"$\tau_{profile,time}$", figure 4.

  e.g. Mark's new position; $\tau_{analyst, 20-07-2008}$ ($\tau_{programmer, 10-08-2006}$ (Mark)).

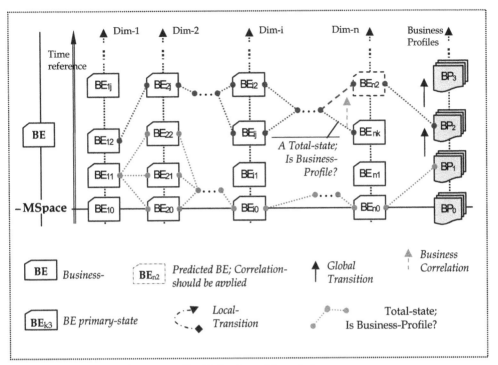

Fig. 4. Entity-States and Business-Profile basis and foundations

However, space designers are incited to identify, during the space modelling phase, at least one business-profile (default profile as well as default primary-states) that each business-entity starts from.

To conclude, The above theory and concepts may mainly be represented either using an algebraic formulation or conceptually by using and adopting the most popular computer-based data modelling techniques, i.e. UML-Like models (next sections).

4.2 BI-like capabilities

MSpace, which we work on, represents a long research project, the validation process refers to business intelligence (BI)-like techniques and practices; pattern-based analysis, business prediction. More capabilities are also integrated; business conduction and entity evolution correlation, etc.

However, the evolution capabilities, in MSpace, are mainly materialized by means of business transitions, especially Global-transitions that express entities progress and evolution. Business-transitions should agree, indeed, to some pre-elaborated management rules, they are directed, predicted and may be correlated and/or encouraged.

E.g. in figure 4 and 6, the current n-pstates $<BE_{12}, BE_{2j}, ..., \{BE_{ij}, BE_{i2}\}, ..., BE_{nk}>$ *couldn't be considered as significant Total-states, neither* $<BE_{12}, BE_{2j}, ..., BE_{ij}, ..., BE_{nk}>$ *nor* $<BE_{12}, BE_{2j}, ..., BE_{i2}, ..., BE_{nk}>$. *The insignificance is due to the last pstate* "BE_{nk}".

Observation: *In this case, the current business-profile "BP$_1$" for the considered entity remain applicable.*

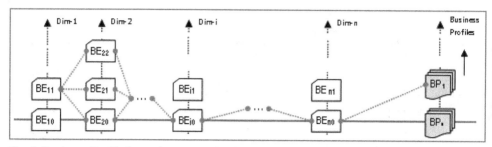

Fig. 5. Business-Profile basis; having multiple values on one aspect "Dim-2"

Direction - first attempt; *estimate the distance (pstates one by one, e.g. "BE$_{nk}$" vs "BE$_{n2}$") between the current Total-state and the nearest significant total-state (next profile). In case of an optimistic assess, the recommendation is to conduct the transition to the nominated profile "BP$_2$" by encouraging the local-transition from "BE$_{nk}$" to "BE$_{n2}$" (figure 4 and 6).*

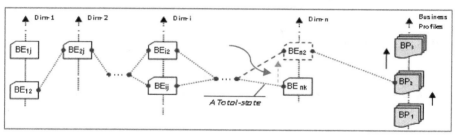

Fig. 6. Business-Profile basis; prediction issues

As shown before, there is a crucial need to introduce and elaborate some BI-like business rules such as "how could auto-conduct business-transitions", etc. However, profile-based analysis, business conduction and correlation, etc. are just now initiated by an experimented operator; they should be enhanced and improved more and more.

4.3 Adaptive software solution

The software model that we adopt looks like a dedicated enterprise manager; transitions as well as pattern-based methodological analysis are Omni-incorporated.

Practically, we opted for component-based client/server software architecture (figure 7); it consists of:

- an Online-Repository-Manager (OMR) applying and emerging a dedicated data-model (next section),
- and two basic front-end modules:
  - an Online-Transition-Processing (OTP) module incorporating functionalities such as: setting-up space features (dimensions, etc.), building business entities, reworking entities, applying transitions, conducting and correlating entity's transitions, etc.

- and an Online-Analytical-Monitoring (OAM) module; here we have two inter-related analytical components:
  - a business-entities' summarizer and explorer, this component leads to re-examine, review (play-back), etc., entity's states (scenarios) and all evolution related transitions. It, also, consists of regrouping, re-organising, re-connecting (semantic connectivity), etc., business entities.
  - and an open and dedicated Business-Intelligence (BI) component emerging and incorporating BI-like tools and functionalities.
    This component represents a curial analytical tool, it helps on conducting and directing entities' transitions, it also helps in correlating entities' evolution. Correlation is almost done according to applied business profiles. It, finally, helps in predicting and expecting entities' future states.

MSpace seems to be a framework intended to assume and emerge BI functionalities as well as analytical monitoring and exploration of the business-space.

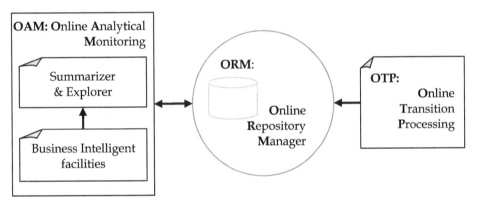

Fig. 7. Adaptive software Architecture

However, MSpace should undergo some building processes. The process aims to build the basic elements, for example, defining the space, building the dimensions and specify their types (discrete or continuous) and domains. Also build the business profiles and their domain intervals. Concerning the business-entities, each entity has its entity state, which describes the values taken at each dimension at a certain time. The business entity profile is the pattern that the entity could follow. Note that business entity could follow many business-profiles along its life cycle, but simultaneously only one is allowed.

4.3.1 The repository data model

The above theory and concepts may mainly be represented either using an algebraic formulation or conceptually by adopting the most popular computer-based data modelling techniques; UML-Like or ER models.

Practically, the proposed data-model incorporates and inherits concepts and theory from the so known multidimensional star schema (diagram in figure 8; BEntity, BEntityState). It also stimulates and materializes our two fundamental bases: (1) multi-sates business entities shown as aggregation of *BEntityState*, (2) and pattern-based analysis referring to *BProfile* (Business Profiles) *and BEntityProfile* conceptual elements that should conduct business-entities evolution.

Finally, setting-up a space, it leads to:

- Generic solution – that instantiates as needed the MSpace and all related features; BProfile, BDim, etc. and the BEntity, BEntityProfile, etc.
- e.g. Employees(named collection) is a set of BEntity.
- or Extendible and case related solution (framework oriented) - allow an engineering procedure leading to initiate (hard coding) and name new domain-related conceptual elements;,
- e.g. Employee ISA BEntity…, Employees (named collection) is a set of Employee.

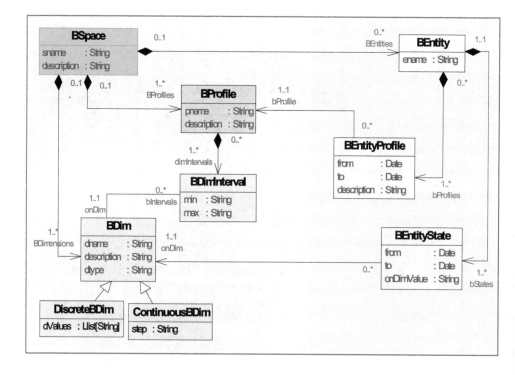

Fig. 8. UML-like multidimensional/state conceptual data model

The above solutions both are valid and applicable. Consequently, the adopted software model allowed an easy setting up and validation of the above data model.

4.3.2 BL Like End-User interface

The end-user interface model supports navigational as well as analytical functionalities; it consists of two main software components (figure 9):

- *Tree-like area* (left side) - it consists of an expandable/collapsible tree that emerges space instances, space aspects/dimensions, business entities, entity states, named business profiles, etc. End users should be able to setup spaces and navigate and explore business features.
- and a *Workspace home area* (right side) – it consists of a large run-time area emerging business-analysis, monitoring, etc. This component plays a crucial role; it should constantly support the analytical approach.

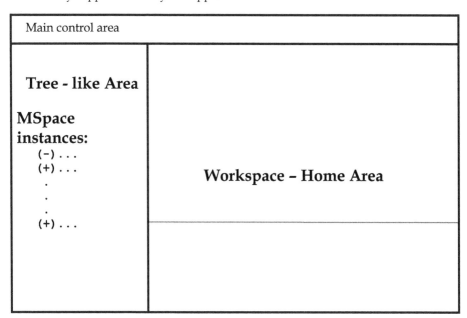

Fig. 9. End user interface

The interface model is intended to be simple, interactive and easy to use; our main goal is to express and demonstrate the above approach and theory. Java APIs (JPA, JPQL, etc.) and facilities provided by Microsoft platform are/have-been used in the validation and prototyping phase.

4.4 Validation and criticism

We are going, in the next section, to deeply consider one typical case study. The study is about employee life cycle analysis "Human Resource Management (HRM)" in the "Lebanese University", the space that we consider is simple and contains single business-entities type. The second case is about city evolution analysis, here the space is complex and partitioned into subspaces, and each subspace could have different type of business-entities.

4.4.1 Case study – Human resource tracking

Human resource (HR) in public sector or in private companies faces enormous challenges in dealing with the growing complexity of managing vast amounts of employee information. Large amounts of employee's historical data and other processes, such as: adding new employees, change the employee state, and even prediction of new employee's state or position, can be managed in business intelligent (BI) system that collect active (on-line) data to make pattern-based-analysis to monitor the employee's life cycle. Improving HR process management can result in significant advantages, especially lower costs, reduced risk, enhanced productivity, and a more comprehensive, reliable and efficient means of managing employee information.

By applying MSpace approach that provides Business Process Management capabilities to HR operations, companies can rise in a progressive strategy for employee lifecycle management, whereby the HR department can effectively manage all relevant employee documents and transactions from "hire to retire". MSpace can enable an organization to eliminate inefficient manual processes that waste valuable employee time. Also, it can provide consistency in executing business processes, and ensure that processes are executed according to industry or governmental requirements.

Mapping case study about the employees' life cycle in the Lebanese University, it is hard to establish analysis about each employee by HR and make analysis about his state, and prediction about his future state, especially when we have a large amount of employee, it takes a lot of effort and time, and it may cost too much, also it may not be accurate. So it is more efficient if we build a BI system with pattern-based-analysis to manage the employee life cycle

Building process: In this case study, we consider that each employee has certain dimensions, such as *gender, age, years of duty, education* degree, *marital status, job specification*. For each of these dimensions, employees can take values from a predefined set of domain indicators that restrict the values at each dimension. Evolution of employee's state at a certain dimension can have an impact on his values of at other dimensions.

Dimensions:

Age: *The length of time that one has existed. Values: positive integer ε [18, 64].*

Marital status: *the condition of being married or unmarried. Values {single, married, divorced}.*

Education level: *the certificates that a person must have in order to apply for a certain job. Values {baccalaureate, BS, BA, MA, MBA, PHD}.*

Years of duty: *the experience that a person had in a certain job. Domain: positive integer ε [18, 46].*

Job specification: *a statement of employee characteristics and qualifications required for satisfactory performance of defined duties and tasks comprising a specific job or function. Job specification is derived from job analysis. Values: {manager, professor, accounter, data entry, supervisor, assistant, secretary}.*

Personnel behaviour: *The actions or reactions of a person in response to external or internal stimuli. Values {Bad, Fair, Good, Very good}.*

As shown in the figure 10, there is a set of dimensions that specify the employee life cycle, here the employee known as business entity (BE), these BSs navigate in this multi-dimensional space taking a range of allowed values along dimensions. BEs can follow certain patterns based in order to reach a goal; these patterns offer a range of values at each dimension for those BE, later we will see a set of patterns in the multi-dimension diagram, that draw a road map for BEs to navigate along it.

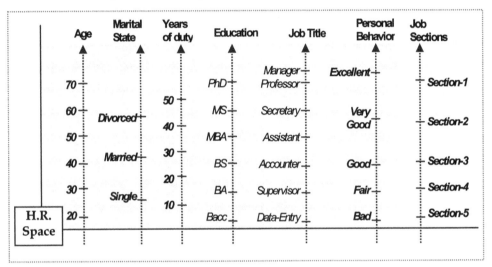

Fig. 10. HR space; business features – dimensions and profiles

Employee Profiles (Named patterns) - As follows, all the business patterns will be mentioned in order to have a clear idea about the allowed employee state transitions:

Job section (salary dependent): each employee has a degree that merges his/her education level and job specification, this degree has an effect in salary, social security level, and employee's state evolution. Values {Section 1, Section 2, Section 3, Section 4, Section 5}.

Employee Profiles and evolutive rules:

Transition to job section 3: if an employee held baccalaureate certificate and he/she is in job section 4 could not be able to transits to job in section 3, unless he/she has at least BA/BS certificate nor has more than 10 years of duty. In both cases, the employee must have good/very good personal behaviour. Note that, changes along all other dimensions will not affect the employee state.

Manager position : if an employee is in section 3 and held MBA/MS certificate or a professor can transits into manager position, in both cases, employee/professor should has more than 5 years in duty and good/very good personal behaviour. Transition occurs only when the position at a certain job section is available.

Transition to section 4: if an employee is in section 5 and wants to become in section 4, he/she wants to hold the baccalaureate certificate and has more than 5 years in duty and considered as fair personal behaviour or above.

Employee Database (instances are compacted):

In the following table, there are some data collected from online database of the Lebanese university faculty of science. Note that each distinct record considered as a single Business Entity (BE), has its set of values along each dimension that combine to formulate business entity state.

Name	Age	Marital status	Educ-ation	Years of duty	Job specification	Job Section	Personal behavior
S. Harb	35	Married	BA	6	Accounting	Section 3	Good
F. Soloh	40	Married	BS	11	Supervisor	Section 3	V.Good
S. Hamoud	45	Single	Bacc	22	Data entry	Section 4	Good
A. Kanj	55	Married	PHD	18	Manager	Section 2	V.Good
R. Bitar	58	Married	PHD	15	Professor	Section 2	V.Good
H. Aloush	40	Married	BS	12	Accouter	Section 3	V.Good
H. Badra	40	Married	BA	15	Secretary	Section 4	Good
S. Sibaia	36	Single	Bacc	6	Data entry	Section 4	Fair

Table 1. HR space; an empirical database for Employees

Employee Evolution Issues - There are a set of business pattern (BP) that constraint the transition of BEs from a state to state, BE cannot transits unless it satisfies the constraints for a certain BP. In our case study (human resource department in the Lebanese university), there are many BPs that constraint the employee evolution along the job specification dimension.

Consider the following case that illustrates the proposed patterns, here there is an employee called "S.Hamoud" <45, Single, **Bacc**, 22, Data entry, Good, **Section 4**>, she is in job section 4 and she held the baccalaureate certificate and she behave well, but later she obtained a BS in science which results to a state transition in job section form 4 to 3.

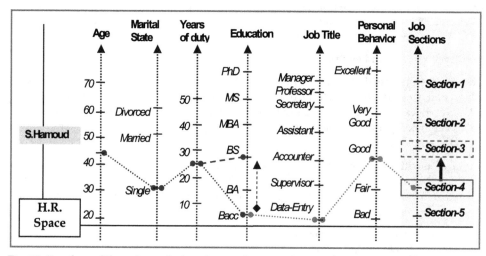

Fig. 11. Employee life cycle evolution; the employee got a new degree!

In the figure 11, we see the dash line that describe the current state of "S.Hamoud", but later on she obtained BS certificate (dashed line), this change leads to evolution at the section level dimension and become at value 3.

Entity values may evolve at any dimension and this evolution may leads to transition to new state based on predefined pattern analysis. Furthermore, certain state transitions need an evolution at more than one dimension to be omitted, for example, if an employee at accounting position held BA in business management and he is 30 years old may not be a manager, unless he complete his master degree and he is above 35.

In this case we have the employee "H.Aloush" <40, Married, BS, 12, Accouter, V.Good, Section 3> in job section 3, an evolution occurred at the education level from BS into MBA, this evolution in addition to the overall state of Ms. Aloush lead to two transitions in the job specification and job section dimensions. By this transition Ms. Aloush may become a manager and in section 3, as shown in figure 12.

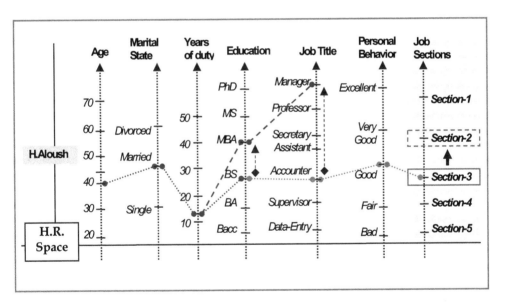

Fig. 12. The employee (H. Aloush) became Manager; *H. Aloush* should be repositioned in his job sections!

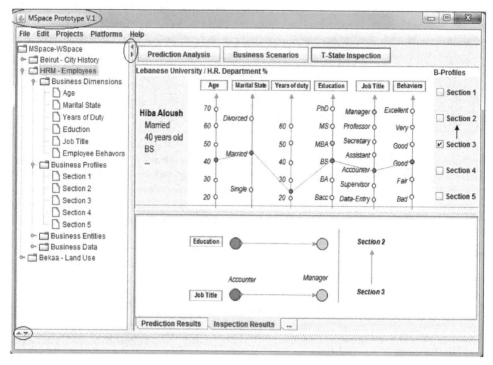

Fig. 13. MSpace software prototype

Otherwise, our business-analysis theory is about to be integrated in the MSpace software prototype (figure 13). The experiments show that the restrictions made on the space (building process; dealing with only one entities type) are so useful and give very good results.

4.4.2 Complex case study and criticism

The idea behind this section is to express the big challenges that we are faced where the space is qualified as complex. Given materials are hypothetical, devised theory is still under validation!

However, we trying, in this section, to analyze and track the evolution in a city, we record and analyze futures, and urbanization from multiple perspectives. We partition the city into a set of adjacent areas (figure 14), these areas are seen as business entities. Those entities take values along a set of dimensions such as: Building, Street, Garden, etc. Here business entities are subspaces that are each one is considered as independent space that has its entities, dimensions and patterns; towards hyper-mspace.

Dimensions - At the first level the space contains set of areas and three dimensions:

Building: Permanent or temporary structure enclosed within exterior walls and a roof, etc. Values {civil building, hospital, school, university}.

Street: a public thoroughfare, usually paved, in a village, town, or city, including the sidewalk or sidewalks. Values {public, private}.

Garden: a plot of ground, usually near a house, where flowers, shrubs, vegetables, fruits, or herbs are cultivated. Values {area, capacity, location}.

etc.

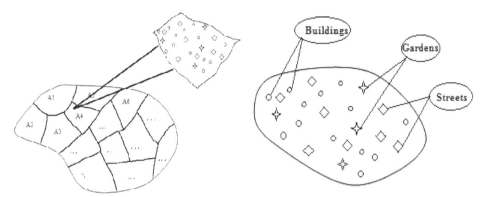

Fig. 14. Space decomposition

Business Patterns/Profiles -

Area is fully constructed: where no other building, street or garden could be added, the ratio of civilians to the number of buildings, streets and gardens used to make decision about the capacity of the area.

Area is not fully constructed: where some building, street or garden could be added.

Only gardens could be added: since the ratio of total area to the number of buildings and streets is fair in order not to have overpopulation.

etc.

As we mentioned the space (city) is partitioned into set of subspaces (areas), each one has its business-entities and patterns. Subspaces have common dimensions and may contain different types of independent BEs, where in some cases evolution in BE's state may influence other BEs. By projection along areas we introduced into subspaces with more dimensions, these subspaces contain BEs with different categories such as building, street, and garden.

Relating to the inner spaces, there are a set of dimensions that describe them and the specification of each categories and their dimension is defined as follows:

Dimensions of Buildings category: Height; Values {real positive number}, Area of the building; Values {real positive number}, Distance from street; Values {real positive number}, Capacity of the building; Values {positive integer}, etc.

Consider, for example, the subspace (area A4 in figure 14) called "Down Town", it contains a set of business entities from different categories: Buildings, Streets, etc. So the transformation of one entity may influence other entities, note that we can trace the state of BE into a diagram and make comparison and analysis with other BE. For example, the presence of building in such place requires the presence of street, and the presence of 20 buildings or more requires the presence of a garden.

As a result, the partition of city into sub-areas facilitates analysis, support decision making and prediction of BEs' states and transitions along dimensions.

4.4.3 Observation and criticism

As we seen in the previous case studies, space may be simple where only one type of business entity could be founded, or complex and composite with different types of business entities.

The experiments show that we are pressed, during the validation process, to decide with what category we are going to deal with; simple and/or complex spaces. Theoretically, the most typical spaces are simple or should be simplified / restricted. Restrictions are indeed about the space constitution itself; they regard the space building process.

Practically, spaces are usually complex, and business-entities could be referred to many different categories, they could interact and influence each other, etc.

To conclude, the model should be applied to all cases; simple or complex, e.g. Marine navigation tracking, Soldiers and lifesaving in risked areas, Biomedical treatments and experiments, etc. As a result, the above approach is still under elaboration, complex cases aren't yet solved. In the next phase, we plan to elaborate a deep theory that deals with such cases; interaction rules, space subdivision rules, hierarchical space constitution (multi-levelling space), vertical navigational rules (summarising, zooming, etc.), etc.

5. Conclusion

Data growth consistently, and day by day, emergent technologies are solicited more and more. Business applications became more intelligent, due to the advance in data computation and integration technologies.

The approach "MSpace" that we proposed represents an initiative leading to provide a flexible modelling framework. We started by elaborating features and foundations that introduce and characterize concepts of evolutive/mutable space and business entities. We stated that business entities are reactive, multidimensional and multi-states. Business entities transit, continually, from one state to another state; entity-states (primary or total) characterize entity-transitions. In MSpace business-entities' transitions are predicted and, usually, conducted, they could be correlated with respect to pre-elaborated patterns (Business Profiles).

Practically, MSpace is end-user oriented tool intended to stimulate business intelligence facilities such as pattern-based analysis and an analytical navigation through space components; it inherits both OLTP and OLAP characteristics. The tool consists mainly of one emergent data model (ORM: Online Repository Manager) and a BI-like Examiner and explorer (OAM: Online Analytical Monitor).

After specifying the software architecture, we opted during the validation process for Java platform; the devised prototype is attractive and hopeful. We started validating the tool through two different and distinguishable space categories; *simple* mono entities type (case study: employee life cycle analysis in the Human Resource department in the Lebanese University) and *complex* without restrictions on the entity types (case study: city evolution analysis).

Rather than the elegant and hopeful outcomes, the experiments show that we need to deploy more efforts regarding especially the second category of MSpace's instances. As a result, we need indeed to state for a complete complex-space building and exploring theory; we need to answer questions like "how the space could be partitioned", "how entities could interact and influence each other", "how could navigate through different levels", etc., such questions outline, finally, our future research.

6. References

Dbouk & Sbeity 2009, Dbouk, M. & Sbeity, I. (2009). *GeoSEMA: A Modelling Platform, Emerging GeoSpatial-based Evolutionary and Mobile Agents.* World Congress on Science, Engineering and Technology (WCSET 2009); Conf. Proceedings ISSN: 2070-3740, March 23-25, 2009, Hong Kong, China.

Erwig et al., 1999, Erwig, M.; Güting, R. H., Schneider, M. & Vazirgiannis, M. (1999). *Spatio-Temporal Data Types: An Approach to Modeling and Querying Moving Objects in Databases.* In Geoinformatica, vol.3 n.3, p.269-296, September 1999.

Pestana & da Silva, 2005, Pestana, G. & da Silva, M. M. (2005). *Multidimensional Modeling Based on Spatial, Temporal and Spatio-Temporal Stereotypes.* ESRI Inter. User Conference July-25-29 (2005), San Diego Convention Centre, California.

Pelekis et al. 2006, Pelekis, N.; Theodoridis, Y., Vosinakis, S. & Panayiotopoulos T. (2006). *Hermes - A Framework for Location-Based Data Management.* In EDBT 2006, Springer Lecture Notes in Computer Science, Vol. 3896, pp.1130-1134.

Praing & Schneider, 2007a, Praing, R. & Schneider M. (2007). *A Universal Abstract Model for Future Movements of Moving Objects.* In AGILE International Conference on Geographical Information Systems, 2007.

Praing & Schneider, 2007b, Praing, R. & Schneider M. (2007). *Modeling historical and future movements of Spatio-temporal objects in moving objects databases.* In proceedings of the 16th ACM Conf. on Information and Knowledge Management (CIKM), p183-192, Lisbon- Portugal, Nov. 6-10, 2007.

Hammam et al., 2004, Hammam, Y.; Moore A., Whigham P. & Freeman C. (2004). *Irregular vector-agent based simulation for land-use modelling.* In 16th Annual Colloquium of the Spatial Information Research Centre (SIRC 2004: A Spatio-temporal Workshop), 29-30 November 2004, Dunedin, New Zealand, pp. 103-116.

Zhang et al., 2007, Zhang, L.; Yin, X. & Liu, Y. (2007). *Multidimensional modelling of marine water body based on time series multi-surfaces.* Society of Photo-Optical Instrumentation Engineers, Bellingham, 2007 SPIE, Bellingham, Wash., ETATS-UNIS (2007)

Part 3

Mobile Applications as Service

7

Designing an Interactive Museum Guide: A Case Study for Mobile Software Development

Dilek Karahoca[1,2] and Adem Karahoca[1]
[1]Bahçeşehir University Software Engineering Department
[2]Near East University Computer Technology and
Instructional Design PhD Program Department
Turkey

1. Introduction

Portable devices disseminate the information sharing without encountering the location barriers. By the great enhancements of mobile phones, it has been changed the direction of computing to the people centric computing (Lane et al. (2006), Shi et al. (2010)). Mobile phones have advantages to support mobile learning (m-learning) through the use of wireless mobile technology to allow learners to access information from anywhere and at any time (Ally, 2009). M-learning can be defined as "using mobile and interactive technologies to transfer information and knowledge with different contexts" (Sharples et al., 2007).

Mobile phone has become a part of the personalized computing. Nowadays everyone has a strong loyalty to use these devices. Personalization helps users to identifying his intentions, and trends about a specific area. In the life-long learning activities, museums have interested to provide information from ancient history to modern ages. This viewpoint emphasizes the importance and role of the museums and their accessibility. By using mobile learning platform and its features, we can share information about the museums not only with audio guides about art objects but also the location of the museums and places located in near environment. Also, interactive tools can provide interfaces for users to access some art objects which located in a specific museum by help of the mobile solutions.

Lifelong learning process (LLP) covers learning knowledge and gaining new skills throughout his life and focuses on the post-educational period. In LLP, individuals have to be self-motivated and voluntary to learn themselves. Lifelong learning materials have to be designed for different age groups and different levels. Visiting a museum and obtaining knowledge from its exhibition is one of the suitable areas for lifelong learning. To provide the efficiency for the museum visiting, mobile museum guide will be a good way to directed learners (Aspin and Chapman, 2000).

The goal of this study is to develop an application that will provide information about museum guide, using smart mobile devices. This chapter presents the architecture and implementation of such a location-based application, called Mobile Museum Guide, with the mobile phone as a platform. Implemented on Android, the system is designed to provide museum guide information services; therefore, people can get museum guidance information that they need anytime and anywhere.

In the beginning of the 2000's, tourist guides or museum guides need to develop specific devices to provide information about art objects, finding a location about an art gallery, and providing detailed information about a particular art object. But now, rapidly increasing mobile phone market provides smarter phones that have abilities to access any portal by using Internet or executing specific software tools to push or pull some important information.

In this study, mobile devices are used for creating a mobile museum guide for exhibition contexts to improve the visiting experience, increase learning, and satisfying interests. In this book chapter, it will be described the design, implementation and deployment of a location-based application, named mobile museum guide for the mobile platform. This application will permit users to get museum guidance information when they need anytime and anywhere. In particular, the users could be browsed or queried through an Internet map service such as Google Maps.

This study includes following functional items:

- Find your current location within the Museum and explore the map.
- Get real-time directions to your next exhibit, a café, or anywhere else in the Museum by using the smallest route.
- Learn more about items from the Museum's collection, during your visit or browse exhibits from anywhere in the world.
- Choose from Museum highlights or in-depth guided tours.
- Plan your own tour before you arrive or on the spot.
- Share an interesting exhibit through email, Facebook, or Twitter.
- Want to learn more? Bookmark an item and receive a link to more information when you get home.

From the functional viewpoint, following manifesto items are the aim of this project for visitors (Chou et al., 2004):

- Mobile application should provide deep information about art objects,
- Mobile application should present information about any art objects or collection without requesting or searching information about it. Information should be provided as location based services.
- Museum exhibition should be enjoyable with accessing different activities and places by mobile application.

Forthcoming sections are considering consecutively about mobile technologies for museums, a mobile museum guide analysis, design, and development stages. Also at last, conclusions and future directions are given.

2. Mobile technologies for museums

Smart phones and tablets take place everywhere as mobile partners. These mobile devices have accessibility to Internet and wireless nets. When we look at the pros and cons of these devices, mobility and accessibility as portability seems to be advantages, but, small screen sizes, prices, heterogeneity in mobile applications, and constraints in presenting multimedia information gives a negative impression. For implementing these devices in museums, smart devices' connectivity features have to be taking into account to providing exhibition, and guide information to visitors. When the mobile devices are concern point, location based services may be taking into account. New generation smart phones have support the GPS functionality. Thus, location based services can be a trigger the visitor to getting any information near to him.

For example, portable devices such as personal digital assistants were used to provide interactive museum guidance. Chou et al. (2004) constructed a platform to support PDAs to give information about special art objects by using text, voice or video clip. Context-awareness is the popular human computer interaction discipline. A context-aware system defined as a system that "uses context to provide relevant information and/or services to the user, where relevancy depends on the user's task" (Dey and Abowd, 2000). The presentation of these services or information brings with it the issue of proactiveness – should the system initiate the presentation of information or should it wait for the user to request information (Lanir, 2011). Context-aware systems might support three categories of features: (1) presentation of information and services to the user; (2) automatic execution of a service; and (3) tagging of context to information for later retrieval (Dey and Abowd, 2000). In a related project, Ghiani et al (2009) propose a multi device, location aware museum guide which able to read RFID tags. Context-dependent information presented to the visitor via his location and historical behaviors. Proactiveness of mobile visitors' guides brings with it a possibility for better service to the user at the cost of taking control out of the user's hand (Lanir et al., 2011)

As emphasized here that, smart phones and tablets can be used to support interactive museum guidance. By using Wi-Fi, 3G or another network connection method, visitors can access to bring exhibition related information and special event notifications. Also, GPS (Global Positioning System) provides mobile user location via satellite. By using the location data, location awareness can be obtained. For instance, "special exhibitions near to you alerts" can be produced for museum visitors. Floor plans of the museum and location information of the visitor may be matched and, some adaptive guidance can be generated. As illustrated in Fig. 1, museum collections and art objects categorization data is located in DB server and business logic related issues located in application server, web server handle the requests which are coming from the web and mobile clients (Xiehao et al., 2009). By using this network topology, geospatial data can be integrated with multimedia data. This architecture can present the location based services to the museum visitors. Location based service creates location and multimedia data relations to provide information.

3. A Mobile application for achieving museums: Mobile museum guide (MMG)

Mobile museum guide development is the main idea of this study. In this section, mobile software development stages are detailed. MMG development project is organized base on the smart phone abilities. Functional and process based analysis is performed consecutively.

Software engineering encapsulates different techniques and models to support successful project management. Models and methodologies describe any system by using different notation, association semantics, and relationship between activities. Software methodology like UML covers all requirements engineering activities by using different diagraming techniques to enforce the software quality assurance. UML diagrams generate different documents and models: requirements specification documents, analysis models, designs, code, testing specifications and reports and so on. These documents and models are the inputs for the related forthcoming and planned activities that reside in software development life cycle (Jacobsen et al., 1998).

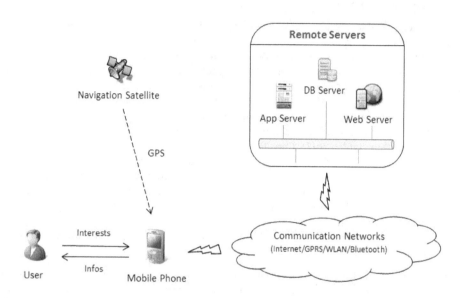

Fig. 1. Mobile users and accessible networks (Xiehao et al., 2009)

Following sub sections have details about mobile software development life cycle and its stages.

3.1 Mobile software development life cycle

Mobile software development life cycle is same as traditional software development and its life cycle. But it has some different aspects such as in duration of the software development time. Rapidly increasing mobile devices and mobile software tools enforce the minimization of the development time of the mobile software. But, common development platforms, such as iOS, Android, Black Berry, Symbian, Windows Mobile, et al., support same capabilities with different efforts.

In this study, activities of the software development life cycle are taking into account as: "Analysis", "Development ", "Testing/Training", "Documentation" and "Project go live".

At the analysis phase, system requirements analysis is performed and detailed the technical requirements of the software. This allows real time update of content, such as exhibition information of the museums, guided tours, special event notification and great flexibility of information. Also, it was decided to using Android platform which is the number one mobile platform for more easily learning and developing mobile applications.

Second work package of the analysis phase covers identifying processes for museum learning system modules. In this stage, design prototypes were prepared by Balsamiq software tool and UML diagrams drawn. At the development phase, we developed all modules for Android devices. At the testing phase, all modules were tested with Android supported device. At the last stage, review and acceptance of the study realized.

In this study, we might summarize following work packages in developing and implementing mobile museum guidance:

- Analyzing and designing context-awareness museum guide principals,
- Developing mobile application,
- Usability Testing to the mockups, resolving problems,
- Acceptance testing,
- Deploying the application.

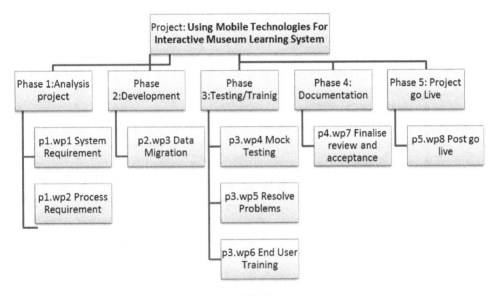

Fig. 2. Example Work Breakdown Structure (WBS)

3.2 Model driven analysis activities for developing MMG

Analysis activities start with investigating end users' (visitors) expectations from the MMG. As described by Richardson et al. (1998), interface development stage can be supported with task analysis and designers need to work detailed specification of requirements for the interface. For satisfying, functional and non-functional behavior of the proposed system, software specification has to be organized based on the hierarchical task analysis (HTA). Stanton (2006) proposes that HTA provides an opportunity to the analyst to plan tasks not only the designer but also end user viewpoint. Annett (2006) emphasize that "*HTA encourages the analyst to consider not only what should happen, but also what does actually happen and how this can go wrong. He suggests that these questions will arise naturally as the analyst seeks to discover the indicators for success and failure of each of the sub-goals*" (Stanton, 2006). In investigating user requirements, task analysis, specially HTA might be a useful tool for system analysts and system designers (Stanton, 2004).

In interactive system design, task analysis has to take into account the end user profile and system usage. Ormerod and Shepherd (2004) proposes sub goal template to obtain requirements specifications by a task analysis.

Here, HTA analysis is performed to obtain the main skeleton of the application. As illustrated in Fig. 3, language selection, museum searching, creating favorites list, and items info are the main tasks for the MMG application. "Search Museum" function is the main task of the application and it has criteria for filtering museums by map, city, type, culture, term, era, or a year.

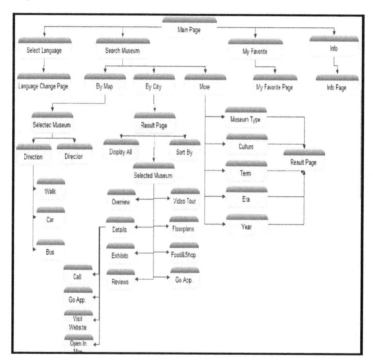

Fig. 3. Hierarchical task analysis and menu items

Use case driven approach is well known and used in the requirements elicitation phase of software development life cycle (Jacobson, 1992).

Hsu et al. (2012) propose a touristic trip forecasting and intelligent recommendation system. Also, they use Google Maps API to allow the user to adjust the geographic data according to personal needs. Google Maps API well accepted for connecting geospatial data with business data. Also in this study, transportation to the museum and directions are provided by using Google Maps API. After the selection process of the museum, extra information and features are presented to the visitors.

In Table 1, fourteen different use cases are listed to show all details of the MMG. In use case model 1, following steps are followed;

- User runs the application,
- User accesses main page,
- User selects "language change" button,
- User browses language change page,
- User selects another language from the list,
- Finally, system sets application language as selected.

Second use case includes museum searching steps:

- User runs the application,
- User goes main page,
- User selects "search museum" button,
- User browses search museum page,
- User selects search by map button,
- User explores via Google map and sets location,
- User selects a museum in this map,
- If user selects direction icon, system draws direction line (user current location with museum),
- If the user clicks car icon, system calculates taxi price,
- If the user clicks bus icon, system gives options bus name for current location,
- If the user clicks walk icon, system calculates the distance (user current location with museum).

Main concept of the designed system listed in the second use case model and illustrated in Fig.4.

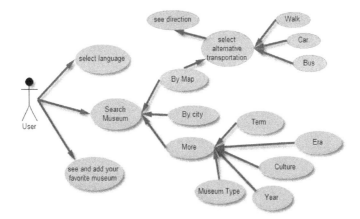

Fig. 4. Use Case Modeling diagram for searching museums

Functional requirements can be best obtained by using use case models (Jacobsen et al., 1992; Jacobsen et al., 1998). Business analysts and system analysts prefer to prepare the use case models which include more practical business rules and descriptive statements of natural language. As mentioned before, use case modeling helps analysts to develop functional requirements and task models such as HTA or sub goal templates (SGT) are feeding user interface design stage. In the specification of use cases, the described activities are performed by entity when interacting with an actor (here end user or visitor).

Use cases, introduced by Jacobsen et al. (1992), versus task descriptions to identify sequences of actions, considering variants to generate a response from system to an actor (Booch, 1999). The definition emphasized that actions performed by system not user. The UML diagram reflects this, showing use cases as bubbles inside the system. Task descriptions don't cover

Quality requirements such as response time and usability, but they point out where quality is crucial (Lauesen, 2003). As Lauesen (2003) declared that, a UML use case diagram, which deals only with the computer system's actions and separate human and computer actions; but the task descriptions, which do not separate human and computer actions. This feature supports the requirements engineering activities based on the object oriented analysis and design side.

Use Cases	Description
Use Case 1	User changes language
Use Case 2	Find your current location and Museum location, explore the map. User get real time direction to museum User get distance to museum User get transportation option (taxi, bus, on foot)
Use Case 3	User search museums with some criteria (this criteria: by map, by city, museum type, culture, term, era, year)
Use Case 4	User adds favorite museums to favorite page.
Use Case 5	User display museum search result with some criteria (display all, A to-Z, area, distance, popularity)
Use Case 6	User display overview about selected museum and rate it.
Use Case 7	User display selected museum's exhibitions.
Use Case 8	User display selected museum's floor plan.
Use Case 9	User downloads selected museum's application.
Use Case 10	User display selected museum's multimedia tours.
Use Case 11	User display museum calendar (what's happening today, tomorrow and this weekend)
Use Case 12	User gets detailed information about selected museum (address, phone, web site address etc.)
Use Case 13	User searches alternative restaurant, café, shops near the selected museum.
Use Case 14	User share museum opinion with social network (Facebook, Twitter etc.)

Table 1. Use cases for MMG

One of the most important components of UML is the class diagram, that model the information on the domain of interest in terms of objects organized in classes and relationships between them. UML class diagrams allow for modeling, in a declarative way, the static structure of an application domain, in terms of concepts and relations between them (Fowler and Scott, 1997).

A UML class diagram represents a set of objects with common features. A class has a rectangle and top the shape consist the name of the class. The attributes of the class diagram are denoted in the second cell of the rectangle. Third cell consists of the operations that associated to the object of the class (Berardi et al., 2005). N-ary association shows more than three connections between classes. Figure 5 illustrates the class diagram for MMG study.

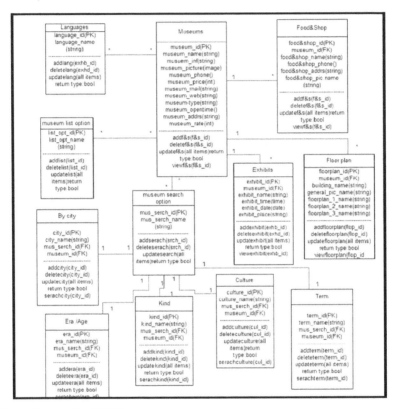

Fig. 5. Class diagram for MMG

Dynamic behavior of a system can be modeled in UML based sequence diagrams and proposed that at least a sequence diagram have to be drawn for per Use Case to describe the behavior of the sub system more efficiently (Jacobsen et al., 1992). By using the Use Case's description, first version of the sequence diagram can be prepared. In the design process, the Use Case diagram or the Sequence diagram might be updated till fine and tuning satisfied (Larman, 1998). A sequence diagram has two parts, the vertical side represents time, and the horizontal side represents the different classes. Time proceeds down the page and, there is no significance to the horizontal ordering of the object types (Jacobsen et al., 1992). In figure 6, sequence diagram of museum search is depicted.

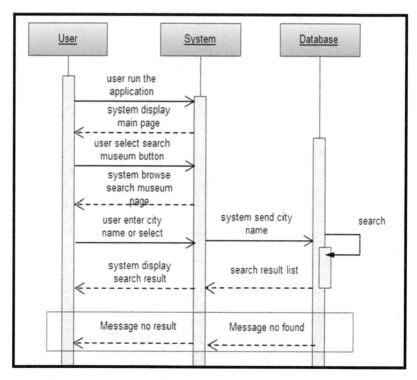

Fig. 6. Sequence Diagram - User searching museum by city name

3.3 User interface designing activities for MMG

Usability of mobile device depends on the size. Shneiderman's "Golden Rules for interface design" covers eight interface design guidelines (Shneiderman, 1998). But four of them can directly be applied to the mobile devices;

- Enable frequent users to use shortcuts,
- Offer informative feedback,
- Design dialogs to yield closure,
- Support internal locus of control.

Gong and Taraswewich (2004) propose modifications on other four design guidelines.

- Consistency (create input/output methodologies which are device independent),
- Reversal of actions (mobile applications should rely network connectivity as little as possible),
- Error prevention and simple error handling,
- Reduce short-term memory load (recognition of function choices instead of memorization of commands),

Following mock-up designs are constructed by considering the modified Golden Rules for interface design.

In the main mockup screen, user can select language information for the mobile application or select the search museum button. User can use action bar.	The user can change mobile application language with this page.	This mockup screen helps for searching museums. The user can enter city name and all museums can be listed which located in that city. Also user can search museums by map.

In this mockup screen, selected city's museums are listed. The visitor displays all museum and sort by selected category.	This mockup screen shows Google map to select museum via map. The user can reach the selected museum in map. MMG offers selections to reach there (car/bus/walk).	In this mockup screen Google map helps visitor to reach museum. Application gets visitors location by GPS and calculates the distance to reach the museum. The user can see selected museum in map. He can see the distance to museum.

This mockup screen has Google map. The user can see selected museum in map. Application offers an option to visitors for go there (car/bus/walk).	This mockup screen helps visitor for searching museum by using criteria. These criteria are museum kind, culture, term, year, era.	This mockup screen shows selected museum by the kind criteria. The user can see some kind of museums if visitor finds a specific museum he finds it very fast withThis searching criterion.

This mockup screen displays selected criteria result. Visitor can find museum's rate and distance.	This mockup screen displays overview about selected museum. User can rate this museum.	This mockup screen displays museum's floor plan.

This mockup screen shows social network page. User can give some comment for visited museum.	This mockup screen shows different alternative places such as restaurant, café, and shop for near the selected museum.	This mockup screen shows selected museum and details information about this museum. User can access the selected museum's overview, details, exhibits, reviews, floor plans.

This mockup screen displays information page of selected museum. User can reach museum address, phone, city, open time and close time, and entry price.	This mockup screen shows multimedia page of museum. Visitor can watch museum's introduction video.	This mockup screen displays culture criteria for searching museum. User can select a culture and list the selected culture's related museum(s).

This mockup screen displays term criteria for searching museum. User can select a term and list selected term's museum.	This mockup screen shows selected era or age criteria for searching museum.	

3.4 Usability analysis based on the ISO9241-11

The development of mobile applications has some important limitations; such as, size of the screen, memory and processing capacities of the smart phones. For these reasons, different design decision for the tasks has to be taking into account (Rauch, 2011). Nielsen (2011) reports that the mobile user experience improving slightly 59% to 62% and these success rates obtained by computing correctly versus incorrectly done tasks. Also, shown that, acceptance of mobile applications are better than mobile site. Even web site is good; success rate of mobile application usage is 76% and 64% for web site success rate.

These feedbacks show that mobile applications may suffer from the usability and design issues. To handle design issues effectively, mobile interface analysis and design stages have to be supported with mock-up usability tests. As Nielsen (2009) reported that, since WAP phones (2000), there is not progress in task performance. He conducted two simple tasks to users and expected that current phones have improvement from usability perspective. But, results show that feature phones (regular cellular phone) have worst user experience when accessing web sites. Smart phones and touch phones have average success rates 55% and 75% respectively when accessing web sites. Bigger screen of the mobile phones provides better user experience (Nielsen, 2009).

Activity	Average Results
1. Time to complete to task	234 seconds
2. Percent of task completed	%86
3. Percent of task completed per unit time	%69
4. Ratio of success to failures	0
5. Time spent in errors	0
6. Percent or number of errors	0
7. Number of competitors better than it	2
8. The number of commands used	10
9. Frequency of help and documentation use	0
10. Percent of favorable/unfavorable user comments	%50
11. Number of repetitions of failed commands	0
12. Number of runs of success and failures	0
13. Number of times interface misleads the user	2
14. Number of good and bad feature recalled by users	2
15. Number of available commands nor invoked	16
16. Number of regressive behaviors	1
17. Number of users preferring your system	3/5
18. Number of time average number of users need to work around a problem	0
19. Number of times the user is disrupted from a work task	0
20. Number of times user loses control of the system	2
21. Number of times user expresses frustration of satisfaction	0

Table 2. ISO9241-11 Usability results

From these viewpoints, here, usability analysis conducted with five expert users with "search museums nearby here" scenario. In ISO9241 usability standard, twenty-one criteria can be used to measuring the usability and the possible ways to set the worst/best case and planned/now-level targets. These measurements are named as usability metrics. We now describe the development and evaluation of usability trails for MMG with five HCI experts to access on smart phones by performing ISO 9241-11 usability standard. Parameters and average trail results of the interfaces are listed in Table 2 for five experts.

4. Conclusion

As a result, best way to provide information to people, seems to be mobile phones. But these devices have some miserable aspects such as screen size. To provide information efficiently and more rapid way, design aspects have to be consider for different sized mobile phones. Even mobile applications have usability advantages when compared with web sites; but also, they have also limitations, because of the design shortcomings. This chapter shows that mobile application development stages can be modeled by model driven software development in software development life cycle. Mobile applications development platforms and programming languages can be different. But, main design idea is same; keep it simple, accessible and minimal. Complex and confused design strategies might be hazardous for mobile applications and web sites.

5. Acknowledgment

The authors would like to thank to Miss Hafize Arabul for designing the prototypes of the MMG.

6. References

Ally, M. (2009). Mobile Learning: Transforming the Delivery of Education and Training, pp. 1, ISSN 1919-4390, Edmonton, Canada.

Annett, J.(1996). Recent developments in hierarchical task analysis, S.A. Robertson (Ed.), Contemporary Ergonomics, Taylor & Francis, London, pp. 263–268.

Aspin, D. N.; Chapman, J.D.(2000). Lifelong learning: concepts and conceptions, International Journal of Lifelong Education, vol. 19, no. 1, pp. 2-19, 2000.

Berardi, D.; Calvanese,D.; Giacomo,G.D.(2005). Reasoning on UML class diagrams, Artificial Intelligence, Vol.168, No:1-2, pp.70-118, ISSN 0004-3702, 10.1016/j.artint.2005.05.003.

Booch, G.; Rumbaugh, J.; Jacobson, I. (1999). The Unified Modeling Language User Guide, Addison-Wesley, Boston.

Chou, L.-D. Lee, C.-C. Lee, M.-Y., Chang,, C.-Y. (2004). A Tour Guide System for Mobile Learning in Museums, The 2nd IEEE International Workshop on Wireless and Mobile Technologies in Education (WMTE'04).

Dey, A.K.; Abowd, G.D.(2000). Towards a better understanding of context and context-awareness, CHI 2000 workshop on the what, who, where, when, and how of context-awareness, pp. 1-6.

Fowler, M.; Scott, K. (1997). UML Distilled – Applying the Standard Object Modeling Laguage, Addison-Wesley, Reading, MA, 1997.

Ghiani, G.; Paternò, F.; Santoro, C.; Spano, L.D.(2009). UbiCicero: A location-aware, multi-device museum guide, Interacting with Computers, Volume 21, Issue 4, August 2009, Pages 288-303, ISSN 0953-5438, 10.1016/j.intcom.2009.06.001.

Gong, J., Taraswewich,P.(2004). Guidelines for handheld mobile device interface design. Proceedings of the Decision Sciences Institute Annual Meeting.

Hsu,F.-H.; Lin,Y.-T.; Ho,T.-K.(2012). Design and implementation of an intelligent recommendation system for tourist attractions: The integration of EBM model, Bayesian network and Google Maps, Expert Systems with Applications, Vol.39, No:3, pp.3257-3264, ISSN 0957-4174, 10.1016/j.eswa.2011.09.013.

Jacobson, I.; Christerson, M.; Jonsson, P.; Övergaard, G.(1992). Object-oriented Software Engineering, a Use Case Driven Approach, Addison-Wesley, Reading, MA.

Jacobson, I., Booch, G., Rumbaugh, J. (1998). The Unified Software Development Process, Addison Wesley, Reading, MA

Lane, N.D. ; Miluzzo, E.; Peterson, R. A. ; Ahn, G.-S.; Campbell, A. T.(2006). Metrosense project: People-centric sensing at scale, In First Workshop on World-Sensor-Web (WSW'2006).

Lanir,J.; Kuflik,T.; Wecker,A.J.; Stock,O.; Zancanaro,M.(2011). Examining proactiveness and choice in a location-aware mobile museum guide, Interacting with Computers, vol.23, No.5, pp. 513-524, ISSN 0953-5438, 10.1016/j.intcom.2011.05.007.

Larman,C.(1998). Applying UML and Patterns, Prentice-Hall.

Lauesen, S.(2003). Task Descriptions as Functional Requirements, IEEE SOFTWARE March/April 2003, pp.58-65.

Nielsen, J. (2011). Mobile usability. Retrieved January 20, 2012 from http://www.useit.com/alertbox/mobile-usability.html

Nielsen, J. (2009). Mobile Usability First Findings, http://www.useit.com/alertbox/mobile-usability-study-1.html

Ormerod,T.C.; Shepherd,A.(2004). Using task analysis for information requirements specification: the sub-goal template method, D. Diaper, N.A. Stanton (Eds.), The Handbook of Task Analysis in Human Computer Interaction, Lawrence Erlbaum Associates, London, pp. 347–365

Rauch, M.(2011). Mobile documentation: Usability guidelines, and considerations for providing documentation on Kindle, tablets, and smartphones, Professional Communication Conference (IPCC), 2011 IEEE International , pp.1-13, 17-19 Oct. 2011, doi: 10.1109/IPCC.2011.6087221

Richardson,J.; Ormerod,T.C.; Shepherd,A.(1998). The role of task analysis in capturing requirements for interface design, Interacting with Computers, Vol.9, No.4, February 1998, pp. 367-384, ISSN 0953-5438, 10.1016/S0953-5438(97)00036-2.

Sharples, M.; Taylor, J.; Vavoula, G. (2007). A Theory of Learning for the Mobile Age, In R. Andrews and C. Haythornthwaite (eds.) The Sage Handbook of Elearning Research. London: Sage, pp. 221-247

Shi, X.; Sun, T.; Shen, Y.; Li, K.; Qu, W. (2010). Tour-Guide: Providing Location-Based Tourist Information on Mobile Phones, Proceedings of IEEE 10th International Conference on Computer and Information Technology (CIT), 2010, pp.2397-2401, Bradford, UK, 29 June-1 July, 2010

Shneiderman, B.(1998). Designing the User Interface - Strategies for Effective Human-Computer Interaction, Addison-Wesley. 1998

Stanton, N.A.(2004). The psychology of task analysis today D. Diaper, N.A. Stanton (Eds.), The Handbook of Task Analysis in Human–Computer Interaction, Lawrence Erlbaum Associates, London, pp. 569–584

Stanton,N.A.(2006). Hierarchical task analysis: Developments, applications, and extensions, Applied Ergonomics, Vol.37, No.1, January 2006, pp.55-79, ISSN 0003-6870, 10.1016/j.apergo.2005.06.003.

Xiehao, B.; Hongxia, B.; Mingxiao, W.(2009). Integration of multimedia and location-based services on mobile phone tour guide system," Network Infrastructure and Digital Content, 2009. IC-NIDC 2009. IEEE International Conference on , pp.642-646, 6-8 Nov. 2009, doi: 10.1109/ICNIDC.2009.5360805

8

Mobile Health – Monitoring of SaO$_2$ and Pressure

Nilton Serigioli, Edgar Charry Rodriguez and Rodrigo Reina Muñoz
Engineering and Applied Social Sciences Center – UFABC,
Laboratory of Integrated Systems of São Paulo University
Brazil

1. Introduction

Use of mobile devices assisting medical practices is acknowledged as Mobile Health (m-Health). M-Health technology involves the mobile telecommunications infrastucture to deliver medical services and medical assistance to patients. Mobile technology is growing up at a fast rate. This rapid development, along with dropping in cost of mobile devices introduces a new scenario where mobile technology is becoming an important tool of information and communication technology (Black et al., 2010). In developing countries, many of those new "mobile citizens" live in poor areas with a scarcity of infrastructure. That is why the use of mobile telephony is a great opportunity to promote health services that could improve the quality of life of those people (Germanakos et al., 2005).

M-Health technologies along with electronic systems are changing the profile of medical services. For example, m-Health technologies has the potential to replace 5% of hospitalizations, 5% of in home visits by nurses (home care), and 20% of home visits by health workers, translating into economic use of both time and money to patients and health professionals (Fishman, 1997). The advantages of m-Health include the possibility of establishing a direct link between professional health workers and patients in order to provide efficient medical assistance, especially to the rural population, saving time. and in addition, patients can follow up with their recovery having major access to information to their illnesses (Istepanean, 2006).

The advance in telecommunications and information technologies, has made possible the rise of new services which can be delivered through mobile telephony. It was practically unimaginable only few years ago that any kind of medical service could be delivered through the mobile telecommunications infrastructure. Realizing that nowadays many people, including people living in rural areas have access to a cell phone, and that the number of people connected electronically is increasing everyday, many researchers around the globe started to develop diverse healthcare solutions supported by telecommunications technology. This has been the driving force behind m-Health development. In this way, we have seen many groups trying to demonstrate the m-Health potential to support assisted medical care, locally or remotely. However, despite this enthusiasm, many of the efforts have faced high resistance coming from several sides of society, from physicians to government authorities.

Looking at this scenario, our group, at the Federal University of ABC undertook a study to explore the high potential of m-health to save lives or at least to improve people´s quality of life, especially for people suffering chronic diseases. It could also bolster confidence in this new technology to attract the attention of those people in authority. Among the many possibilites and with feasibility issues to be explored , we chose a hardware solution involving the acquisition and monitoring of vital signs. Hence, it was chosen to work with arterial blood pressure and oxygen blood saturation applications. Arterial blood pressure was chosen because it is a disease affecting many people in the world, and an oximeter application was chosen because usually equipment involved is too expensive, so the prototype implemented here might contribute to lower costs with more people having access to this technology.

We will discuss here in this report the developtment of an electronic system to acquire biomedical signals. Markedly, arterial pressure and oximetry signals are acquired and processed with this system and sent to a cell phone at a remote location. Data is sent as an SMS message. The main objective is to asssist professional health workers with the patients information in such a way that they can analyze the data collected remotely and return instructions to the patient and also to help the local health worker make the proper decisions in regards to the patients care. System architecture is presented here and the main results are highlighted.

2. Telemedicine and m-Health concept

m-Health is an abbreviation for mobile health. m-Health can be defined as any kind of service which facilitates the flow of information over some form of mobile network (cellular, PDAs, laptops, wireless, etc), that enhance the delivery of appropriate medical support or healthcare solutions (Fong, et al, 2011, Sanderson & Grondlund, 2010).

As pointed out in (Vital Wave Consulting, 2009), tens of millions of citizens that never had regular access to a fixed-line telephone or computer now use mobile devices as daily tools for communication and data transfer. This growing ubiquity of mobile phones is a central element in the promise of mobile technologies for health.

m-Health terminology has emerged as a sub-segment of eletronic health (eHealth). In fact these terms should not be confused. As m-Health can be seen as the access point to capture and enter the remote collected information, providing information to healthcare clinics and health workers, e-Health involves digitizing patient records and creation of electronic systems to standarize access to patient data within a national system (Vital Wave Consulting, 2009).

It is important to mention that m-Health applications are not restricted to remote data collection. There are many other important applications in this field. Besides to remote monitoring, applications and tasks that are related include communication and training for healthcare workers, disease and epidemic outbreak tracking, diagnostic and treatment support, among others.

mHealth applications include mobile devices used to gather information related to community health, providing useful information to health workers and patients. This is crucial as mobile computing allows real time monitoring of vital signs of patients and direct medical care.

Telemedicine involves the use of electronic communications and information technologies to provide clinical services when participants are at different locations. Therefore, it is a tool that can be used by health providers to extend the traditional practice of medicine outside the walls of the typical medical practice (ATA, 2006).

The scope of Telemedicine is vast. As stated by Natalia Pérez et al (Pérez-Ferre N. & Calle-Pascual A., 2011). Telemedicine covers a wide variety of procedures with very different stages of complexity. From a simple telephone conversation between two health professionals sharing information, to complex diagnostic or therapeutic procedures long distance and in real time. As can be infered through the telemedicine definition, m-Health is colsely related with the telemedicine concept, except that the m-Healt definition is conceived when supported by mobile devices.

3. Review of other applications reported in m-Health

m-Health technologies are extremely dynamic and a variety of applicattions that are being conceived are in continous expansion. Applications that can be considered vital to m-Health in developing countries according to (Vodafone Foundation Partnership, 2009) are: education and awareness, remote data collection, remote monitoring, communication and training for healthcare workers, disease and epidemic outbreak tracking, and diagnostics and treatment support.

In the education area, Short Message Service (SMS) are sent directly to user telephones to provide information about treatment methods, health services availability and disease management. According to the Vodafone Foundation (Vodafone Foundation Partnership, 2009), formal studies show that SMS has an important impact and and high capacity to influence people´s behavior than campaigns conducted by radio or television. It happens because the confidentiality involved with SMS, especially in places where certain kinds of diseases are considered as a taboo. Other reasons to use SMS messages comes from the fact that it is totally suited to reach populations in rural areas where medical support and health workers are scarce.

Data collection is an essential component to public health programs. Medical technicians and and goverment officials need precise data in order to make an evaluation of the efficacy of political decisions and ongoing programs as new programs and decisions are drawn up.

Some examples of m-Health initiatives can be found described in the report of Vodafone (Vodafone Foundation Partnership, 2009). One of them is the Project Masiluleke, in Africa. This Project was designed to take advantage of the power of mobile technology as a high-impact, low-cost tool in the fight against HIV/AIDS. In Brazil was conducted the project Data Gathering, which allows the creation of customized questionnaires, which are distributed to the mobile phones of health agents in the field. When the field workers finish their surveys, they send the data back to the server via a wireless connection, from which it can be integrated into the organization's existing systems for immediate analysis. That system also provides GPS location information for each record, which would otherwise require dedicated instruments. Anotther experience was designed in South Africa, as reported in (Murthy, 2008), called Dokoza System, developed to use in HIV/AIDS studies, and can be accessed in real time via PC web, laptop, PDA, Smartphone and Palmtop.

Some years ago, it was pointed out by Istepanian (Istepanian, 2003) some future trends in m-Health, indicating the way this technology could be impacted by 3G technology. Today, we are witnessing the arrival of 4G communication technology. 4G technology should be able to deliver peak download speeds of 1Gbps in stationary environments, and 100Mbps in high mobile environments. The impact of 4G on m-Health will be fantastic because m-Health solutions will introduce video images to the health professionals as they will have in their hands the powerful resources that real time imaging offers. In that direction, as reported in (Green Technology News, 2011), Washington Hospital Center, a teaching hospital in Washington DC, is using a different form of mobile technology. The hospital worked in collaboration with AT&T to develop "CodeHeart," a mobile application that provides real-time video and audio streams that can be used in critical care situations. This system allows physicians and first responders to communicate during an emergency situation working with real time images. Hospital cardiologists, for example, can view vital signs and test results captured through real-time video feed while simultaneously speaking with the patient's first responder or an attending emergency department doctor. Using the mobile application in this scenario, the cardiologist can assess and prepare cardiac treatment before the patient arrives at the emergency department, while emergency departments themselves can better prepare for the patient's arrival.

As can be seen, the progress of m-Health solutions is quite astonishing. In only a few years we have seen a huge amount of research and development in this area including local patient care, video conference systems, in which, a patient can be monitored at home by health professionals through communiction between the hospital and patient using video IP calls, internet communication with a remote server and remote monitoring using a mobile communications infrastucture. Jim Black (Black et al., 2010) reported a system to aid health workers using a hardware platform that can work with some sensors. The results were exibited in a cell phone application. So basically all applications in that system run locally and the whole system, hardware and cell phone, should be provided to the health professional. The applications on that system were developed using C# and the Microsoft .NET framework running on SmartPhones. Jim Black reported the development of applications like respiratory and pulse rate calculator, Gestational dates calculator, formulary/drug dose calculator, drip rate calculator, drug reminder alarm, among others. Joseph Finkelstein (Finkelstein, et al 2010) presented a solution that could also be used locally at home. It is basically an application using internet as patient at home can use. Data are sent to a remote server where a clinician can analyze the information and send back the proper actions for a patient to follow. The system mentioned in that application has been used for management of patients with asthma, COPD, hypertension, inflammatory bowel disease, and multiple sclerosis. Jablonski (Jablonski, et al 2010) reported a system that monitors the patient health at home, and sends the collected data to a remote server via internet Virtual Private Network (OpenVPN) using the HTTP protocol. The telemedical system therein described is dedicated to patients needing a long term monitoring of their lung function. Home monitoring using a local network incorporating a wireless transmission module like ZigBee has also been reported in (Wun-Jin Li, et al, 2010) to monitor blood pressure. David Mulvaney (Mulvaney, et al 2010) developed a system to monitor and collect data on heart diseased and diabetic patient in rural areas. This system is able to send data via internet or using the mobile communications infrastructure (GSM/GPRS)/3G). We are reporting here a system that is like that reported by Mulvaney in collecting patient data and sending it remotely using the installed mobile communication infrastructure (data is sent as SMS via GSM modem). The next section describes the developed system.

4. Hardware conception

Aware of the importance that m-Health represents to provide health care to patients, our Group at *Federal University of ABC* (São Paulo, Brazil) conducted a study to figure out an application that would be able to be implemented in hardware, able to monitor vital signs and sent health data of a patient remotely. Specifically, the objective was to demonstrate the hability of our prototype in capturing data of the patient and sending it immediately to a remote location using SMS. The next step in our our decision making was to choose the signals that could be monitored. Monitoring of these signals should be done in the same electronic module, by just changing a switch position. It was conceived that the electronic module should be able to show data locally and with remote transmission capability. In the following section we describe the conception, and module implementation.

4.1 System architecture

Architecture of the developed system is shown in figure 1.

The system includes two electronic units for signal acquisition. One of these units allows acquisition of arterial pressure signals, and the second one acquires a signal for oximetry analisys. These acquisition blocks include amplification and filtering stages. Signals coming from these inputs are fed into a microcontroller. The microcontroller unit controls signal digitalization, signal processing and transfer of captured samples to a GSM modem, which, in turn, sends processed information to a remote location using text messages (SMS).

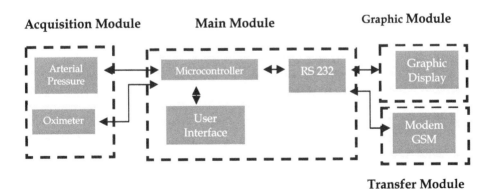

Fig. 1. Block Diagram of prototype implemented.

4.2 Arterial pressure module

The method used to measure blood pressure in this system was the oscillometric method which allows measurements of systolic and diastolic pressure. In this method, the arterial flow is blocked by inflating the pneumatic system (cuff) above the systolic pressure level. Afterwards, the pressure is reduced slowly and blood flows through the artery in an oscillatory way. When oscillations cross the cuff pressure, the systolic pressure is identified. As pressure in the system continues to decrease slowly, to the point it is under the cuff pressure, the diastolic pressure can be measured (Peura, 1998).

During the measurement cycle, the microcontroller activates the inflation and deflation of the pneumatic system. The cuff pressure is detected by a piezoelectric transducer and converted into an electrical signal proportional to the pressure and processed by two different circuits. One of them amplifies and makes a correction of the signal offsetting it before it is passed to an analog to digital converter (ADC). The second circuit consists of a high pass filter and amplifier.

The pressure signal acquisition module includes the acquisition units, the conditioning circuitry, including amplification and filtering. These conditioning subsystems are connected with the microcontroller unit. The microcontroller drives the pneumatic devices and also executes the digitalization of the captured samples to be sent to the communication interface. At this point, all processed information is ready to be sent to a local database bank, or to a remote location.

To measure the arterial pressure, a commercial sensor (MPX2050) was used. This sensor has a linear output proportional to the applied pressure (Freescale Semicondutor,2010). The sensor output has two signals, the pressure signal and a signal that contains the blood oscillation information (see figure 2a). The pressure signal is amplified and sent to the microcontroller to be digitalized, while the oscillations component is filtered out and then amplified (see figure 2b). In this way the continuous components contained in the oscillation signal are eliminated and adequately conditioned to be processed by the microcontroller.

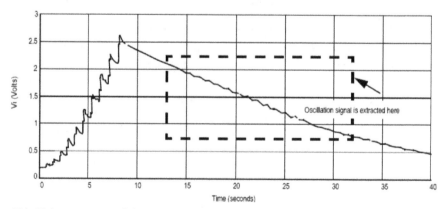

Fig. 2(a). Voltage output of the pressure sensor. (Freescale Semiconductor. Application Notes).

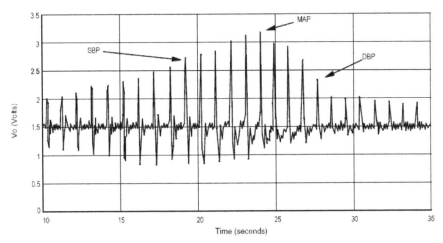

Fig. 2(b). Oscillations at amplifier output. (Freescale Semiconductor. Application Notes).

Figure 3 illustrates the complete schematic of the arterial pressure meter. The pressure sensor (MPX2050) provides an output signal in the range of 0 mV to 40 mV, which corresponds to a pressure range of 0 mmHg to 375 mmHg. To amplify this signal, an instrumentation amplifier with a 100 voltage gain, allows an output range within 0 V to 4 V. The instrumentation amplifier output is connected to the microcontroller for processing.

As mentioned before, the inflation and deflation system is formed by a pneumatic pump and an electro valve. The pneumatic pump inflates the system, while the electro valve drains this system.

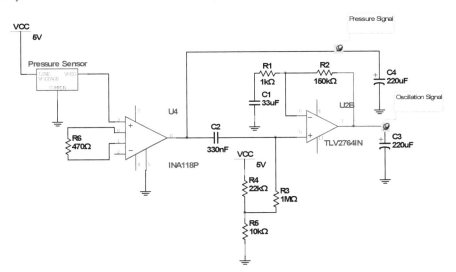

Fig. 3. Schematic of the Electronic Blood Pressure Meter. (Adapted from: Freescale Semiconductor).

As mentioned before, the inflation and deflation system is formed by a pneumatic pump and an electro valve. The pneumatic pump inflates the system, while the electro valve drains this system.

The filter consists of two RC networks from which two cut off frequencies can be obtained (0,48 Hz and 4,8 Hz). These two poles (see equation 1) were chosen to guarantee that the oscillation signal does not have distortion or signal lost.

$$F_{c1} = \frac{1}{2\pi R_1 C_1} \qquad F_{c2} = \frac{1}{2\pi R_3 C_2} \qquad (1)$$

The sensor output, once amplified, is divided in two different components. One of them identifies the pressure signal of the pneumatic system (continuous component) and other signal identifies the oscillations that takes place in a pressure detection process (alternating component), coming from a heartbeat (aproximatelly 1 beat per second, corresponding to a frequency of 1 Hz).

The pressure signal is sent directly to channel 1 of an A/D converter input and at the same time the oscillatory signal is passed through a band pass filter to eliminate the continuous component and any noise coming from the electric network. After filtering, this signal is sent to channel 2 of the A/D converter. As soon as these signals are digitilized, the digital processing is executed by the microcontroller, and pressure data, systolic and diastolic pressure are left available for visualization in a display as well as sent to a GSM modem in text format message.

4.3 Oximeter module

A pulse oximeter is a medical instrument for monitoring blood oxygen concentration of patients in a non invasive way allowing measurement of heart beats. Oximeter operation is based on blood oxygen saturation identification, measuring the difference in absorption in two wavelenghts of light. When hemoglobin gets bonded with oxygen, oxygenated hemoglobin is formed and it becomes red. Otherwise, when dissociation of oxygen occurs in the hemoglobin, it becomes darker.

The variable that determines the hemoglobin oxygenation level in the bloodstream is called Oxygen Saturation, and is also known as SaO_2. It is defined as the relationship between the oxygenated hemoglobin (HbO_2) and total hemoglobin (Hb) in the blood. It is calculated with next equation (equation 2):

$$SaO_2 = \frac{HbO_2}{Hb + HbO_2} \qquad (2)$$

The pulse oximeter is built with a probe placed on a peripheral part of the body as a finger or ear. The probe is constructed using two led emitter diodes (LEDs), one of them operating with red light in the 660 nm light spectrum and the other one operating with infrared light in the 940 nm light spectrum. These LEDs are placed over one side of the probe, and a photodiode is placed on the opposite side of the probe (Wukitsch et al. ,1988).

The light beam emitted by the red and infrared diodes pass through the tissues, bones, veins and arteries, reaching the photodiode on the other side of the probe. The light absorbed by tissues and bones does not suffer significant variations during short time periods, and basically can be considered as a constant component of the signal (DC component). On the other hand, the signal associated with the arterial blood changes during short time intervals due to cardiac pulsation characterizing an AC component. With the DC and AC components identified it is possible to isolate the arterial blood component (Baura, 2002).

The oxygen saturation can be calculated accordingly with the next equation (equation 3):

$$SaO_2 = \frac{\varepsilon_{d\lambda 1} - \varepsilon_{d\lambda 2}\ R}{[\varepsilon_{d\lambda 1} - \varepsilon_{0\lambda 1}] - [\varepsilon_{d\lambda 2} - \varepsilon_{0\lambda 2}]R} \qquad (3)$$

Where: λ_1 and λ_2 are the wavelengths corresponding to the two wavelengths passing through the vascular body. $\varepsilon_0\lambda_1$ is the absorptivity of oxygenated hemoglobin related with the wavelength λ_1, $\varepsilon_d\lambda_1$ is the absorptivity of desoxygenated hemoglobin. Similar nomenclature is valid for λ_2 wavelength.

Factor R in equation (3) can be found taking the ratio between AC component and DC component of the signal for both wavelengths ($\lambda 1$ e $\lambda 2$) as follows:

$$R = \frac{log_{10}\left(\frac{i_{ac}}{i_{cc}}\right)\lambda_1}{log_{10}\left(\frac{i_{ac}}{i_{cc}}\right)\lambda_2} \qquad (4)$$

Where: $i_{ac}\ \lambda_1$ is the current detected in the photodiode corresponding with the AC component of signal related with wavelenght λ_1, $i_{cc}\ \lambda_1$ is the DC photodetected current related with wavelength λ_1. Similar analysis is applied to the wavelength λ_2 parameter.

Equations (3) and equation (4) are the key to oximeter design and are calculated in the algorithm implemented in the microcontroller.

Figure 4 describes the architecture of the oximeter used to implement the prototytpe. An Oximeter signal, as usually done, is recovered using a transimpedance amplifier topology as shown in figure 5. This system includes biomedical signal acquisition units, signal conditioning unit (including amplification and filtering). The conditioning unit is connected with a microcontroller which, after signal digitalization, processes the signal and transmits the samples to a GSM modem. The modem sends processed information as text messages (SMS) to a cell phone or a remote database.

The transmitting and LED light intensity control is done via microcontroller that turns on and turns off the red and infrared LEDs in a frequency of 500 Hz. This frequency was chosen in order to extract the maximum power of the LEDs so they would have sufficient intensity to cross the exposed tissue with the probe. Thus, it is possible to apply maximum voltage to the LEDs in a short time interval.

The LEDs current is adjusted by a microcontroller in such a way that the photodiode current can be adjusted accordingly with the tissue sample of the patient. This situation might take place depending on the patient, making it neccessary to increase the LEDs current and therefore the photodetected current. The larger the tissue thickness is between emitter and receiver, the stronger the current through the LEDs should be. The LEDs luminosity is controlled by two PWM (Pulse Width Modulation) micronttroller outputs. The conditioning circuitry used to process the photodetected signal is shown in figure 5.

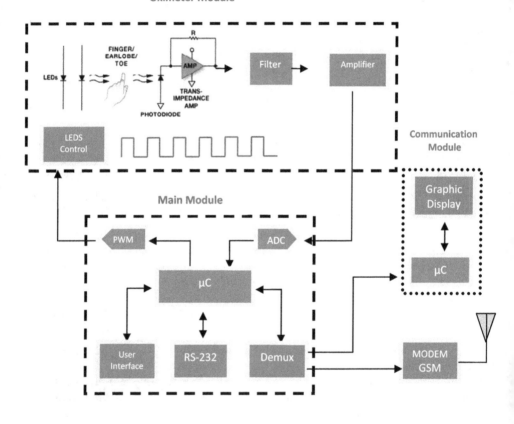

Fig. 4. Diagram of the oximeter system architecture.

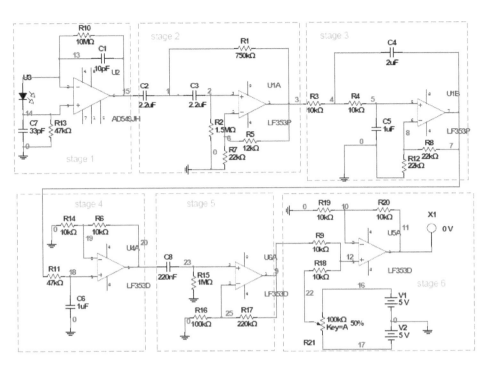

Fig. 5. Schematic diagram of the processing stages used to recover the oximeter signal.

This final schematic was obtained after the necessary adjustments were done in order to have the oximeter signal totally conditioned before entering to the microcontroller A/D converter. All signal processing was simulated with Multisim usign this schemathic.

Stage 1 illustrates the photodetection and electonics for amplification. A transimpedance amplifier was used to amplify the generated current and to convert this current signal in a voltage signal. The cut off frequency was about 6 KHz (Feedback resistor and capacitor shown in stage 1 were tailored to get that frequency). This bandwidth is above the frequency of interest which is in the order of some Hertz, but it was decided to work with this frequency range to avoid using impractical values of R_f. The penalty with this approach is the need for additional filters to get the desired oximeter signal.

Second and third stages are Butterworth filters to eliminate the DC signal component as well as the LEDs modulation frequency (500 Hz). An additional low pass filter was included (stage 4) to avoid any noise influence into the system. Finally, there were included two stages (stage 5 and stage 6) for amplification and level shifting purposes, in such a way to make compatible the processed signal level with the analog to digital converter input of the microcontroller.

To illustrate the oximeter Multisim simulation that was conducted, simulation at first and last stages of circuit of figure 5 is presented. Figure 6 shows the simulation at stage 1.

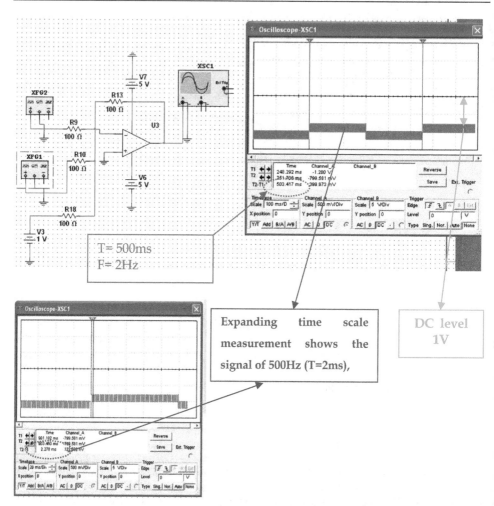

Fig. 6. Plot from Multisim simulation at stage 1 of figure 5.

Photodiode signal was represented using an operational amplifier configured as a weighted adder with three input signals. A 100 mV - 500 Hz signal for LEDs driving. The second signal, a 100 mV - 2 Hz signal that represents the heart beat (120 beats per second), and a third signal representing a constant value, e.g., the non pulsating part of the arterial blood, corresponding to the signal through the bones and tissues as reported in Philips Electronics report (Philips Electronics, 2002).

Multisim simulation (figure 7) at stage 6, shows the signal obtained that finally goes into the microcontroller A/D input. Figure 7 show two traces. The trace in blue corresponds to the signal at stage 5 of figure 5, while the trace in yellow is the signal at stage 6. The only difference between these signals, is a level shifting introduced so yellow trace signal can be compatible with microcontroller A/D converter input.

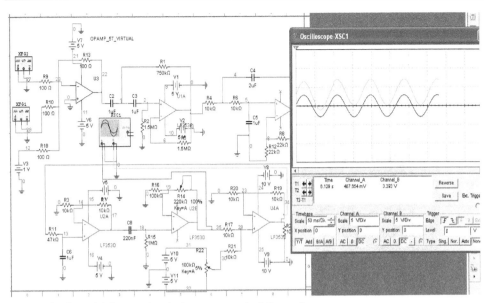

Fig. 7. Plot from Multisim simulation at stage 6 of figure 5.

The system implemented is shown in figure 8. The prototype includes the following modules:

- **Acquisition and processing module:** This is the oximeter module that includes the probe containing the LEDs and photodiode, and the electronic circuitry previously described to adequate the signal before being processed into the microcontroller. The probe used in this system was a commercial probe (Oximeter probe from Nellcor). The signal processing unit includes a pre-amplifier (AD549 from Analog Devices). This amplifier was configured as a transimpedance amplifier. AD549 amplifier was chosen due to its low current detection capability (about 26 fA rms at a bandwidth of 16 Hz). Finally, electronic blocks in this unit include filtering blocks (second order Butterworth high pass filter with 0,07 Hz cutoff frequency, and second order Butterworth low pass filter with 3,4 Hz cutoff frequency).

- **Main module:** In this module the information is processed according to equations (2) and (3). This module includes the microcontroller to make up the processing and communication tasks (used here was the PIC18F4520 from Microchip).

- **Communication module:** This module uses a GSM modem (Global System for Mobile Communications) and a graphic interface (LCD display along with microcontroller to control the LCD display). The GSM modem delivers the results obtained with the microcontroller to the LCD display (local mode), or remotely to a cell phone. Used was an 8 bits microcontroller (PIC16F877A from Microchip) and a graph display (YB12864ZB, 128 x 64 dots), as well as a GSM modem from Motorola (Motorola G24).

System operation can be described as follows: The conditioning circuit after proper filtering allows the capture of the oximetry signal which is then passed to main microcontroller. This microcontroller also has the task of driving the red and infrared LEDs of the probe in a frequency of 500 Hz.

After processing with the main microcontroller, processed information is sent to the GSM modem using the serial port of the prototype, as well as to the local display.

A second microcontroller (figure 9) was included in this system and is responsible for user interface tasks, allowing commutation between arterial pressure signals or oximetry signals measurements. Results regarding arterial pressure measurements with this prototype were published in (Serigioli, 2010). Also, this microcontroller controls all processing of the LCD display. Communication between microcontrollers is done through a communication protocol.

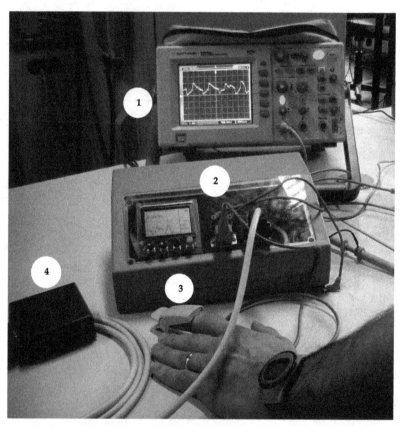

Fig. 8. Biomedical signals prototype: (1) Signal captured with oscilloscope; (2) Measurement of the signals with the prototype mounted inside a module; (3) Commercial oximeter probe used; (4) GSM modem used in experiment.

The GSM modem sends data using SMS to a cell phone for information management and communication. In this way, information can be sent as a text message using wireless networks to any cell phone that can be found in the area under covering. To establish communication between microcontroller and modem, AT commands were used. These commands are instructions used to control the modem (AT Commands Reference Manual, 2006).

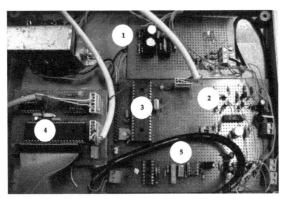

Fig. 9. Illustration of the prototype implemented in a printed circuit board: (1) DC power supply; (2) circuit for LEDs driving; (3) main microcontroller; (4) microcontroller to command the LCD display; (5) circuitry for oximetry signal processing.

Figure 10 illustrates the algorithm flowdiagram implemented in the microcontroller.

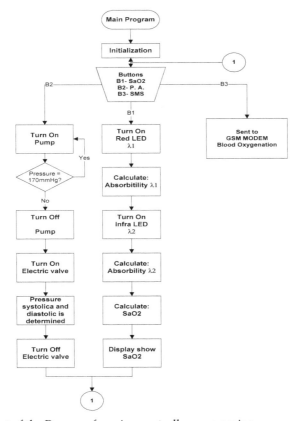

Fig. 10. Flowchart of the Program for microcontroller programing.

The user can select the biomedical signal of interest by pressing the proper button available. Button B1 selects the oximetry mode, and button B2 selects the arterial pressure mode. Button B3 enables the communication path to send the signals to the GSM modem. By selecting the oximetry mode, the microcontroller energizes the LEDs to initiate the oxygen blood saturation, SaO_2 as was already described above in this section. When the arterial pressure mode is selected, the microcontroller makes the pressurization, depressurization of the pneumatic system as systolic and diastolic pressures can be determined as described in section 4.2. Then results can be visualized in the display, in local mode, or in a cell phone remotely.

Regarding microcontroller programming, code was written using the MPLAB IDE V8.36 environment from Microchip.

5. Modem GSM

The GSM model (Global System for Mobile Communications) is a wireless solution that accesses the GSM network in the same way cell phones do. The GSM modem does not have the entire peripheral accompaniments that a cell phones might, for instance, keyboard, display, microphone, and speaker. With the lack of these kinds of resources, it is necessary to include other devices like the microcontroller.

The modem was used in this prototype to send biomedical signals that were captured to a cell phone using SMS messages available in a GSM network. Messages, as defined in the standard GSM 900/1800/1900, can have up to 160 ASCII characters. Text includes letters, numbers and alphanumeric characters. Modem used was the G24 from Motorola (Module Hardware Description - Motorola G24 Developer's Guide).

Main technical specifications of the modem are:

Quad band (850, 900, 1800 e 1900 MHz);
Voltage: 3.3 to 4.2V
Operation temperature: -20 to + 60 °C;
Currrent: up to 2,5mA;
Connections: USB 2.0 and RS232 (300 bps a 460800 bps);
Transmission speed: up to 85.6 Kbps;
SMS: text mode and PDU;
Commands AT (GSM 07.05, GSM 07.07 and GSM 07.10)

Communication between modem and prototype was done via serial communication. The configuration and resources utilization of G24 modem were implemented with commands called AT commands (AT Commands Reference Manual,Motorola G24 Developer's Guide). These commands can be written using a set of characters of the ASCII table, starting with an "AT" prefix. The prefix "AT" is derived from the word *attention*, and requests the modem to pay attention for a solicitation (command).

An AT command line might have one or more commands, separated by delimiters according to the structure shown below:

Prefix	Command 1	Delimiter	Command 2	Delimiter	...	Command N	Suffix

Each AT command has an "AT" prefix and a suffix <CR>, called *Carriage Return*. The delimiter can be a comma or a space.

When a command is launched, the modem answers with a message, so called, *Result Code*.

An example of the writting of these commands, is as follows. See (table 1).

Command	Comment
AT+CMGS= "81358659", 145	// number of destination cell phone.
> test message <CTRL+Z>	// write message and finalizenwith CTRL+Z.
+CMGS:222 OK	// Message succesfully sent. modem returns a number corresponding with the reference of the message.

Table 1. Example of commands composition.

Among different commands available, it were used the commands set necessary to modem configuration, message composition and sending of messages. These commands are described below (table 2).

Command	Description
AT	Basic command to test the communication. Return 'OK' or 'ERROR'
AT&K0	Disables controle flow of serial communication.
AT+CMGF=1	Configure the SMS messages to text mode.
AT+CMGS= Destination phone number <CR> > text of the message <CTRL Z>	This command sends SMS message from modem to network.
AT+CMGR=<mem1> +CMGR:"status","n° telephone", test message OK	This command allows reading of SMS message stored in memory <mem1> modem return status of the message. It can be: read, unread, sent, and unsent.

Table 2. Examples of commands used in this experiment.

The source code implemented in the microcontroller to establish serial communication between the microcontroller and the GSM modem is shown in the appendix.

6. Results

The initial step in the prototype implementation was a simulation with Multisim for each stage and for each subsystem (arterial pressure or oximeter circuit). Next, the electronics for the entire system was implemented in a board.

Signals corresponding with arterial pressure and oximetry are shown in figure 11 and figure 12 as obtained in tests conducted in the laboratory.

Figure 11(a) corresponds to the prototype for arterialpressure signal acquisition. It includes the MPX2050 pressure sensor, pump and electro valve. By activating the pump, the cuff is presurized up to the maximum pressure is achieved and when the electro valve is activated, the cuff is depressurized. With this cycle systolic and diastolic pressure is meassured.

Figure 11(b) corresponds to the arterial pressure signal, where the green trace (signal with negative slope) corresponds to the pressure sensor output when the pneumatic system is in deflation mode. The yellow trace is the oscillation corresponding to the pressure without the constant component (continuous component) that was extracted by filtering and amplified, as comparisons can be made by the microcontroller. These signals are connected individually with the channels of ADC conversion of the microcontroller.

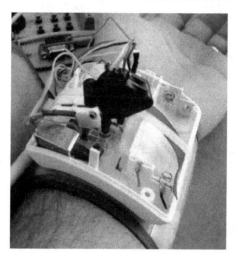

Fig. 11(a). Arterial pressure Prototype for arterial pressure acquisition.

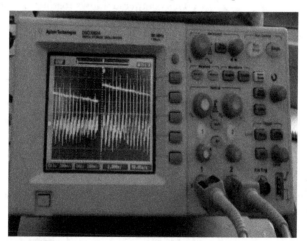

Fig. 11(b). Cuff Pressure Signal at the Output of the Pressure Sensor and Extracted Oscillation signal at the Output of the Amplifier.

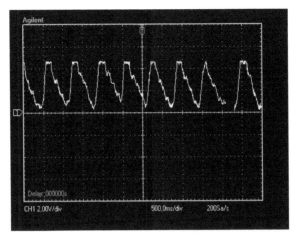

Fig. 12(a). Waveform of the oxymeter output as obtained in an oscilloscope

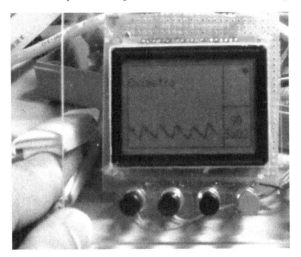

Fig. 12(b). Waveform of the oxymeter output.

Figure 12(a) corresponds to the oximetry signal observed in an oscilloscope. Results are available in a LCD display of the prototype in numerical format or as a waveform providing easy result interpretation for the health care workers (figure 12b).

After testing the functionality of the prototype, there were some tests conducted in order to verify the proper operation of the communication interface, especially the remote communication with a cell phone using the communication infrastructure available in our country. Results obtained indicated that the communication worked according to expectations with the oximetry and the arterial perssure data that were processed with the electronic module. Data sent via modem to a cell phone as an SMS message was received as intended. Figure 13 shows the results displayed on a cell phone for both, pressure and oximetry signals.

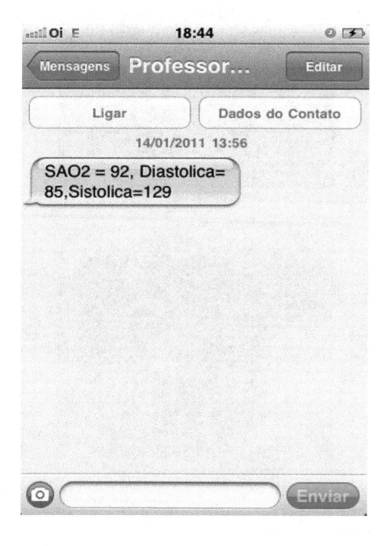

Fig. 13. Oxymeter and blood arterial pressure data sent to a cell phone via GSM communication.

7. Conclusion

We presented implementation of a prototype to acquire, process and transmit biomedical signals. It was designed eletronics for signal processing to accommodate arterial pressure signals as well as blood oxygen saturation.

Quantitative results for SaO$_2$ calculations were processed in a microcontroller from which, the results were made available using a LCD display to local visualization, or sent to a remote location, where results can be obtained in a cell phone.

The electronic module implemented is able to monitor two different kinds of biomedical signals, markedly, arterial blood pressure, and blood oxygen saturation.

Results obtained with this prototype demonstrates that it is quite possible to construct an infrastructure based on mobile communication, where data coming from biomedical equipment, can be made available remotely to medical specialists, to readily obtain precise diagnostics of a patient's health. In this way, proper decisions can be drawn as preventive diagnostics, or as a diagnostic tool in a real emergency situation where a patient should be taken to a hospital for adequate medical assistance.

We hope this experiment will draw the attention of the government agencies of our country to give support to this kind of initiatives that could be benefical for many people, especially for people living in rural areas, or areas with scarce medical support.

Besides other vital signs that could be included in this system, it is necessary to develop other important part of an m-Healt system. For instance, the organization of a database in a server where patient's collected information can be viewed and managed by clinicians.

From the point of view of global m-Health's progress and trends, the trends of m-Health, are changing as pointed out in a study of Manhattan Research: "information gathering — either from simply searching for health information or news — remains the most common m-Health behavior. However, that trend is shifting. The study found that three percent of consumers used prescription drug refills or reminders on their mobile phones in 2010, a number that inched to eight percent in 2011". The report also found that about 56 million U.S. consumers had accessed their medical information electronically by utilizing an electronic health record (EHR) system maintained by their physician. An additional 41 million people expressed an interest in accessing EHR's in the future.

The progress of m-Health as can be accessed through different demonstrations worldwilde is astonishing. First demonstrations took advantage of 3G communication technologies to deliver care services and information to the patient. In the coming years m-Health will benefit from 4G data rate transfer allowing applications with image and voice as medical teams will interact with first responders to take proper decisions and at the same time, make the necessary preparations for the treatment before the patient's arrival. Also, 4G technology will allows reaching rural areas and will make easier the m-Health Programs implementation in less developed parts of the world.

GPS-based directions to the closest, and most appropriate, medical facility for the patients condition is another benefit in todays's m-Health services.

8. Appendix

Described below is part of the microcontroller source code responsible for communication between the microcontroller and GSM modem. This code was written in C programming language and implemented in MPLAB IDE V 8.36 with C18 compiler.

```
#include < P18f4550.h >
#include < delays.h >
#include < usart.h >
void ()
{
char cm_ini[]="AT"; // matrix type CHAR that stores AT command
char cm_texto[]="AT+CMGF=1"; // matrix type CHAR that stores the command of
                             // configuration of messages in text format.
char cm_sms[]="AT+CMGS=81199644,145" // matrix type CHAR that stores the command
                                     // to send a message to destination phonenumber

// Configuration of serial communication of microcontroller to work in asynchronous mode
//with 8 bits and with speed of 9600bps.
```

$$\text{OpenUSART}\begin{pmatrix} \text{USART\_TX\_INT\_OFF \& USART\_RX\_INT\_OFF \&} \\ \text{USART\_ASYNCH\_MODE \& USART\_EIGHT\_BIT \& USART\_CONT\_RX \& USART\_BRGH\_HIGH , 25} \end{pmatrix};$$

```
//************* Modem startup*******************
putsUSART (cm_ini);          // Send to the modem the "AT" command;
while (BusyUSART());         // Wait until all data is sent.
putcUSART (0x0D);            // Send to the modem the command CR (carriage return)
while (BusyUSART());
Delay1KTCYx(1);              // Wait for 1ms

putsUSART (cm_texto);         //Sends to the modem the command "AT+CMGF=1"
while (BusyUSART());
putcUSART (0x0D);            // 0D in ASCII table corresponds to CR
while (BusyUSART());
while(1)
{
//*************************** Send to the modem ************
if(b3)                       // IF button b3 is pressed
{
putsUSART (cm_sms);          // Send to the modem the command"AT+CMGS=81199644,145"
while (BusyUSART());
putcUSART (0x0D);
Delay1KTCYx(1);

// Send to the modem the content of two variables, minimum and maximum,
corresponding to oximeter and arterial pressure signals.
fprintf(stdout,"SAO2 = %d, Diastolica= %d,Sistolica=%d",sao2, minima,maxima);
while (BusyUSART());
putcUSART (0x1A);            // Send to the modem thecommand CTRL+Z
while (BusyUSART());
}}}
```

Initially it was criated CHAR type matrices to store the AT commands after the USART configuration, asynchronous mode, with 8 bits of data and 9600 bps. To initialize the modem, it was sent through the serial interface of the microcontroller the "AT" characters followed by the CR command. After this, it was sent the "AT + CMGF = 1" command followed by the CR command. These commands are necessary for proper text mode modem configuration. After startup, the program remains in an infinite loop until the moment that the B3 button is pressed. At that moment, the microcontroller sends through the serial interface, a command with the destination telephone number ("AT +CMGS= ") and finally, the variables containing the desired information (data of the patients health) are sent. To close the process for sending the message, the command CRTZ+Z is used.

9. References

ATA-American Telemedicine Association (2006). Telemedicine, Telehealth, and Health Information Technology.

AT Commands Reference Manual (2006). *Motorola G24 Developer's Guide*. Motorola Inc.

Baura G. D. (2002). *System Theory and Practical Applications of Biomedical Signals*. Wiley Interscience. San Diego, USA.

Black, J., Koch, F., Sonenberg, L., Scheepers, R., Klandoker, A., Charry, E., Walker, B. & Soe, N. (2010). Mobile Health Solution for Front-Line Workers in Developing Countries. *IEEE Xplore*. University of Melbourne. Austrália.

Finkelstein J., Wood J., Cha E., Orlov A., Dennison C. (2010). Feasibility of Congestive Heart Failure Telemanagement Using a Wii-based Telecare Platform, *32nd Annual International Conference of the IEEE Engineering in Medicine and Biology Society*, pp. 2211-2214, ISSN 978-1-4244-4124-2. Buenos Aires, Argentina, November 2010.

Fishman, D.J. (1997). Telemedicine: bringing the specialist to the patient, *Nursing Management*.

Fong B., Fong A.C.M., Li C.K., (2011). *Telemedicine Technologies, Information Technologies in Medicine and Telehealth*, John wiley & Sons Ltd., ISBN 9780470745694, United Kingdom.

Freescale Semicondutor. (2010). MPX 2050 Datasheet, In: *Application note AN1571*, February 2010, Available from
http://www.alldatasheet.com/datasheetpdf/pdf/188298/FREESCALE/MPX2050.html.

Germanakos, P., Mourlas, C. & Samaras, G. (2005). A Mobile Agente Approach for Ubiquitous and Personalized eHealth Information Systems.

Green Technology News, (2011). "Washington Hospital Center develops CodeHeart in collaboration with AT&T", October 2011, Available from http://green.tmcnet.com/news/2011/10/25/5880838.htm.

Istepanean R., Lacal C. Jose, (2003). Emerging Mobile Communication Technologies for Health: some Imperative notes on m-Health, EMBC 2003.

Istepanean R., Laxminarayan S., Pattichis C. S. (2006). *M-Health Emerging Mobile Health Systems*. Springer Science.

Jablonski I., Glomb G., Guszkowsky T., Kasprzak B., Pekala J., Polak A.G., Stepien A.F., Swierczynski Z., & Mroczka J. (2010). Internal Validation of a Telemedical System for Monitoring Patients with Chronic Respiratory Diseaes, *32nd Annual International Conference of the IEEE Engineering in Medicine and Biology Society*, pp. 2172-2175, ISSN 978-1-4244-4124-2. Buenos Aires, Argentina, November 2010.

Li W., Luo Y., Chang Y., & HsianY. (2010). A Wireless Blood Pressure Monitoring System for Personal Health Management, *32nd Annual International Conference of the IEEE Engineering in Medicine and Biology Society*, pp. 2196-2199, ISSN 978-1-4244-4124-2. Buenos Aires, Argentina, November 2010.

Manhattan Research, (2011). Available in http://manhattanresearch.com/News-and-Events/Press-Releases/ehr-consumer-online-medical-records.

Murthy, M.V. Ramana, (2008). Mobile Based Primary Health Care System for Rural India, (2008), Available from http://www.w3.org/2008/02/MS4D_WS/papers/cdac-mobile-healthcare-paper.pdf.

Mulvaney D., Woodward B., Datta S., Harvey P., Vyas A., Thakker B., & Farooq O. (2010). Mobile communications for Monitoring Heart Disease and Diabetes, *32nd Annual International Conference of the IEEE Engineering in Medicine and Biology Society*, pp. 2208-2210, ISSN 978-1-4244-4124-2. Buenos Aires, Argentina, November 2010.

Pérez-Ferre N. & Calle-Pascual A. (2011). Overview of Telemedicine Applications in the Follow-Up of the Diabetic Patient, In: *Advances in Telemedicine: Application in Various Medical Disciplines and Geographical Regions*, pp. 71-86, ISBN 978-953-307-161-9, Madrid, Spain.

Peura R. A. (1998). Blood Pressure and Sound. *Medical Instrumentation: application and design*, pp 287-329, ISBN 0-471-15368-0. USA.

Philips Electronics North America Corporation. (2002). Understanding Pulse Oximetry SpO_2 Concepts. *Philips Medical Systems*, 2002.

Sanderson David, Gronlund Jay, (2010). The future of mHealth – About to Explode But Key Challenges Remain, Global Partners Inc, Feb. 2010.

Serigioli N., Muñoz R. R. & Rodriguez E. C. (2010). Biomedical Signals Monitoring Based in Mobile Computing. *32nd Annual International Conference of the IEEE Engineering in Medicine and Biology Society*, pp. 3868-3871, ISSN 978-1-4244-4124-2. Buenos Aires, Argentina, November 2010.

Vital Wave Consulting. (2009). *mHealth for Development: The Opportunity of Mobile Technology for Health care in the Developing World. Washington*, D.C. and Berkshire, UK: UN Foundation-Vodafone Foundation Partnership.

Wukitsch, M. W.; Petterson, M.T.; Tobler D.R. & Pologe, J.A.(1988) Pulse oximetry: analysis of theory, technology and practice. J Clin Monit. pp-209-301.

9

Mobile Technologies Applied to Hospital Automation

Cicília Raquel Maia Leite[1,2], Glaucia R.M.A. Sizilio[2], Anna G.C.D. Ribeiro[2],
Ricardo A.M. Valentim[2], Pedro F.R. Neto[1] and Ana M.G. Guerreiro[2]
[1]Laboratory of Software Engineering, State University of Rio Grande do Norte
[2]Laboratory of Hospital Automation and Bioengineering,
Federal University of Rio Grande do Norte
Brazil

1. Introduction

Industrial automation has been the focus of many studies owing to the need for increased production in the market and constant technological developments. Thus, the concepts of industrial automation have been incorporated into the medical area for some time, and are now being used in hospital automation. However, the hospital environment still not being properly automated and the automation that does exist is only found in a few processes. Several studies have been developed and are usually addressed most of the problems involved in processes with automation potential, such as: security, communication, reliability and performance of applications, biomedical devices, systems usability, logical and temporal consistency, among others.

With all the technological advances and current devices available, large and good projects are not only restricted to the invention of new technologies and concepts but also, and mainly, to the merging of existing technologies resulting in new ideas and devices that address problems not yet solved.

Mobile computing and portable devices, for example, are changing the relationships between human and computers, and are introducing a new form of communication based on context. According to Figueiredo (Figueiredo & Nakamura, 2003) this new form of communication allows people to interact seamlessly with objects, computers, environments, etc. Such technological advances are a significant departure from the existing computational paradigm in which users need to interact explicitly with the systems in order to achieve the expected results.

This new paradigm, known as ubiquitous computing, named by Weiser (Weiser, 1991), has the ability to foster a different computer vision, focusing on people's daily life (and daily tasks). Its current applications and future possibilities can be utilized in an almost invisible way, allowing the user to communicate with technology without even realizing it. Thus, the processes occur for the user, as the services and interfaces are hiding the complexity of the system.

In particular, ubiquitous medical environments are those in which technological advances such as mobile devices and wireless networks bring new opportunities for access and interaction of its users, such as access of patient information. And medical ubiquitous environments must support the mobility of its employees, given that mobility is inherent in the medical profession.

The medical field, in its constant pursuit for finding new methods of healing and improving patients' quality of life, has been, and will continue to be, a major beneficiary of Ubiquitous Computing. Although not a substitute for the direct contact between physician and patient, is increasingly becoming an essential and indispensable factor for doctor's decision-making. The current telemedicine systems provide global integration, which enables the sharing of data, images and voice from different sources and applications.

Thus, the aim of this chapter is to present new hospital automation technologies, specially, mobile techniques and a survey of a number of state of the art studies. Additionally, we will present an example of architecture for processing, monitoring patient's vital signs using artificial intelligent technique as logic fuzzy.

This chapter is organized as follows: Section 2 describes a brief introduction of the technologies involved with the state of art and mobile technologies applied in hospital automation. In Section 3 presented the architecture and its components by for example of an architecture with Intelligent and Mobile Technology. In Section 4 presented all the valdation of the architeture with focus on the constraints that must be obeyed when it comes to patient monitoring. Finally, in the Section 5 the conclusions are presented.

2. Mobile technologies applied in hospital automation

2.1 An overview of hospital automation

The automation can be considered a multidisciplinary area involving: programming languages (software), electronic platforms (hardware) and actuators (mechanical). This factor means that studies in automation are comprehensive and therefore involve a wide range of knowledge (Nof, 2009).

The hospital automation is a subfield of automation that seeks to promote the automation of processes relevant to the hospital environment, looking for efficiency and productivity and considering mainly the features and constraints peculiar to the medical environment (eg, the acquisition of data should be provided with privacy in order to ensure the ethics of the medical act and preserve the integrity of the patient) (Feng, 2007).

Typically, the hospitals make use of technologies that provide greater security, reliability, robustness to the daily tasks, mainly because they deal with human lives. As an example, we can mention applications (hardware / software), relating to Fig. 1.

- management and control: electronic medical records, appointment scheduling, control of pharmacy, hospitalization, laboratory, among others;
- communication: tracking patients, staff and materials;
- medical equipment and laboratory devices: cardiac monitors, pulse oximeter, stethoscopes, thermometers, surgical tools, magnetic resonance, scanner, among others;
- monitoring: patients, staff and materials;
- helping medical diagnosis: according to each specialty.

Integrating the hospital environment are the ICUs, defined as hospital units for the care of critically. The scope of work includes the monitoring of vital signs of patients in the ICU, aiming at the realization of pre-diagnostic to help medical decision and providing information to send alerts when needed.

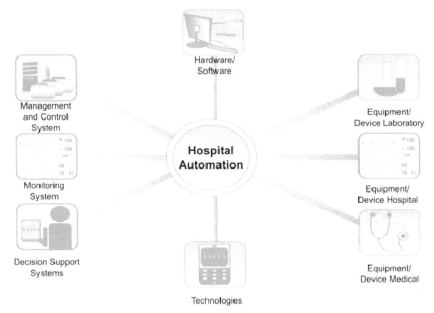

Fig. 1. Hospital Automation

According to Hoerr (Mosby's, 2010) "the patient is any individual under medical care." Particularly, patients in the ICU need care, company and continuous monitoring of vital signs, aimed at early detection of risk situations, allowing timely intervention by health professionals monitoring of vital signs, to early detect risk situations, allowing timely intervention by medical staff. Some patients are admitted because they present a severe clinical manifestation and others are admitted only for monitoring of vital signs because they underwent surgery, for example. So, the automation process of the ICU becomes necessary in order to minimize errors and maximize available resources to the medical team for the patients' care and monitoring.

Vital signs are measurements that provide physiological data indicating the health conditions of the person, demonstrating the functioning and changes in body function. Thus, the vital signs guide the initial diagnosis and the monitoring of patients' clinical evolution. So, their main objective is to help in the health assessment of the person, as well as equip the decision making process related to specific interventions. The vital signs monitored that help the medical diagnosis are: systolic blood pressure, diastolic blood pressure, mean arterial pressure, heart rate, respiratory rate, body temperature and partial oxygen saturation, as shown in Table 1 (Jauch et. al, 2010). The correct measurement of vital signs is extremely important for the clinical assessment of patients that are, in this work scope, in the ICU.

Name	Abbreviation	Normal Value
Pressure (Systolic / Diastolic) *	Bp	04 years old -85/60 mmHg; 06 years old-95/62 mmHg; 10 years olsd - 100/65 mmHg; 12 years old - 108/67 mmHg; 16 years old - 118/75 mmHg; Adults - 120/80 mmHg; Elderly - 140 a 160/90 to 100 mmHg.
Heart rate (The objective is to evaluate whether the heart is beating, and if he does so with appropriate pace and frequency.)	Hr	Newborn - 100 a 160 bpm Children - 80 a 120 bpm Adult - 60 to 100 bpm
Respiratory Rate (Through rhythm, sound and depth, it reflects the metabolic state of the body, the condition of the diaphragm and chest muscles, supplying oxygen (O2) to the respiratory tract and alveoli.)	RR	Newborn- 30 to 60 mrpm Children- 20 to 30 mrpm Adult- 12 to 20 mrpm
Body Temperature (It represents the balance between heat production and heat loss.)	Bt	Axillary: 36 0C to 37 0C Oral: 36,2 0C to 37,2 0C Rectal: 36,4 0C to 37,4 0C
Partial oxygen saturation (It represents the partial oxygen saturation in the blood.)	POS2	Low- 0 - 94 % Normal- 95 - 100 %

*MBP - Mean Blood Pressure

Table 1. Key parameters for patients' vital signs analysis Sample table title

2.2 Technology trends for hospital automation

The development of technologies for health care are becoming a recurring term in the research field, whether the field of Engineering, Exact Sciences, Health or Human Sciences. This aspect characterizes the development of technology in health as a transversal element, or even transdisciplinary, for whose purpose is to study innovation in health usually permeate the border areas of knowledge, a factor that almost require interdisciplinary or transdisciplinary (Guimarães, 2004).

Technological innovation in health for emerging countries can be a significant tool for socioeconomic development, for two primary reasons (Marziale, 2004):

Instrumentation in order to encourage improvements in the quality of population health, democratizing and universalizing access to health care;

Generation of products with high added value. This represents a very important artifact because it can help to improve the balance of trade balances, with the reduction of royalty payments, increase of exports and job creation.

In this sense, it is important to be delimited by prospective studies that may indicate demands actually required for the productive sector in the health area, this at the local and global sense. Thus, it becomes more consistent the strengthening of research, as well as the integration of these in the market for technological innovation in health, which is fundamental to ensure the economic sustainability of investments in research in this area (ABDI, 2008).

Technological innovation in health has many nuances and therefore can be classified in several areas, but essentially there are two sectors that are gaining greater space and visibility in the academic and corporate: The Health Informatics and Biomedical Engineering.

- Health Informatics: This is a field where the study is focused primarily on research and development and technological innovation in health from the perspective of computing applied in the medical field.
- Biomedical Engineering: is more focused on the development of medical equipment. Indeed, one can say that it is application of some areas of engineering (Mechanical and Electrical) in the health system.

In this context, there is a set of latent demand for health, and some emerging countries have realized that state. Thus, raising prospects in the following strategic areas (ABDI, 2008):

- Medical Imaging, focusing on Digital Radiology and Ultrasound;
- Hemodialysis, focusing on machines and filters;
- Neonatal, focusing on incubators for newborns;
- Medical Equipment based in Optics: Scopes and similar.

These demands are positioned as strategies because they generally take based on the trade balance and is guided by national policies for industrial development. For example, in the countries of Latin America, especially Brazil, in the year 2011 have been developed papers with following topics (R-BITS, 2011):

- Hospital Automation;
- Hospital Management;
- Telemedicine and Telehealth;
- Medical Equipment;
- Biomedical Signal Processing;
- Intelligent Systems Applied to Health;
- Medical Image Processing;
- Neuroscience;
- Rehabilitation and Assistive Technologies;
- Biomaterials and Implants.

The World Health Organization (WHO) (OMS, 2009) definition of Telemedicine involves the provision of services related to health care, where distance is a critical factor; such services are provided by professionals at health institutions using Information and Communication Technology (ICT) for the exchange of information valid for diagnosis, prevention and treatment of diseases and the continuing education of health services providers, as well as for research and evaluation.

The telemedicine applications can be classified into five main types: telemonitoring, teletherapy, teledidactics, social telephony and telediagnosis (EDUMED, 2008) and(Shen et al, 2007).

Telediagnosis, object of this work, is characterized by remote transmission of data, from vital signs to laboratory data and medical images, among others, as well as remote consultations to patients with the objective of diagnostic decision-making among medical specialists. In this area can be envisioned remote collaborative diagnosis and second opinion scenarios, which can be defined as an additional consultation with another physician or medical group, requested by the patient or the doctor who is seeing the patient, in order to guarantee the correct diagnosis.

Noting, therefore, important advances in health, especially when it comes to innovation, perhaps the greatest challenge is to automate processes without losing the axis of the humanization of health services, i.e. automating to humanize. This is because innovation in health care is already doing this in contemporary societies, research has expanded and is contributing to the breaking of paradigms in this area, bringing to light new knowledges, and therefore the biggest concern is not losing focus on patient.

2.2.1 Intelligent systems techniques

Because of the globalization, technological revolution, fast acess to information and efficient management, the market and companies start to demand the development of intelligent computational systems. Thus, the technology becomes the central attention of this revolution with the internet, softwares, hardwares and communications. Some challengers start to appears because of the needs listed in the previous sections, as:

- Acess to relevant data;
- Identify opportunities;
- Fast Action and re-action;
- Manipulation of high amount of data and information;
- Simulation of new methods, process and technology.

The advances in artificial intelligence, in parallel computation and the evolution in the communications, as the internet, have contributing for the development of new ystems capable of bring new way of processing. Adding value and advantages to this systems.

Intelligent Systems (IS) have important characterisitcs, as: ability to store, adapt and modify their context to solve problems, tasks in an automatic way, the capacity to make associations and inferences to solve complex real problems (Rezende, 2003).

For a system to be consider intelligent, the architecture of the system should have some characteristics as:

- It should have a set of abilities;
- Models specifics tasks.

The intelligent systems have some special techniques that can be used together or not. Artificial neural networks, fuzzy logic, evolutionary computation are some of the main techniques used in SI (Hanson, C. e Marshall, 2001). There are three sub-areas (supervised learning, evolutionary and hybrid) that are the core of intelligent systems. There are others importants paradigms as unsupervised learning, reinforced learning, simbolic learning and cognitive sciences (Shavlik e Dietterich, 1990). The Fig. 2 shows the relation between this three sub-areas and their core. They were develped in the beginning of the sixties as the perceptron (Rosenblatt, 1958); the fuzzy logic (Zadeh, 1965, 1973; Zadeh et al, 2002.); and genetic algorithms (Barricelli, 1954; Fraser, 1957).

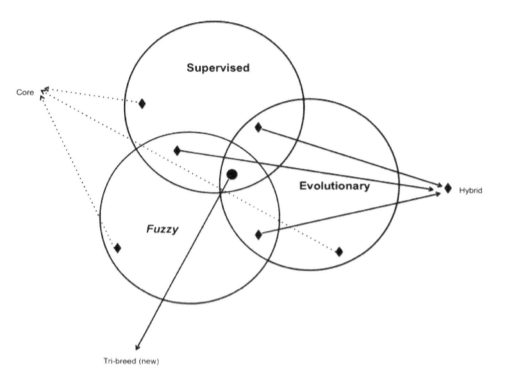

Fig. 2. The main paradigms of computational intelligence. Begg (2007)

It is already known that intelligent systems are efficent tools to deal with high amount of data, and these systems have been used in healthy systems and in pre-diagnostic systems.

2.2.2 Mobile and wireless techniques

Ubiquitous computing aims to make human-computer interaction invisible, i.e., integrating computing with personal actions and behavior (Sousa, 2002).

Ubiquitous computing (Fig. 3) is defined as the junction of two other concepts that are: Mobile Computing, where a computing device and its services can be relocated while they are connected in a network or the Internet. The other is the Pervasive Computing, in which computing devices are distributed in the environment in a seamlessly way (Weiser, 1996). And the Fig. 4 represents the users ubiquitous interfaces.

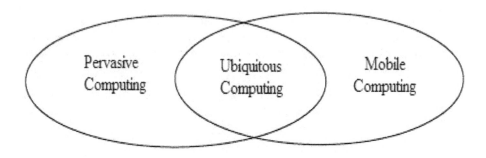

Fig. 3. Ubiquitous computing.

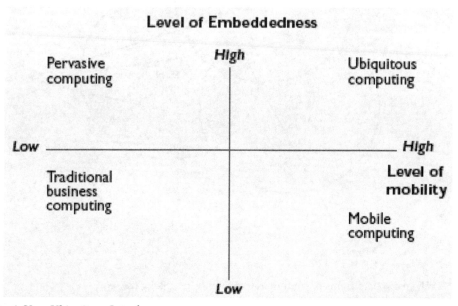

Fig. 4. User Ubiquitous Interface

Mark Weiser (Weiser, 1996) proposal is becoming a reality, through technologies such as PDAs, smart-phones, and the consolidation of wireless networking standards such as Bluetooth and IEEE 802.11. With ubiquitous computing, the relationship between users and computing devices changes compared to personal computers, what it was one to one, happens to be one to many (one user to multiple devices).

In addition to mobility, ubiquitous systems support interoperability, scalability, among other things to ensure that users have access when they want (Fig.5). According to Saha and Mukherjee (Saha & Mukherjee 2003), advances in technology necessary to build a ubiquitous computing environment are: devices, interconnection network, middleware, and applications.

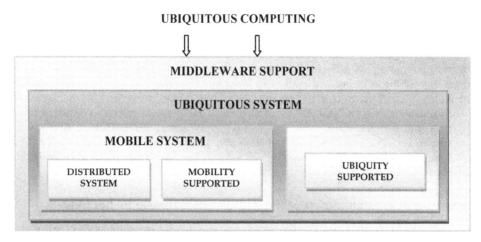

Fig. 5. Ubiquitous Computing (Saha and Mukherjee 2003).

2.2.2.1 Ubiquitous medicine

Health care seems to be an ideal application field for ubiquitous computing. Where else is the paradigm of "getting the right information at the right time at the right place of greater importance than in health care? Scenarios for application of ubiquitous computing are home care and monitoring, assistance for health professionals, and the self organization of health care institutions. Wearable systems and especially new man-machine interfaces are key technologies of ubiquitous computing in health care . Another key technology, namely RFID chips (Radio Frequency Identification) (Stanford, 2003), useful for realizing context awareness of ubiquitous computing solutions is already available and in use in several domains. These miniaturized chips allow the wireless transfer of data within a limited area around a special RFID reader and can be used to identify nearby people and objects.

Ubiquitous medical environments are those in which technological advances such as mobile devices and wireless networks bring new opportunities for access and interaction of its users, such as access of patient information. This information makes up the so-called Electronic Patient Record (EPR), allowing data about tests, facts and situations concerning the health of a patient to be accessed through multiple devices and heterogeneous networks.

Ubiquitous in medicine can be made to PEPs access to consolidated information on patients from anywhere in the network, allowing also cooperation between professionals regardless the time and space. In particular, medical ubiquitous environments must support the mobility of its employees, given that mobility is inherent in the medical profession. In addition to this nomadic nature of the doctor, it is important to consider that the medical activity is highly fragmented, i.e., shall be subject to interruptions during execution, as doctors spend little time at each location or activity. Thus, mechanisms that facilitate the professional's activities tend to improve their productivity. The importance of ubiquitous computing occurs not only when the main actor is the doctor, it can also be applied in the "world" of the patient, optimizing, for example, their monitoring system. Therefore the proposal shown in this chapter is not only a PEP system modernized but also the implementation of a unique module for tracking and monitoring patients.

2.2.2.2 Patient monitoring

Patient monitoring systems comprise sensors, data communication, storage, processing, and presentation of medical data. These functions are performed both near the patient, in local surgery, or remotely at a health care infrastructure, e.g., a medical centre or a hospital. Patient monitoring systems can be used in a variety of health care scenarios ranging from paramedic, diagnostic, surgical, post-operative, and home surveillance situations. The systems must meet a high demand of flexibility since data may be produced outside a health care enterprise (Maghsudi et. Al, 1999) (Raffloer & Wiggens, 1997). This requires specific measures in order to fulfill security, availability, privacy, and Quality of Service (QoS) demands. The properties are: a) mobility; b) outside hospital infrastructure; c) biomedical sensor networks in use; d) wireless channel.

3. Example of an architecture with intelligent and mobile technology

As an alternative to monitoring vital signs and conducting pre-diagnosis, object of this work, we consider that the systems for medical decision support using intelligent systems techniques combined with technologies that integrate mobility and portability in accessing processed information. The effects of this architecture can be significant, allowing a better interface, especially in the aspect of expert knowledge, communication and usability, important features for applications in medicine.

Thus, the specification of the application architecture considered environments with heterogeneous architectures and was based on: the acquisition of data from patient's vital signs monitoring; the use of intelligent systems techniques, especially fuzzy logic; information processing; and sending alerts through mobile devices.

The monitored environment, entitled Intelligent System for Monitoring Patients (ISMp) (Fig. 6), consists of: acquisition of data through a network of sensors placed in the patients' beds; pre-processing, where the preparation (filtering) and data selection are carried out; data processing and classification, where process is done through fuzzy logic in order to implement a pre-diagnosis to help the medical staff; data post-processing and preparation for sending alerts if any abnormality was detected; the information is sent to mobile devices that are registered in the environment, to support medical staff in decision making and implementation of relevant actions.

a.   Data acquisition

To simulate the physiological data acquisition of patients (vital signs), we used the MIMIC (Multi-parameter Intelligent Monitoring for Intensive Care), which is a public database available on the Internet by the Physionet (PhisyoNet, 2010), in order to assist the work development facing the automation of hospital systems related to multiparametric monitoring of patients.

We used the software MATLAB (MathWorks) to read and load the data acquired from the biomedical devices.

The MIMIC has 74 records, with 20 to 40 hours of continuously recorded data each, related to patients admitted for medical, surgical and / or cardiac treatment in the ICU of Beth Israel Hospital in Boston. The data was obtained directly from the heart monitors installed in the beds and each record typically consists of hundreds of individual files.

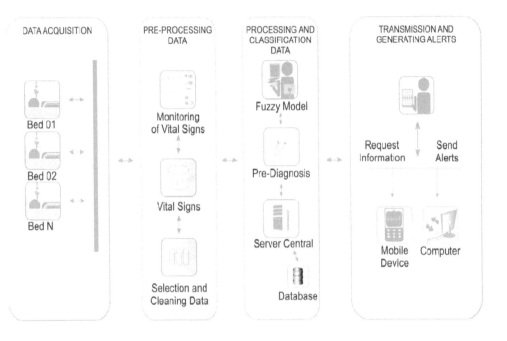

Fig. 6. Architecture of intelligent system for monitoring patients

It was observed that there are other notes in most of the records in the MIMIC database, including the QRS complex (which compose the ECG signal), as well as periodic alarms related to changes in the patient's condition, including heart and respiratory rate, oxygen saturation and systolic, diastolic and mean pressure shown in Fig. 7. In some records data from temperature sensors and cardiac output were also presented.

b. Pre-processing data

We carried out the extraction of the major physiologic signals that interfere directly in the clinical condition of patients with a stroke diagnosis (mean blood pressure, systolic blood pressure, diastolic blood pressure and oxygen saturation). It was observed that there are other physiological signals in the records of MIMIC database, such as the QRS complex (which compose the ECG signal) periodic alarms related to changes in the patient's condition; heart and respiratory rates; temperature; and cardiac output. The process of acquisition and validation of knowledge was done through weekly interviews during 2 (two) years, at the Promater Hospital, with the ICU medical staff. Thus, by pre-analysis performed together with medical specialists (general practitioner, cardiologist and neurologist) and nurses, the patients for validating the fuzzy model were selected.

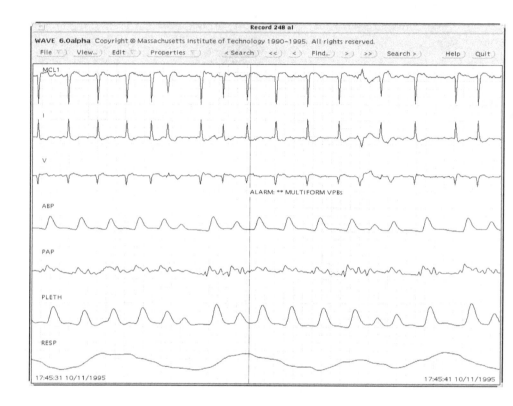

Fig. 7. A MIMIC sample (record 248)

c. Processing and classification data

In complex systems and processes, are required mechanisms for dealing with inaccurate information and reasoning and processing procedures to make them tractable. An effective strategy in these circumstances involves the acquisition, representation and processing of concepts described linguistically using fuzzy logic. In the literature studied and towards the proposed problem was found that the strategy of applying fuzzy logic could provide more benefits (acquisition of specialist's knowledge, generation of rules base, the process automation and increased accuracy of the pre-diagnosis) and satisfactory results. The implementation of intervention and control actions, in the model developed uses fuzzy logic, considering that it enables the capture of specialists' knowledge in the same way that lets you check the precise timing of the intervention and alarm. We developed a flowchart to assist the creation and use of a fuzzy system, called medical fuzzy system, shown in Fig. 8.

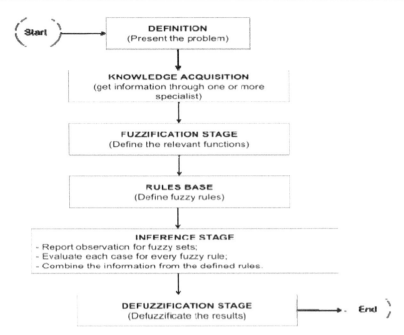

Fig. 8. Flowchart of creation and use of the fuzzy medical system

The fuzzy medical system definition and its stages (Fuzzification Stage, Inference Stage, Defuzzification Stage and Rules Base) are presented below.

1. **Definition of fuzzy medical system:** conditions of vital signs analysis, considering the parameters of normality and the defined fuzzy rules base, inferences in vital signs are made generating alarms from pre-diagnosis indicating abnormalities.

2. **Obtain information from one or more specialists:** the role of a specialist in the application to be modelled is of fundamental importance to collaborate in the construction of membership (relevants) functions for the entries description.

3. **Define the fuzzy sets (membership functions) - Fuzzification Stage:** in this stage the input variables are defined identifying to which fuzzy set(s) they belong to by assigning the respective degree to each relevance. The fuzzy sets represented by relevance functions should be set on the discourse universe in order to understand it completely. Thus, before the creation of fuzzy system, it is necessary to assemble the fuzzy sets (relevance functions) to be used in both fuzzification and defuzzification stages. The inputs of fuzzy system in question are the main vital signs (mean blood pressure and partial oxygen saturation) that were defined by the following relevance functions.

3.1 **Mean Blood Pressure (MBP) Membership**: MBP normal (N_{MBP}) considering a domain (80-130), by the linguistic terms low (L), normal (N) and high (H), respectively representing the bands, as illustrated in Fig. 9.

Fuzzy set of MAP:

Low MBP (L_{MBP}) <80 → L_{MBP}= {(0, 1), (60, 1), (80, 0)};

Normal MBP (N_{MBP}) 80-130 → N_{MPB} = {(75, 0), (105, 1), (130, 0)};

High MBP (H_{MBP}) > 130 → A_{MPB} = {(126, 0), (138.7, 1), (200, 1)}.

3.2 Partial Oxygen Saturation Membership POS$_2$: POS$_2$ normal (N$_{POS2}$) considering a domain (94-100), by linguistic terms, low (L) and normal (N), respectively, representing the bands, as illustrated in Fig. 10.

Fuzzy set of POS$_2$:

POS$_2$ baixa (B$_{POS2}$) < 94 → B$_{POS2}$ = {(0, 1), (90, 1), (94, 0)};

POS$_2$ normal (N$_{POS2}$) 94 - 100 → N$_{POS2}$ = {(89.2, 0), (96.2, 1), (100,0)}.

For this purpose, relevance functions were built from the direct method, the specialist informed all relevance functions data (values that represent each function and the degree of relevance, within the function of each) in order to set them explicitly. It is noteworthy that there are many relevance functions, but the most used in this fuzzy system were the triangular and trapezoidal as they better represent the functions according to the context.

4. **Fuzzy rules definition (Rules Base):** the rules base is assembled with the following structure: If <premises> Then<conclusion>. For the rules definition of the fuzzy medical system concerned, we could standardize the following structure:

- R: {R$_1$, R$_2$, R$_3$,...,R$_n$} → Set of rules;
- SV: {SV$_1$, SV$_2$, SV$_3$,..., SV$_n$,} → Set of vital signs;
- D: {D$_1$, D$_2$, D$_3$,..., D$_n$} → Set of possible diagnoses;
- P: {n, l, h}→ Parameterization of signals (normal, low and high).

  # Definição das Regras:

  #Rule: IF <(SV$_1$, SV$_2$, SV$_3$,..., SV$_n$,)> <{n($\downarrow\uparrow$), a ($\uparrow$), b ($\downarrow$)}> And/Or <(SV$_1$, SV$_2$, SV$_3$,..., SV$_n$,)> <{n($\downarrow\uparrow$), a ($\uparrow$), b ($\downarrow$)}>
  THEN <D$_1$, D$_2$, D$_3$,..., D$_n$>

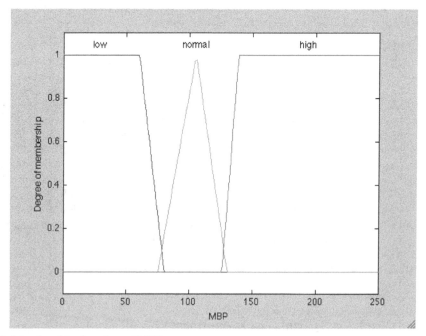

Fig. 9. Membership function of MBP

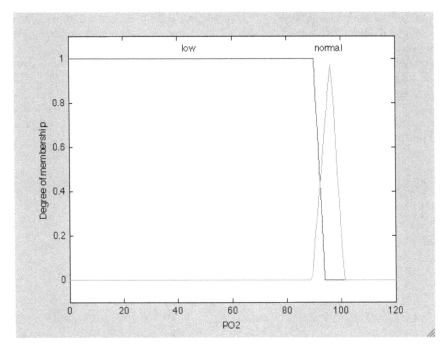

Fig. 10. Membership function of PO2

To exemplify, some rules for fuzzy medical system were set up, using two vital signs <premises>and 6 (six) situations as pre-diagnosis.

Rule 1: If *low* MAP and *low* POS2 then there is clinical instability.
IF MBP ↓ AND POS2↓ THEN UNSTABLE
Rule 2: If *low* MBP and *normal* SPO2 then low MBP.
IF MBP ↓ AND POS2↓ ↑ THEN ↓ MBP
Rule 3: If *normal* MBP and *low* SPO2 then hypoxemia.
IF MBP ↓ ↑ AND POS2↓ THEN HYPOXEMIA
Rule 4: If *normal* MBP and *normal* SPO2 then stability in clinical condition.
IF MBP ↓ ↑ AND POS2↓ ↑ THEN STABLE
Rule # 5: If *high* MBP and *low* SPO2 then instability in the clinical condition.
IF MBP ↑ AND POS2↓ THEN UNSTABLE
Rule 6: If *high* MBP and *normal* POS2 then high MBP
IF MBP ↑AND POS2 ↓ ↑ THEN ↑MBP

At this stage it is important that the amount of rules defined can cover all possible combinations of inputs and outputs of the problem proposed and that the consistency of the rules is reviewed to avoid contradictions. The rules base was developed from several meetings, discussions and interviews with the Promater hospital medical staff.

5. **Reporting the comments to the fuzzy sets - Inference Stage**: At this stage, the inputs are analyzed to generate the output fuzzy set with its respective degree of compatibility. In the proposed fuzzy medical system, we used the controller model

proposed by Mamdani (Mamdani, 1974), where the activation function of each rule is set in and the inference system determines the degree of compatibility with the premise of the rules contained in the rules base. After that, it is determined which rules were activated and the relevance output function is applied, joining all activated output fuzzy sets and their degrees of compatibility in a single Output Set (OS). This OS represents all actions that are acceptable to the input set, each one with their level of compatibility. It is also assessed at this stage, each case for all fuzzy rules and the information combination is performed from the rules already defined in the Rules Base, as illustrated in Figure 11.

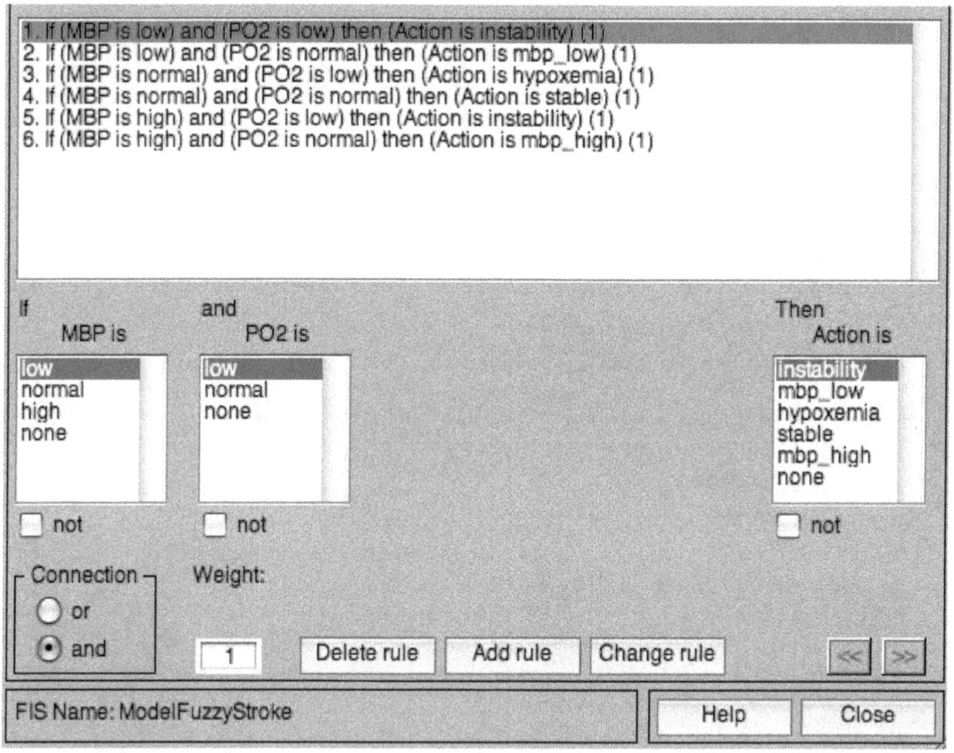

Fig. 11. Rules Base

6. **Defuzzificate results - Defuzzification stage:** this stage is used to generate a single numerical value, from all possible values contained in the fuzzy set obtained from the inference stage, to generate the control action. As a consequent action of the relations and variability of vital signs, was adopted for defuzzification the field (0-10), as illustrated in Table 2.

6.1 **Action Relevance Function (A) - Defuzzification:** representing the bands [<2.5; 2.5-4.5; 4-6, 5, 5-8 and> 8] by linguistically terms instability, low MBP, hypoxemia, stable and high MBP.

Cases	MBP	SPO2	Situation	Message	What should be done	Level of urgency
1	Low	Low	Unstable clinical situation (Instability)	The patient's vital signs are altered	Send alert to the doctor	High priority
2	Low	Normal	Low MBP	The patient's blood pressure is low		Low priority
3	Normal	Low	Hypoxemia	Patient with hypoxemia – abnormal deficiency of oxygen concentration in arterial blood		High priority
4	Normal	Normal	Normal clinical situation (stable)	No alert	No abnormality	
5	High	Low	Unstable clinical situation	The patient's vital signs are altered	Send alert to the doctor	Medium priority
6	High	Normal	High MBP	The patient's blood pressure is high		Low priority

Table 2. Diagnostics and levels of urgency of clinical cases

d. Alert generation and transmission

From the level of urgency set in the rules base already defined, messages are sent to the medical team from the issuance of alarms for devices (mobile or not) and may, according to pre-defined settings, be sent to desktop screen, via email, SMS and others. The post-processing and alerts sending is the architecture mechanism responsible for the control, sending and receiving messages between users and the architecture. This way, it is possible to create an effective communication system between a user (doctor) and the station (ICU). The main idea is that medical staff can connect to the centre with wireless network coverage in the hospital and thus receive on their device the alerts of possible changes in vital signs of monitored patients, as defined by Araujo (Araujo, 2009).

4. Validation

The simulations and validations of the proposed architecture have been conducted using MATLAB 2009a (student version) because of the tools available in this application for the development of models and the rapid visualization of the results obtained in the fuzzy system.

The fuzzy model developed for pre-diagnosis of patients in the ICU performs the interaction between the captured values, operated by the inference rules in fuzzy expert system, triggering control actions, monitoring and helping to medical diagnosis. The model indicates the alarms in accordance with the Guideline (Jauch et al., 2010), prescribed and developed by the American Heart Association, playing the main features defined for issuing alerts. After obtaining the definition of normal values of vital signs, the relevance functions of the main variables that directly influence the clinical condition of ICU patients were acquired. For the generation of rules base was asked to physicians, considering the parameters of normality and abnormality, to indicate the diagnosis of each clinical case and their level of urgency as already illustrated in Table 2.

To validate the ISMp the patient's condition was monitored and classified in five situations that can significantly alter the clinical condition of ICU patients: 1-clinical instability (all signs altered), 2- low MBP; 3-hypoxemia; 4-stable, and 5- high-MBP.

We adopted the basis of fuzzy rules taking as background a normal MBP, considering a domain [80, 130], representing the bands [<80, 80-130] and [> 130] by linguistic terms low, normal and high, respectively; and partial oxygen saturation, considering a domain [94, 100], representing the bands [<94 and 94-100] by linguistic terms low and normal, respectively.

As the consequent action of signs relations and variability, it was adopted for defuzzification the domain [0, 10], representing the bands [<2.5; 2.5 - 4.5; 4-6; 5.5 - 8 and> 8] by linguistic terms: instability, low MBP, hypoxemia, stable, high MBP, respectively.

Therefore, we used the vital signs selections required for the entry of fuzzy model constructing inference by relevance functions, rules base and already defined alarm conditions of vital signs for monitoring and support medical diagnosis in ICU inpatients.

An important step in this process was the extraction of data relevant to the model functioning, since the record is composed of many signs that are not used, which could interfere with the results and performance of the model. In the processing and sorting stage the results of the clinical diagnosis of patients' records were obtained through the model, as illustrated in Fig. 12.

In Fig. 12, we obtained the monitoring extract (query) of the patient identified by ID: 1662426 - 254NM, from 14h: 06m: 37s of the day 24/11/1995 to 14h: 06m: 57s of the day 24/11/1995. It was noted that monitoring is conducted every second and that in this interval the patient started unstable and passed to the state of Low MBP.

In the implementation of the model for monitoring and supporting the medical diagnosis of the clinical situation of the ICU patients was obtained a satisfactory result, with 96% accuracy (including the five situations planned) and 4% false alarms (due to various causes: from calibration of the equipment itself to body movements), according to analysis conducted by medical experts through the inferences made.

To this outcome measurements were available 100 (one hundred) inferences through forms (with patients' vital signs) so that physicians involved in this project could validate the pre-diagnosis provided by the proposed architecture and the fuzzy model.

```
                              ISMp
ID: 1662426
PATIENT: 254NM

     TIMESTAMP (TSR)          MEP     PDS2     PRE-DIAGNOSIS
   [14:06:37 24/11/1995]      35      91      Instability
   [14:06:38 24/11/1995]      34      91      Instability
   [14:06:39 24/11/1995]      35      91      Instability
   [14:06:40 24/11/1995]      35      91      Instability
   [14:06:41 24/11/1995]      34      91      Instability
   [14:06:42 24/11/1995]      34      91      Instability
   [14:06:43 24/11/1995]      34      91      Instability
   [14:06:44 24/11/1995]      34      91      Instability
   [14:06:45 24/11/1995]      34      91      Instability
   [14:06:46 24/11/1995]      33      91      Instability
   [14:06:47 24/11/1995]      34      91      Instability
   [14:06:48 24/11/1995]      35      93      Low MBP
   [14:06:49 24/11/1995]      35      95      Low MBP
   [14:06:50 24/11/1995]      35      95      Low MBP
   [14:06:51 24/11/1995]      36      95      Low MBP
   [14:06:52 24/11/1995]      36      95      Low MBP
   [14:06:53 24/11/1995]      36      95      Low MBP
   [14:06:54 24/11/1995]      36      95      Low MBP
   [14:06:56 24/11/1995]      39      95      Low MBP
   [14:06:57 24/11/1995]      39      95      Low MBP
```

Fig. 12. Diagnosis of Register 254N

It should be noted that medical Specialists are part of the Promater Hospital who promptly answered the questionnaire separately and later joined together to discuss the results, they are both critical care physicians.

Analyses were performed by the answers provided by medical forms and discussions of results. In Fig. 13 you can view the overall performance evaluation of the model through the fuzzy output and results of three specialists. It was obtained from 100 hundred inferences: 92 (ninety-two) with similar diagnoses and 8 (eight) with different diagnoses.

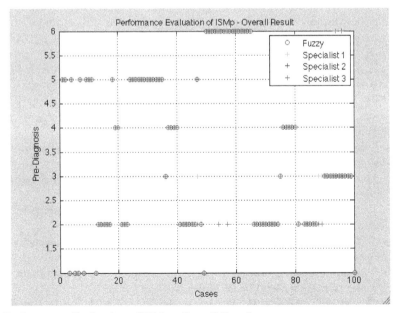

Fig. 13. Performance Evaluation of ISMp - Overall Result

After discussing the results with the specialists it was verified that between the 8 (eight) with different diagnoses: 4 (four) the fuzzy inferred correctly, and 4 (four) diverged from each other.

5. Conclusions and future plans

This chapter presented a fuzzy model able to monitor and classify the condition of the vital signs of hospitalized patients, sending information to an alerts system according to the pre-diagnosis done helping the medical diagnosis.

Monitoring, processing, validation and testing of the fuzzy model were carried out using database with real data. It was also presented a simulation in order to evaluate its effectiveness, taking into account the pre-adjustment of the relevance functions in the pursuit of reducing false alarms. The use of fuzzy logic proved be for to the medical area very useful as a tool to assist specialists in this area.

Finally, from this study numerous possibilities for future work arise, such as: validation of the model in a real scenario and environment, confronting the real-time alarm generation and reception of messages being evaluated by the patient's physician, an increase of vital signs in the model, inclusion of specific alarms for each patient.

6. References

ABDI. Estudo Prospectivo: Equipamentos Médicos, Hospitalares e Odontológicos. / Agência Brasileira de Desenvolvimento Industrial, Centro de Gestão e Estudos Estratégicos. – Brasília: Agência Brasileira de Desenvolvimento Industrial, 2008.

Araújo, B.G.de, Leite, C.R.M., Valentim, R.A.de M., Brandão, G.B., Guerreiro, A.M.G. Middleware for remote healthcare monitoring. In Proceedings of the 6th international conference on Innovations in information technology (IIT'09). IEEE Press, Piscataway, NJ, USA, 66-70, 2009.

Begg, R.; Lai, Daniel T. H.; Palaniswami, M. Computational Intelligence in Biomedical Engineering (1st ed.). CRC Press, Inc., Boca Raton, FL, USA. 2007.

Barricelli, N. A. Esempi numerici di processi di evoluzione. Methodos, 45–68. 1954.

Fraser, A. Simulation of genetic systems by automatic digital computers I. Introduction. Australian Journal of Biological Sciences 10, 484–491. 1957

EDUMED, Projeto. URL: http://www.edumed.net/projetos/projeto-edumed.html (disponível na Internet, capturado em 10/12/2008).

Feng, D.D. Biomedical Information Technology. Series-Academic Press Series in Biomedical Engineering. Hardcover, Academic Press, 2007. ISBN:0123735831.

Figueiredo, C., Nakamura, E. (2003) "Computação Móvel: Novas Oportunidades e Novos Desafios". T&C Amazônia.

Guimarães, R. Bases para uma política nacional de ciência, tecnologia e inovação em saúde. Ci Saúde Coletiva 2004 abril- junho; 9(2):375-87. 2.

Hanson, C. William; Marshall, Brayan E. "Artificial Intelligence applications in intensive care unit", Crit Care Med Vol. 29, No. 2, 2001.

Jauch, E.C., Cucchiara, B., Adeoye, O., Meurer, W., Brice, J., Chan, Y., Gentile, N., Hazinski, M.F. Journal of the American Heart Association. 2010 American Heart Association

Guidelines for Cardiopulmonary Resuscitation and Emergency Cardiovascular Care. Circulation 2010: 122; S818-S828, Dallas, TX, USA. 2010.

Maghsudi, M., Hente, R., Neumann, C., Schachinger, U. and Nerlich, M. "Medical communication from emergency scenes using a notepad computer," J. Telemed. (1999) Telecare, vol. 5, pp. 249-252.

Mamdani, E. H. Application of fuzzy algorithms for control of simple dynamic plant, Procedings of IEEE 121(12), 1585-1588. 1974.

Marziale, MHP. Diretivas para o desenvolvimento de pesquisas em saúde no Brasil. Rev Latino-am Enfermagem 2004 julho- agosto; 12(4):1-2.

Mosby's - Medical Dictionary, 8th Edition, © 2009, Elsevier. Source: http://medical-dictionary.thefreedictionary.com/diagnosis. Accessed 8/04/2010.

Nof, S.Y. Springer Handbook of Automation. 1st. Springer Publishing Company, Incorporated, 2009.

Organização Mundial De Saúde - Oms. Disponível em: http://www.who.org. Acesso em: 18 de ago. 2009.

PhisyoNet. Disponível em: www.physionet.org. Accessed 8/04/2010.

Raffloer K. S. and Wiggens R. A. (1997), "Video in an ambulance (VIA): wireless multimedia for mobile ambulatory applications," in Proc. Amer. Telemed. Assoc. 2nd Annu. Meeting, Atlanta, GA, Apr. 3-6.

R-BITS. Revista Brasileira de Inovação Tecnológica em Saúde. Disponível em http://www.incubadora.ufrn.br/incubadora/index.php/reb/. 2011.

Rezende, S.O. Sistemas Inteligentes - Fundamentos e Aplicações. Manole, Barueri, SP, Brasil. 2003.

Rosenblatt, F. The perceptron: a probabilistic model for information storage and organization in the brain. Psychological Review 65, 386-408. 1958.

Saha, D.;Mukherjee, A. (2003) "Pervasive computing: A paradigm for the 21st century." Computer, IEEE Computer Society Press, Los Alamitos, CA, USA, v.36, n.3, p.25-31,2003. ISSN 0018-9162.

Shavlik, J. and T. Dietterich. Readings in Machine Learning. The Morgan Kaufmann series in machine learning. San Mateo, CA: Morgan Kaufmann Publishers. 1990.

Shen, Y.; Xi, N.; Methil-Sudhakaran, N.; Mukherjee, R.; Zhu, D.; Cen, Z.; Mutka, M. W., Slomski, C. A., Apelgren, K. N. Internet based Tele-Diagnostic Interface for Breast Pathology. From Proceeding (564) Telehealth 2007. Montreal, QC, Canada: May 31 - Jun 1, 2007.

Stanford V. (2003) "Pervasive computing goes the last hundred feet with RFID systems." IEEE Pervasive Computing; 2: 9-14.

Sousa, J. P., Garlan, D. (2002) "Supporting User Mobility in Ubiquitous Computing Environments". Carnegie Mellon University.

Zadeh, L., T. Lin, and Y. Yao Data Mining, Rough Sets, and Granular Computing. Studies in Fuzziness and Soft Computing, vol. 95. Heidelberg: Physica-Verlag. 2002.

Zadeh, L.A. Fuzzy sets. Information and Control v. 8 ed .(3), p. 338-353. 1965.

Zadeh, L. Outline of a new approach to the analysis of complex systems and decision processes. IEEE Transactions on Systems, Man, and Cybernetics 8, 28-44. 1973.

Weiser, M. (1991) "The Computer for the 21st Century". In: Scientific American. Volume: 265, Number: 3, Pages: 94-104, February.

Weiser, M.; Brown, J. (1996) Designing Calm Technology. PowerGrid Journal. Volume: 1, Number: 1, July.

10

CARS-AD Project: Context-Aware Recommender System for Authentication Decision in Pervasive and Mobile Environments

João Carlos Damasceno Lima[1,2], Cristiano Cortez da Rocha[3], Iara Augustin[2]
and Mário Antônio Ribeiro Dantas[1]
[1]*Federal University of Santa Catarina*
[2]*Federal University of Santa Maria*
[3]*MobilEasy Technologies Ltda*
Brazil

1. Introduction

Recommender Systems (RS) emerged as an independent research area in the mid 90s, and they have been proved in the recent years to be a valuable approach for coping with the information overload problem (Ricci, 2011). In general, recommendation systems manage the overload of information by helping a user to choose among an overwhelming number of possibilities. In another point of view, we argue that the underlying concepts of Context-Aware Recommendation Systems are also useful to build supporting software (infra-structure) for mobile, pervasive and ubiquitous environments, which have requirements such as invisibility of computing, follow-me semantics (Augustin et al., 2006), context-awareness, adaptation, user-centric personalization, everyday human activities.

A pervasive environment is characterized by a richness of contexts in which users, devices and agents are mobile in several places and with several entities, including services, applications and resources. These elements can be available or not in a particular time and space. In fact, information regarding this time-space scenario can be used to develop a behavioral pattern of an entity in several contexts (Munoz-Organero et al., 2010).

To achieve ubiquity, the support system, which runs the environment management, must be designed to find the right balance between the user individuality and the system proactivity. In mobile and pervasive computing, we consider that the user's tasks must be personalized, while functionalities associated with security must be designed proactively. In mobile environment, the user moves constantly and wants to maintain access and to continue with the activity that he was performing (follow-me semantics). While traveling, the user can be served by different context (networks, systems, resources), which require authentication services periodically. Thus, proactive support system must know when to perform the authentication so implicitly or explicitly, seeking to reduce the user interference. We propose adopting a Context-Aware Recommender System (CARS) to help in this decision making process.

On the other hand, it is known that mobile devices can be easily lost, stolen, or used by several users, enabling sensitive information to become inappropriately available and could be stolen or broadcasted without permission. To avoid this situation, there is the need to adopt an authentication process, given that standard security policies allow that a second form of user validation can be used to complement the traditional alphanumeric passwords.

In pervasive computing, in which the majority of mobile devices has a reduced size, users face difficulties on providing (safe) passwords with too many characters. Considering that the pervasive space is rich in additional information, captured by sensors such as location, time, temperature, security camera images, which compose the environmental context. Therefore, it is possible to use this information, associated with the user behavior as a component of the authentication process. The challenge of this solution lies on the complexity of modeling the individual behavior, as there is the need to develop models to deal with different user behavior.

To address this issue, we present a user behavioral model based on activities, environmental contexts, and user profile. These three elements form a tri-dimensional matrix of a CARS to the authentication in a pervasive system. We also will discuss the processes of (i) content-based filtering, (ii) collaborative filtering and (iii) hybrid filtering. A relevant factor of the behavioral model is the spatial-temporal modeling, which allows us to compute the conditional probability of the occurrence of a given activity. This factor allows to consolidate user implicit authentications in the pervasive space or to launch a challenge question to determine the user authenticity.

2. Implicit authentication

2.1 Motivation and proposal

With the popularization of mobile devices (smartphones and tablets), there is a gradual user migration to the use of pervasive computing environments. The most common use of such devices is the storage and the retrieval of information that is relevant to the users, such as financial services, social networks, electronic messages, and e-commerce.

However mobile devices add disadvantages regarding the safety and privacy of information that is stored. Now new security mechanisms should be concerned about the loss of the devices and where they are being used, since it can be easily lost, stolen or used by multiple users, allowing confidential information may be used inappropriately.

The standard security policies allow the use of a second alternative for user validation that can be used to complement the traditional alphanumeric passwords and minimize the disadvantages of loss of information in mobile devices. The password-based authentication has the advantage of being simple to implement and use few resources (no additional hardware is usually needed). However, usual password discovery methods (phishing, keyloggers, and social engineering) has been successfully applied in breaking many passwords.

The use of an additional validation as part of the authentication provides a more secure process. There are several services (e.g. google authenticator) that already implement it, but they still have problems regarding usability and cost. The choice of enterprises for the use of SecureID tokens that are displayed by auxiliary devices and have characteristics related to desktop-based computing, where information is restricted to safe environments (business and home) are very different from the pervasive environment where mobile devices not have these limiting safety.

The implicit authentication is an approach that uses observations of user behavior for authentication. Since people are creatures of habits - a person goes to work in the morning, perhaps with a stop at the coffee shop, but almost always using the same route. Once at work, she might remain in the general vicinity of her office building until lunch time. In the afternoon, perhaps she calls home and picks up her child from school. In the evening, she goes home. Throughout the day, she checks her various email accounts. Perhaps she also uses online banking and sometimes relies on her smartphone for access away from home. Weekly visits to the grocery store, regular calls to family members, etc. are all rich information that could be gathered and recorded almost entirely using smartphones. (Shi et al., 2011).

With the migration of users to pervasive computing, mobile devices begin to collect the information produced by daily user activity: user schedule, calls users, messages, and add additional data (eg time and location) in the information produced. This set of data and information that is collected daily defines a profile that woks as a reliable criterion for authenticating users.

According to Shi et al. (2011) the implicit authentication is able to: i) act as a second factor for authentication passwords and supplements for greater assurance of a profitable and easy to use, ii) work as the primary authentication method to completely replace passwords, and iii) provide additional security for financial transactions such as credit card purchases, acting as an indicator of fraud. We note that in the latter scenario, the act of making the transaction does not require any user action on the device.

2.2 Research in authentication for pervasive environment

We present a set of related approaches for context-aware authentication with the goal of comparing this work with the state-of-art in this area:

1. **Implicit Authentication with User Behavior Learning** - Shi et al. (2011) propose an implicit authentication mechanism through user behavior learning. The mechanism focuses on the use of mobile devices (PDAs) and presents a technique to determine the computation of an authentication score based on the user recent activities. To compute such score, the positive (habitual) events are identified; the score increases whenever an habitual event is observed, as buying coffee always in the same store, in a similar period of time, daily. The score decreases when negative (sporadic) events are detected, such as the call to an unknown number or sudden changes of expected places (an event associated with the theft or the inappropriate use of the device). The passage of time is treated as a negative event in which the scores gradually decrease. When the score reaches a lower limit, the user must authenticate explicitly, inserting a code. The successfully authentication will boost the score. The limits can vary for different applications, depending on security needs.

2. **Transaction Level Authentication** - Sathish Babu & Venkataram (2009) present an authentication schema to mobile transactions, named TBAS (Transaction-Based Authentication Scheme), which aims to classify user-operated transactions in the application level in mobile computing environments. Through this classification, the

system (i) is able to interfere and to analyze user behavior using cognitive (intelligent) agents, and (ii) can determine the security level needed, predicting, thus, the cost associated with the authentication process delay, given the application of cryptography algorithms. TBAS uses two kinds of cognitive agents: a mobile cognitive agent (MCA) and a static cognitive agent (SCA). In this approach, the SCA creates the MCA and sends this mobile cognitive agent to the mobile device. This procedure is done while the user is being authenticated.

3. **Authentication based on Activity Recognition** - Hassan et al. (2008) propose an activity-based security mechanism that aims to help in the user activities in ubiquitous environments. Such mechanism is composed of an authentication system based on the human identification of images (Jameel et al., 2006) of an activity oriented access control module. The proposed model supports several kinds of devices, including mobile devices (PDAs), laptops, and desktops. In the mechanism, the activity recognition manager (ARM) provides information regarding user activity to the authorization system, through low level data collection related to the activity and the production of high-level contextual information. This way, the ARM can conduct the process of reasoning about user actions.

4. **Context-based Authentication** - Corradi et al. (2004) propose a security middleware, named UbiCOSM (Ubiquitous Context-Based Security Middleware). Such approach adopts the context as a basic concept to the specification and the execution of security policies. Therefore, the permissions are associated directly to the contexts, instead of being associated with the identities and with the user roles. The information about contexts and resources is provided by the CARMEN middleware (Bellavista et al., 2003). The UbiCOSM access control manager works with two context classifications: physical and logical context. Physical contexts identify physical spaces delimited by specific geographical coordinates. This way, a user operates in a given physical context, depending on his current location; thus, the user can only belong to a physical context. Additionally, the physical contexts define specific boundaries to the access control manager, as each physical context has references to the resources which must be protected.

2.2.1 Analysis of the approaches

In this section, we conduct an analysis of the previously presented approaches considering the essential requirements to the authentication on pervasive environments. As shown on Table 1, the majority of the approaches present a weak contextual modeling, as they consider only aspects regarding the characteristics of the devices used by the user and his spatial context. In this way, such systems have an incomplete vision of the scenario, hurting the decision making process. The proposal 1 works with a limited spatial-temporal model, because time is modeled though a simplification that does not allow the inference of weekly or biweekly activities (for example, on every Saturday the user plays tennis with new adversaries and needs to contact them to schedule the game).

A small part of these analyzed approaches presents some mechanism to dynamically analyze and model user behavior. The proposals presented on 3 and on 4 are static, i.e. they do not offer mechanisms that the system can use to dynamically aggregate the knowledge and the skills acquired by the user during his interactions with the system. In 3, despite the proposition of an activity recognition mechanism, the user must explicitly inform the activity that he is executing. In 4, although a proposal for using profiles to determine the user

Characteristics	Implicit AuthZ with User Behavior Learning	Transaction Level AuthZ	AuthZ based on Activity Recognition	Context-based AuthZ
Contextual Model	Spatial and Temporal	Spatial	Spatial	Spatial
Behavioral Model	Dynamic Profile through scores	Cognitive Agents	Explicit	Static Profile
Atomicity and Dinamicity	Yes	Yes	No	No
Flexibility	No	Yes	No	Yes
Privacy	Yes	No	No	Yes
Authentication control	Client	Client	Client	Server

Table 1. Approaches for Context-Aware Authentication (AuthZ)

permissions is presented, the user must explicitly determine which activities he intends to perform on the system.

As the battery life time is a major usability concern in mobile devices (Rahmati & Zhong, 2009), it is desirable that the authentication mechanisms take into account aspects related to the consumption of computational resources in an intelligent way, when they execute their security procedures. Thus, the validation of the proposal in 2 is based on the categorization of mobile transactions, considering the security level needed to perform such operations. Although there is this cost categorization associated with the authentication process, such categorization is only used to determine the impact of the delay associated to the cryptography algorithm used, and to define which will be the authentication methods (challenges) used. On the other hand, in 1 and in 3, despite the authors cite that the proposed architecture is lightweight, no experiments or additional details are presented to describe how such architecture deals with the mobile devices energy constraints. The architectures having the authentication control in the server do not interfere in the applications and in the mobile device operational system, making its dissemination easier and reducing battery consumption.

The possibility of managing the security policies by the users has become steadily more important in the design of security solutions that aim to align the usability to the capacity of maintaining acceptable levels of integrity, reliability and availability in mobile applications (Toninelli et al., 2009). However, security and usability have been rarely integrated in a satisfactory way in the design and in the development of mobile systems (Hong et al., 2007).

Therefore, we aimed to analyze the proposed approaches in terms of privacy and flexibility of authentication mechanisms and policies. In 2 and 4 it is presented another authentication mechanism. In 2, different challenges are provided to the user in order to ensure his identity, depending on the security level needed by the requested transaction and the user behavioral anomaly level. On the other hand, in 4, the user defines its preferences through profiles, which are used by the system in the user authentication and authorization processes. In 1 it is not presented a validation mechanism nor the generation of challenges, the authors inform that this can be performed by the applications, in different levels. In 3, the proposed architecture provides only one authentication way for the user, which is the process of identifying images proposed before by the same authors in Jameel et al. (2006).

3. Context-aware recommendation systems

We adopt Burke's taxonomy (Burke, 2007) to provide an overview of the different types of RS, which has become a classical way of distinguishing between recommender systems and referring to them. He distinguishes six different classes of recommendation approaches:

- Content-based filtering: recommends items that are similar to the ones that the user liked in the past;

- Collaborative filtering: recommends to the active user the items that other users with similar tastes liked in the past;

- Demographic: recommends items based on the user demographic profile. The assumption is that different recommendations should be generated for different demographic niches;

- Knowledge-based: recommends items based on specific domain knowledge about how certain item features meet users needs and preferences and, ultimately, how the item is useful for the user. Notable knowledge-based recommender systems are case-based or constraint-based systems;

- Community-based: recommends items based on the preferences of the user's friends. This technique follows the epigram "Tell me who your friends are, and I will tell you who you are".

- Hybrid recommender systems: based on the combination of the above mentioned techniques. A hybrid system combining techniques A and B tries to use the advantages of A to fix the disadvantages of B.

Many resources in ubiquitous environments can be available and the users want to share them. However, the situations and the preferences of users are different, even if the users are in the same environment. Therefore, we want to have a proper RS for sharing the available resources. These and other possible models for recommendation systems may be adequate for current uses, but perhaps not for future ubiquitous computing.

Ubiquitous computing systems with knowledge of more than locations - say, the tools a person is using - could greatly benefit that person by recommending others who have expertise with those tools. Although it may be impossible to optimally anticipate the needs of each user at any place at any time, ubiquitous computing will enable such systems to help people to cope with an expanding array of choices (McDonald, 2003).

Therefore, the recommendation approach, which proved to be successful to PC users, cannot be straightforwardly applied for mobile users due to the obstacles that are typically present in mobile usage environments, such as: limitation of mobile devices and wireless networks, impact from external environment, and behavior characteristics of mobile users (Ricci et al., 2011).

3.1 Mobile recommender systems

Mobile recommendation systems are systems that provide assistance to the users as they face decisions "on the go", or, in other words, as they move into new, unknown environments.

Examples include consumers making purchasing decisions in retail stores, or students having ad hoc meetings to decide on assignment workload van der Heijden et al. (2005).

As mobile devices are popular and are becoming a primary platform for information access and business applications, recommendation techniques can increase the usability of mobile and pervasive applications, providing more focused content and tailoring the information to the needs of the user. Ricci et al. (2011) reviews the major techniques that have been proposed in the last years and illustrates the supported functions by Mobile Recommender Systems (MRS).

As we have observed, in the most mobile recommender systems, the recommendation target is Internet content, multimedia (videos, music, films, books), product promotions, tourist experiences and traffic information. The data sources are users and Internet transactions. For those MRS that add context-awareness, the more commonly context information is the user location (location-aware applications).

Context-based applications pro-actively retrieve content of interest based on the user current task or his profile. Roberts et al. (2008) describe the implementation of a mobile recommender system for leisure activities, named Magitti, which was built for commercial deployment under stringent scalability requirements. Ricci & Nguyen (2007) exploit the recommendation by proposal and critiquing techniques in the MobyRek system, that has been designed to run on a mobile phone with limited user input. It searches functionality, lets the user to formulate both must and wish conditions, and returns a ranked product list. The result of an empirical evaluation of the system shows that it can effectively support product selection processes in a user friendly manner.

Although the systems target different needs, they share a common design: the system collects different types of (contextual) information characterizing the user (such as preferences, activities, location, device) and uses it to filter and to rank relevant content items and trying to anticipate the needs or the products in which the user may be interested, while he is moving himself.

3.2 Pervasive security and recommender systems

Security problems in RSs are addressed with two goals in mind: (i) to control malicious users (Ray & Mahanti, 2009), and (ii) to ensure user privacy (Zhan et al., 2010). Thus, we are interested in recommender systems for security in mobile and pervasive environment.

The goal of research in Mobile, Pervasive and Ubiquitous Security is to understand and to analyze the new security and privacy issues arising from the high mobility, context-awareness and invisibility of these systems, that begin to be available, and to propose solutions to safely deploy applications, services and appliances anywhere, anytime, on any device, on any network, running on background.

According to Johnson (2009), pervasive environments need context-aware security mechanisms because the context changes allow these mechanisms to be adjusted on the basis of the current situation. Therefore, the mechanisms using this approach are able to effectively deal with traditional security systems limitations that are designed for static environments. Nevertheless, most of the research regarding the development of context-aware authentication systems is limited or vague (Ricci & Nguyen, 2007). Usually, these systems only consider traditional aspects, e.g. the user location. As a result, they provide an abstract and weak view of a certain situation. Thus, the decisions made within these systems are poor, because they are based on an incomplete scenario.

Few works address issues about pervasive security and context-aware recommender systems. Kim et al. (2009) propose a new authenticated key management method, called 3DE_sec, to minimize the load of the authenticator, even with mobile nodes or the insertion or deletion of nodes. The proposed system generates personalized profiles (using inference of data captured from RFID systems) containing user preference and various lifestyles and uses of recommendation service, it updates based on past history and currently available services. The system architecture is composed by profile collector, profile aggregator, collector resolver, and service manager. The evaluation results indicate that the method can set a shared key faster and more securely using a multiple-key ring assigned to each node before deployment secure and efficient recommendation service in RFID.

Romero-Mariona et al. (2008) propose a recommendation system for helping developers to choose among security requirements approaches. As part of their ongoing research, they identified ten key characteristics (elicitation support, level of customer involvement, unambiguity level, completeness level, clarity level, traceability level, overall security level, update difficult of the security specifications, automation support level, scalability level) that are used to recommend which of the 12 approaches surveyed better suits a specific project. In a different direction of these approaches, we aim to recognize the suitable moment to renew the user authentication automatically or to ask the user for information to explicitly authenticate him.

4. CARS-AD architecture

The pervasive space exists in an environment where situations or contexts surround the user. In particular, these contexts are relevant for the adaptive process of services and information offered to the user through context-aware applications (Dey, 2001). Therefore, the situations that a user can experienced in a pervasive environment are personal, complicating the representation of the user's context and its parameters.

We analyzed the resources offered by mobile devices to identify contexts and properties relevant to the users and their behaviors in pervasive environments. Consequently, the following authentication-relevant contexts were identified (Uden, 2007):

- Operational context: describes the goals, tasks and activities of the user;
- Interpersonal context: describes the social aspects of the user, such as the relationships and communication channels between the user and his community;
- Spatial context: considers attributes regarding the use's location;
- Environmental context: captures the situations surrounding the user, such as services, people and information accessed by the user.

The temporal property was integrated with the context model to improve the decision-making process (Uden, 2007). Specifically, this model considers historical data, such as the user learning capacity, including the acquisition of skills and knowledge, and the evolution of activities and behaviors (see Figure 1).

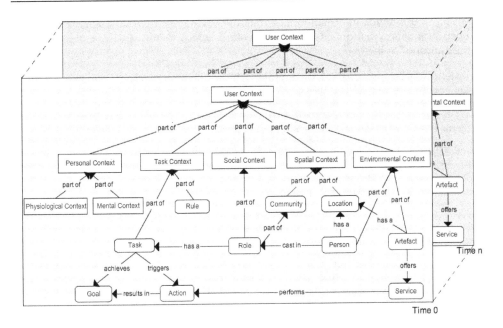

Fig. 1. Contextual Modeling adapted from Cassens & Kofod-Petersen (2006)

4.1 Context model

The proposed context-aware authentication architecture attempts to use resources that are commonly found in mobile devices, such as smartphones, to monitor the behavior of the user in different situations and events where the user is immersed in the pervasive space. These devices are considered as special artefacts that are commonly used by the users to perform tasks and activities, and consequently, to achieve their goals in mobile environments (Uden, 2007). Specifically, these devices offer access to resources such as (Lima et al., 2010):

- User calls: provide information considering the interpersonal context, which is comprised by the community in which the user is inserted and the environmental context, that is regarding the people surrounding the user;

- User schedule: one of the richest resources in terms of context, as it provides information about the relationship between the user and the members of his community. It can help to determine the user location, the people surrounding him and the activities that the user wants to execute in a given time frame;

- GPS: provides information regarding the user spatial situation;

- Device battery level: can indicate the interaction form between the user and the environment, as well as the intensity of such interaction;

- User applications: provide information related to the operational and the environmental context: in particular, such applications indicate which artifacts the user needs to achieve his goals through the performed activities;

- Sensors: can provide information regarding the environment, visual authentication and other information that define the environment in which the user is interacting with the authentication system.

The architecture has additional modules that allow the recommendation system implementation, described as follows:

- Group profile: a pre-defined profile which considers the standard characteristics of the agents (users, applications, use sessions and environment) which interact with the system.

- Explicit profile: created during the first interaction of the system with the user through an interactive interface; contains the events made explicit by the user and extracted from their contacts and the personal agenda stored in the mobile device. This profile can be customized and synchronized at any time;

- Implicit profile: created through the processing of user events and his explicit profile; it has the relevant information about frequent events, the actions taken by the users, and their spatial-temporal characteristics.

- Recommendation filter: an adaptive filter according to the approach (based in content, collaborative, or hybrid) which uses the vector space model to compute the information relevance, and uses a formal treatment through the vectors to compute the similarity between the profiles being analyzed.

The context-aware authentication architecture is illustrated in Figure 2. The context subsystem, or, user context, is responsible for capturing all the situations that determine the occurrence of a new event through the resources previously described. Thus, this subsystem sends the event description e_i to the belief analyzer subsystem.

Belief Analyzer: The Belief Analyzer is responsible for the definition of behaviors or beliefs, as well as for the classification of events and the inference of behaviors through the activities, the stored profiles, and the perceived and registered events. The behaviors are analyzed by similarity or probabilistically in order to define new occurrences and to determine the attitude to be adopted by the system, as well as the actions that must be taken in a new occurrence. The beliefs database works with a knowledge repository (storing beliefs and profiles).

Recommendation Filter: The Recommendation Filter aims to determine the new implicit profiles, i.e. for each combination of an event with the explicit profile, a new orthogonal vector is determined. This vector is used to compute the similarity: if the similarity degree is higher than a defined threshold, the profile is considered relevant and, then, it will be stored in the system as a new implicit profile, with a weight equals to the similarity degree.

Probability Analyzer: The subsystem which analyzes probabilities (Probability Analyzer) is responsible for the user categorization, based on the conditional probabilities of his behavior. This classification is divided in three categories: normal, suspect and abnormal.

Challenger: The subsystem determines how the user will be questioned in order to prove his identity on the system, based on the categorization made by the Probability Analyzer and on the authentication level needed for the desired operation. The response to the challenge proposed to the user is, then, stored for future queries.

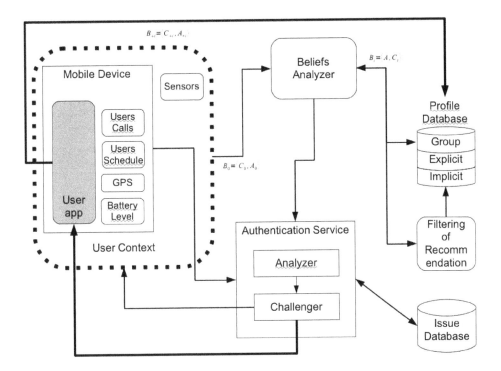

Fig. 2. Proposed Architecture

4.2 Behavioral model

Given the habitual tendencies of individuals, time correlations are important for the determination of successive events (Rocha, 2010). Hence, the prediction of events defines the actions and behaviors that the user will adopt. This work uses the following definitions to formally define the concepts of event and behavior:

- Event: situation of a given entity, in a given location, in a certain time space. An event can be determined as $E_i = \langle id_{entity}, situation_{entity} \rangle$
- Context: a set of events with relevant knowledge to the context definition of recommendation systems. Defined as $C_i = \langle time, location, E_1, E_2, E_3, E_4, .., E_n \rangle$
- Activity: set of actions for realization of a task, defined as $A_i = \langle a_1, a_2, a_3, a_4, ..., a_n \rangle$
- Behavior: the set of events or context related to an activity execution or set of actions (e.g. prescription for patients). It can be defined as $B_i = \langle A_i, C_i \rangle$

In the first moment we used the cosines of vectors to calculate the similarity between contexts and activities. However due to the diversity of domains that exist between the elements of each of these vectors was necessary normalization of values, similar case was reported in Su & Khoshgoftaar (2009). To solve this problem was adopted Pearson's correlation.

The similarity between two different contexts is established by the equivalence of events and it is determined by the possibility that activities in these contexts may occur again. The similarity between context is defined as

$$Sim(C_i, C_j) = \frac{C_i \times C_j}{|C_i| \times |C_j|} \tag{1}$$

When applying the normalization values through Pearson's Correlation Coefficient (PCC) in equation 1. The new similarity between contexts will be

$$PCCc_{i,j} = \frac{\sum_{u \in U} (c_{u,i} - \overline{c_i})(c_{u,j} - \overline{c_j})}{\sqrt{\sum_{u \in U} (c_{u,i} - \overline{c_i})^2} \sqrt{\sum_{u \in U} (c_{u,j} - \overline{c_j})^2}} \tag{2}$$

The equivalence between two activities can be determined by reusing actions or by the similarity between the activities. Can be defined as

$$Sim(A_i, A_j) = \frac{A_i \times A_j}{|A_i| \times |A_j|} \tag{3}$$

When applying the normalization values through Pearson's Correlation Coefficient in equation 3. The new similarity between activities will be

$$PCCa_{i,j} = \frac{\sum_{u \in U} (a_{u,i} - \overline{a_i})(a_{u,j} - \overline{a_j})}{\sqrt{\sum_{u \in U} (a_{u,i} - \overline{a_i})^2} \sqrt{\sum_{u \in U} (a_{u,j} - \overline{a_j})^2}} \tag{4}$$

The presented definitions represent the behavioral modeling and the way to compute the similarity between contexts and between activities. Using these definitions the processes of Recommendations System filtering are defined and characterized.

4.3 Spatio-temporal permutation model

The observed events in the execution of activities form a database for the process of detecting information clusters, which translates to the habits of users. These clusters can be classified into three broad categories: purely spatial, purely temporal or spatio-temporal. In purely spatial clusters, the occurrence is higher in some regions than it is in others, and purely temporal clusters feature the occurrence of events as being greater in a certain period than it is in others. Finally, spatio-temporal clusters occur when events are temporarily higher in certain regions than they are in others. Among the models used to predict events in a spatio-temporal context, we propose the use of spatio-temporal permutation, which allows the incorporation of covariate information found in other contexts within the pervasive space.

According to Kulldorff (2005), the spatio-temporal permutation model is based on three characteristics: i) detecting data clusters in space and time simultaneously; ii) working with only events or cases; and iii) applying the probabilistic model in a null hypothesis to conclude that the events follow a hypergeometric distribution.

Assuming the count of events e, in the timeline set in t, located in a region, z, with circular features according GPS coordinates, is defined as e_{zt}. The total number of observed events, E, and the total number of conditioned events, M_{zt}, are expressed by the following formulas:

$$E = \sum_z \sum_t e_{zt} \quad M_{zt} = \frac{1}{E}\left(\sum_z E_{zt}\right)\left(\sum_t E_{zt}\right)$$

The prediction of an event encompasses the following assumption: the conditional probability of an event $P(E_a)$, in the region z was observed at the time t_1 and t_2, defined in a particular cylinder a, which reflects a possible cluster; therefore, E_a has an average M_a and follows the hypergeometric distribution determined by the following function:

$$M_a = \sum_{(z,t)\,\in\,A} M_{zt} \tag{5}$$

$$P(E_a) = \left(\sum_{t\,\in\,(t_1 \vee t_2)}\sum_{z\,\in\,A} E_{zt}\right)\frac{\left(\left(\sum_{t\,\in\,(t_1 \vee t_2)}\sum_{z\,\in\,A} E_{zt}\right) - \dfrac{E - \left(\sum_{t\,\in\,(t_1 \vee t_2)}\sum_{z\,\in\,A} E_{zt}\right)}{E_a}\right)}{\left(\sum_{t\,\in\,(t_1 \vee t_2)}\sum_{z\,\in\,A} E_{zt}\right)} \tag{6}$$

The SaTScan tool developed by Kulldorff (Kulldorff, 2005) is used to determine the regions of the clusters and the statistical significance is validated by the use of a Monte Carlo hypothesis test.

The conditional probability of the user $P(E_a)$ provides an estimation of the user's past and present activities. Thus, there are four cases that can occur: normal execution, abnormal execution, and two cases of suspicious execution. Normal execution entails the same activity in the same spatio-temporal context, and abnormal execution involves different activities in different spatio-temporal context.

The two cases of suspicious execution occur when the same activity is performed in a different spatio-temporal context or when different activities occur in the same spatio-temporal context. In the first case, the security-relevant context of the activity will define the authentication policies.

4.4 Filtering for recommendation system

In this project, we work with the development of 3 (three) recommendation filters:

Content-Based Filtering: The recommendation system uses the definitions of user behavior to establish their guidelines, if a particular activity in a temporal context was last conducted ($Time_0$ in Figure 1), there is a reasonable probability that this same activity can be executed again ($Time_{+1}$ in Figure 1). The temporal context that can be represented similarly to Oku et al. (2010):

$$\langle \ldots, \underbrace{(A_{-1}, C_{-1})}_{B_{Past}}, \overbrace{(A_0, C_0)}^{B_{Present}}, \underbrace{(A_{+1}, C_{+1}), \ldots}_{B_{Future}} \rangle \tag{7}$$

Collaborative Filtering: This filtering process uses the information from other behavior of users $\left\langle \underbrace{(B_1 = (A_1, C_1))}_{User_1}, \overbrace{(B_2)}^{User_2}, \underbrace{(B_3)}_{User_3}, \ldots \right\rangle$ to predict the users being implicit authentication $\left\langle \underbrace{(B_0 = (A_0, C_0))}_{User_{Predict}} \right\rangle$. Therefore, the similarity can be applied to the user behavior. And can be defined as:

$$
\begin{aligned}
Sim(B_0, B_1) &= Sim\Big((A_0, C_0), (A_1, C_1)\Big) \\
&= Sim(A_0, A_1) \times Sim(C_0, C_1)
\end{aligned}
\tag{8}
$$

$$
\begin{aligned}
Sim(B_0, B_2) &= Sim\Big((A_0, C_0), (A_2, C_2)\Big) \\
&= Sim(A_0, A_2) \times Sim(C_0, C_2)
\end{aligned}
\tag{9}
$$

Hybrid Filtering: The proposed model uses a hybrid filtering which explores the space-time perspective to define clusters of events and user behaviors. It is performed to predict the need of authentication. Regarding the user knowledge base expansion, it uses a similarity vector to expand and to redefine the user profile.

5. Cases and results

5.1 Content-based filtering

The presented experimental results are related to the content-based filtering process. The data from testing and the content-based filtering process results are preliminary. They were collected using two mobile devices during two weeks, with a total of 96 events, which were contextualized through their location, device and the time of their occurrence. The case study will refer to the content based filtering as shown in Figure 3. The analysis was conducted through complete authentication cycles, as follows:

1. The behavior B_0 is captured in the mobile device producing the B_0 vector.

2. The event is analyzed through the content based filtering process, which uses a clustering algorithm similar to k-means, where the clusters are formed by devices and other information that compound the event. The average values of the events define the centroid of the cluster, shown in Figure 4. The centroids are calculated through a normal distribution and their values are updated every time the user needs to authenticate explicitly. Every new event is calculated the distance to the centroid, which will be called the rank of similarity.

3. The need to challenge the user is analyzed, based on the authentication level required by the application, rank of similarity and statistical information the centroid of clusters (represented by the Centroid D1 in Figure 4); and

4. if the authentication process is completed with success then the user behavior is stored in the profile database.

In content-based filtering, the clusters of devices are defined as parameters because:

- Mechanisms are used massively by the User to carry out their activities;

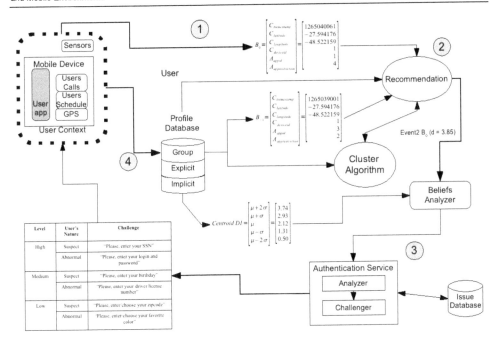

Fig. 3. Experimental Results to the Content Based Filtering

Fig. 4. Cluster of Devices

- Users work with a limited number of devices that enables the creation of statistical models for each user; and

- Filtering processes work with different parameters, which enables its completeness. The spatio-temporal parameters have already been evaluated in the hybrid filter, the focus in this filter is to study another parameter that incorporates the context of the user;

The authentication process begins with the first user interaction with the system. In this interaction, the user alphanumeric password is explicitly requested and the behavior vector B_0 is defined.

The authentication recommendation process starts being performed in the second user interaction. When the second interaction is requested, the behavior vector B_0 is redefined to B_{-1}, preserving previous user authentication information.

Level	User's Nature	Challenge
High	Suspect	"Please, enter your SSN"
	Abnormal	"Please, enter your login and password"
Medium	Suspect	"Please, enter your birthday"
	Abnormal	"Please, enter your driver license number"
Low	Suspect	"Please, enter/choose your zipcode"
	Abnormal	"Please, enter/choose your favorite color"

Table 2. Challenge for Authentication Level

In the second interaction, the request was done in the same mobile device, from the same location of the first interaction. However, such request was done to other application with different restrictions, represented by the B_0 vector in Figure 3.

The content based filtering does the execution of the cluster algorithm to determine the rank of similarity, which indicate if this application is being executed by the same user. In the case of *Event2*, shown in Figure 4, the rank of similarity is equal to 3.85, this value is calculated through the Euclidean distance between centroid $D1$ and the *Event2*. Thus, the user category is determined (normal, suspect, abnormal). We assumed the following definition:

- Normal user: the distance of the new event must be until one standard deviation from the centroid;

- Suspect user: the distance of the new event must be until two standard deviation from the centroid; and

- Abnormal user: values higher than the defined above.

Given the intervals defined above, there is the need of testing the user with the challenge corresponding to a abnormal user and to the authentication level required by the application (high level), as shown in the Table of Figure 3 and Table 2. When the user responds the challenge correctly, he is authenticated in the system, executes the desired operation and the requested event is inserted in the user profile, which contains the history of his interactions with the system.

5.2 Collaborative filtering

The presented experimental results are related to the collaborative filtering process. The data from testing and the collaborative filtering process results are preliminary. They were collected using three mobile devices during six weeks, with a total of 160 events, which were contextualized through their location, device and the time of their occurrence. The case study is related to the collaborative filtering as shown in Figure 5. The analysis was conducted through complete authentication cycles, as follows:

1. The behavior B_0 is captured in the mobile device producing the B_0 vector of the $User_0$.

2. The behavior B_0 is analyzed under the collaborative filtering process that uses Pearson's correlation coefficient to determine the rank of similarity between B_0 and the behaviors available in database of other users, represented generic by B_1 and B_2, shown in Figure 5.

3. The analysis of the need to challenge the user is based on the authentication level (defined on the Table 2) required by the application and rank of similarity (represented by the PCC B_0 in Figure 5); and

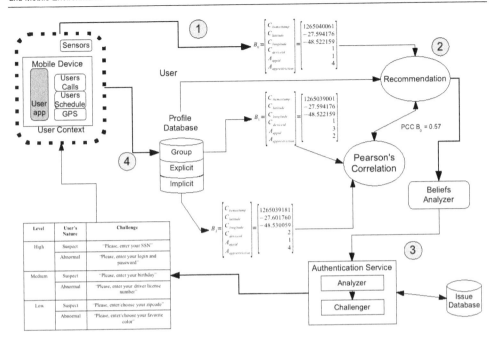

Fig. 5. Experimental Results related to the Collaborative Filtering

4. if the authentication process is accomplished with success then the new user behavior is stored in the profile database.

This filter aims to find other users who have a similar behavior (profile) to that of the User who is being authenticated. Thus, it is possible to determine that user behavior B_0 has similar behavior to that stored in database. The use of this filter requires that users decrease your privacy and allow their behaviors to serve as a basis for the definition of ranks of similarities (PCC).

The authentication process begins with the User performing the first authentication through an explicit process (typed password). The information collected in his first iteration are stored in the user profile. In the second interaction the system will try an implicit authentication using the Content-Based Filtering, in case the rank of similarity are below of the desirable level, the system performs Collaborative Filtering.

The Collaborative Filtering performs the search in a three dimensional matrix ($User \times Context \times Activities$) that formally is represented by: $R : U \times C \times A \rightarrow S$, where S is the value of evaluation in space result with expected value of $[0 , 1.00]$. In this project, the S was replaced by PCC aiming to standardize values and transform the relation between the behaviors in a linear relation which can be represented on a Cartesian plan, shown in Figure 6.

Those expect values to the PCC possess values between $[-1.00 , 1.00]$, and the nearest to 1 will be most similar behavior among users. If values are negative represent opposite behaviors among users. Thus, the user category is determined (normal, suspect, abnormal). We assumed the following definition:

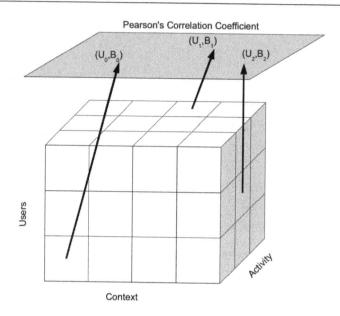

Fig. 6. Person's Correlation apply in Collaborative Filter

- Normal user: PCC above 0.85;
- Suspect user: PCC between 0.70 and 0.85;
- Abnormal user: PCC below 0.70.

Given the intervals defined previously, there is the need of testing the user with the challenge corresponding to a abnormal user and to the authentication level required by the application (high level), as shown in the Table of Figure 5 and Table 2. When the user responds to the challenge correctly, he is authenticated in the system, executes the desired operation and the requested event is inserted in the user profile, which contains the history of his interactions with the system.

5.3 Hybrid filtering

The experimental results presented in this section are related to the hybrid filtering. We conducted an analysis of the architectural core (Beliefs Analyzer) and its interaction with other modules, through complete authentication cycles (see Figure 7), as follows:

1. the behavior (B_0) is captured in the mobile device;
2. the event is analyzed under the spatio-temporal perspective;
3. the conditional probability determined by the spatio-temporal permutation model is used to verify the similarity degree of the event with the user behavioral profile;
4. the need to challenge the user is analyzed, based on the authentication level required by the application; and
5. if the authentication process is completed with success then the user behavior is stored in the profile database.

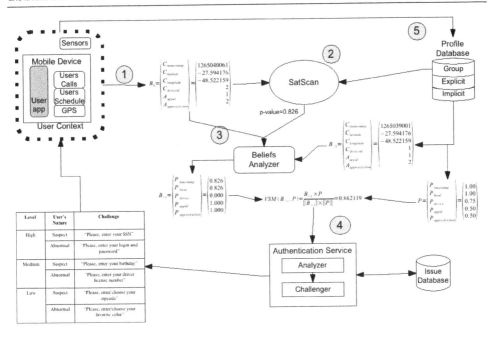

Fig. 7. Experimental Results of Hybrid Filtering

Based on this analysis, it is possible to determine the capacity of the context sensitive authentication system to aggregate new user knowledge and abilities, enabling system autonomicity. With this purpose, firstly, we defined which are the behavioral attributes to be considered according to the proposed target scenario.

We opted for the following parameters: the mobile device used, the location of the event occurrence, the timestamp of the event occurrence, the application being executed and the constraints of the executed application. Next, we defined the weights associated with each behavioral attribute, to set different priority levels to the analysis of the different comparative attributes. Therefore, the following weights were used: $P = (P_{timestamp} = 1.00, P_{location} = 1.00, P_{device} = 0.75, P_{appid} = 0.50, P_{apprestriction} = 0.50)$

When the user accesses the system for the first time, he enters personal information (e.g. authentication in the medical clinic). When he provides such information, he is authenticated on the system. After such information is provided, the system is able to extract the explicit profile and the user session profile, which in the first interaction are the same.

Therefore, the proposed authentication process is performed from the second user interaction. In the second interaction, the same application was requested, from the neighborhood location of the first interaction. However, such request was performed from another available mobile device. To determine the vectors used to compute the similarity degree, we need to use the weights previously defined to VectorP. On the other hand, to determine VectorE, the attribute values must be compared, which is performed comparing the captured behavior B_0 and the session profile (behavior B_{-1}). The attributes values that remained unchanged received one (1) as its value, and those that changed received zero (0) as its value. In the case of the spatio-temporal attributes (location and timestamp) the value to be received is the minimum value of the spatio-temporal permutation model considering the spatio-temporal cluster used as reference, determined using the SaTScan tool (Kulldorff, 2005).

The base to the analysis, in the SaTScan tool, is composed of 280 previously collected events. Thus, when comparing the p-value of the two executions of the spatio-temporal permutation model (with co-variables and without co-variables), the system finds the minimum value between them to analyze the worst case (the case that represents a higher risk to the authentication process). Therefore, the system uses the p-value of 0.826, determined by the spatio-temporal analysis without co-variables, which is represented in Figure 8. Such value is used to compute the similarity degree between the captured event and the session profile, which represents the user execution context, and, therefore, exists only during the interaction of the user with the application being considered. The remaining models shown on Figure 8 are presented to demonstrate the efficiency of the spatio-temporal permutation in the detection of anomalies in pervasive systems.

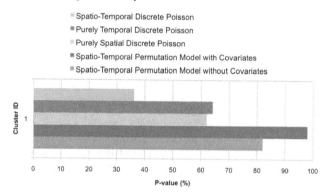

Fig. 8. Results of SaTScan analytical models

After the definition of these two vectors, it is possible to determine the similarity degree between the captured vector and the session profile. However, as there is the need to determine which are the intervals of values for similarity degree, which determine each user category (normal, suspect and abnormal). Thus, we assumed the following definition:

- Normal user: a similarity degree above 90%;
- Suspect user: a similarity degree between 70% and 90%;
- Abnormal user: a similarity degree below 70%.

According to the definition of these intervals, there is the need to test the user with the challenge regarding to a suspect user and regarding to the authentication level required by the application (medium level), according to table presented in the Figure 7 and Table 2. When the user responds the challenge correctly, he is authenticated in the system, executes the desired operation and the requested event is inserted in the user profile, which contains the history of its interactions with the system.

As Figure 9 illustrates, it is perceptible that the proposed context sensitive authentication architecture enables the evolution of its behavioral parameters, through the incorporation of

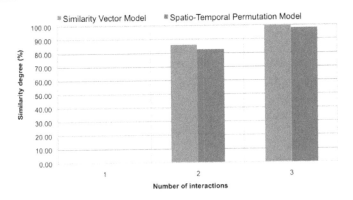

Fig. 9. System evolution according to the number of interactions

user events (activities) to the explicit profiles, implicit profiles and user session. Interactions of the system with the authentication module are represented in the X-axis, the first interaction is a traditional authentication, i.e., through password without graphical representation.

Consequently, the system is able to widen its knowledge base, and, thus, aggregate the user actions, which reflect its knowledge and abilities, refining the authentication process according to the number of interactions with the user. Through the dynamism offered by the proposed architecture, it is possible to provide a higher autonomicity to the user, i.e., the authentication system continually reduces the need for explicit data input to the system (response to challenges).

6. Conclusion and research agenda

Through this research, regarding the determination of user behavior in mobile computing environments, we confirmed the importance of considering two fundamental attributes in the user context: space and time. Such properties are relevant, as human beings have habits and the time correlations determine successive events that define a behavioral profile. Thus, in this work, an event is defined as the situation of an entity defined by one of more contexts that compose the user total context, in a given location and in a given time frame.

Therefore, a research was needed to analyze behavioral models considering both attributes (time and space) simultaneously, aiming to obtain a more precise evaluation of user behavior, identifying conformity in the behavior standard and possible behavior anomalies, which would characterize a suspicion attempt of automatic authentication. We proposed the use of a context-aware recommendation system model which allows the user of three filtering approaches: i) content based filtering, ii) collaborative filtering and iii) hybrid filtering. The experimental results comprising the content based filtering, and its respective analytical model, present a significant efficiency in the detection and analysis of anomalies in the authentication process.

Beyond that, the proposed architecture fulfills the autonomicity and dynamicity requirements, as through the behavioral profiles defined by the vector space model, the system is able to aggregate the skills and the knowledge acquired by the user during his interaction with the system. Additionally, our proposal provides flexibility as it allows different authentication forms, according the security levels required by the executed applications. Thus, we consider that the proposed approach was able to circumvent the lack of existent alternatives in the literature to fulfill simultaneously the requirements of context-awareness, computational efficiency, flexibility, autonomicity and dynamicity.

Future work will focus on conducting the impact analysis of the number of users on the context-aware authentication mechanism, i.e. the system capacity to maintain an acceptable rate of success in the authentication process even in the presence of an increasing number of users registered in the system. Another future work is a case study for each recommendation filter, aiming to evaluate their performance in terms of knowledge acquisition and of portability of mobile devices in the authentication of information and of the device itself.

7. Acknowledgments

This work was partially supported by CNPq (National Counsel of Technological and Scientific Development) of MCT (Ministry of Science and Technology), Brazil.

8. References

Augustin, I., Yamin, A., da Silva, L., Real, R., Frainer, G. & Geyer, C. (2006). ISAMadapt: abstractions and tools for designing general-purpose pervasive applications, *Software: Practice and Experience* 36(11-12): 1231–1256.
URL: *http://onlinelibrary.wiley.com/doi/10.1002/spe.756/pdf*

Bellavista, P., Corradi, A., Montanari, R. & Stefanelli, C. (2003). Context-aware middleware for resource management in the wireless Internet, *IEEE Transactions on Software Engineering* 29: 1086–1099.
URL: *http://www.computer.org/portal/web/csdl/doi/10.1109/TSE.2003.1265523*

Burke, R. (2007). Hybrid web recommender systems, *in* P. Brusilovsky, A. Kobsa & W. Nejdl (eds), *The adaptive web*, Vol. 4321 of *Lecture Notes in Computer Science*, Springer-Verlag, pp. 377–408.
URL: *http://portal.acm.org/citation.cfm?id=1768211*

Cassens, J. & Kofod-Petersen, A. (2006). Using activity theory to model context awareness: a qualitative case study, *Proceedings of the 19th International Florida Artificial Intelligence Research Society Conference, Florida, USA, AAAI Press*, pp. 619–624.
URL: *http://scholar.google.com/scholar?hl=en&btnG=Search&q=intitle:Using+Activity+Theory+to+Model+Context+Awareness+:+a+Qualitative+Case+Study#0*

Corradi, A., Montanari, R. & Tibaldi, D. (2004). Context-based access control management in ubiquitous environments, *Network Computing and Applications, IEEE International Symposium on* 0: 253–260.
URL: *http://www.computer.org/portal/web/csdl/doi/10.1109/NCA.2004.1347784*

Dey, A. (2001). Understanding and using context, *Personal and ubiquitous computing* 5(1): 4–7.
URL: *http://portal.acm.org/citation.cfm?id=593572*

Hassan, J., Riaz, A. & Raazi, S. (2008). Activity-based Security Scheme for Ubiquitous Environments, *IPCCC 2008.* pp. 475–481.
URL: *http://ieeexplore.ieee.org/xpls/abs_all.jsp?arnumber=4745102*

Hong, J., Satyanarayanan, M. & Cybenko, G. (2007). Guest Editors' Introduction: Security & Privacy, *IEEE Pervasive Computing* 6(4): 15–17.

Jameel, H., Shaikh, R., Lee, H. & Lee, S. (2006). Human identification through image evaluation using secret predicates, *Topics in Cryptology–CT-RSA 2007* 4377: 67–84.
URL: *http://www.springerlink.com/index/EVL6JGT546674294.pdf*

Johnson, G. (2009). Towards shrink-wrapped security: A taxonomy of security-relevant context, *Pervasive Computing and Communications, 2009. PerCom 2009. IEEE International Conference on*, IEEE, Galveston, TX, pp. 1–2.
URL: *http://ieeexplore.ieee.org/xpls/abs_all.jsp?arnumber=4912819*

Kim, J., Song, C., Kim, T., Rim, K. & Lee, J. (2009). Secure and Efficient Recommendation Service of RFID System Using Authenticated Key Management, *Ubiquitous Information Technologies & Applications, 2009. ICUT'09. Proceedings of the 4th International Conference on*, IEEE, pp. 1–5.
URL: *http://ieeexplore.ieee.org/xpls/abs_all.jsp?arnumber=5405678*

Kulldorff, M. (2005). SaTScan: software for the spatial, temporal, and space-time scan statistics, version 5.1 [computer program], *Inf Manag Serv* .
URL: *http://scholar.google.com/scholar?hl=en&btnG=Search&q=intitle:SaTScan:+Software +for+the+Spatial,+Temporal,+and+Space-Time+Scan+Statistics#0*

Lima, J., Rocha, C. & Dantas, M. (2010). An authentication approach based on behavioral profiles, *Information Systems and Technologies (CISTI), 2010 5th Iberian Conference on*, IEEE, Santiago de Compostela, Spain, pp. 1–4.
URL: *http://ieeexplore.ieee.org/xpls/abs_all.jsp?arnumber=5556601*

McDonald, D. (2003). Ubiquitous recommendation systems, *Computer* 36: 111.
URL: *http://www.computer.org/portal/web/csdl/doi/10.1109/MC.2003.1236478*

Munoz-Organero, M., Ram\'\iez-González, G., Munoz-Merino, P. & Kloos, C. (2010). A Collaborative Recommender System Based on Space-Time Similarities, *IEEE Pervasive Computing* pp. 81–87.
URL: *http://www.computer.org/portal/web/csdl/doi/10.1109/MPRV.2010.56*

Oku, K., Nakajima, S., Miyazaki, J., Uemura, S., Kato, H. & Hattori, F. (2010). A Recommendation System Considering Users' Past/Current/Future Contexts, *ids.csom.umn.edu* pp. 3–7.
URL: *http://ids.csom.umn.edu/faculty/gedas/cars2010/OkuEtAl-CARS-2010.pdf*

Rahmati, A. & Zhong, L. (2009). Human-battery interaction on mobile phones, *Pervasive and Mobile Computing* 5(5): 465–477.

Ray, S. & Mahanti, A. (2009). Strategies for effective shilling attacks against recommender systems, *Privacy, Security, and Trust in KDD* 5456: 111–125.
URL: *http://www.springerlink.com/index/d6v15h1276872265.pdf*

Ricci, F. (2011). Mobile recommender systems, *Information Technology and Tourism* 12(3): 205–231.
URL: *http://www.ingentaconnect.com/content/cog/itt/2011/00000012/00000003/art00002*

Ricci, F. & Nguyen, Q. (2007). Acquiring and revising preferences in a critique-based mobile recommender system, *IEEE Intelligent Systems* 22: 22–29.
URL: *http://doi.ieeecomputersociety.org/10.1109/10.1109/MIS.2007.43*

Ricci, F., Rokach, L. & Shapira, B. (2011). Introduction to Recommender Systems Handbook, *Recommender Systems Handbook* pp. 1–35.
URL: *http://www.springerlink.com/index/X8622U506942LU28.pdf*

Roberts, M., Ducheneaut, N., Begole, B., Partridge, K., Price, B., Bellotti, V., Walendowski, A. & Rasmussen, P. (2008). Scalable architecture for context-aware activity-detecting mobile recommendation systems, *World of Wireless, Mobile and Multimedia Networks, 2008. WoWMoM 2008. 2008 International Symposium on a*, IEEE, pp. 1–6.

Rocha, C. C. (2010). *A Context-Aware Authentication Approach Based on Behavioral Definitions*, Master's thesis, Federal University of Santa Catarina, Florianopolis, SC, Brazil.

Romero-Mariona, J., Ziv, H. & Richardson, D. (2008). SRRS: a recommendation system for security requirements, *Proceedings of the 2008 international workshop on Recommendation systems for software engineering*, ACM, pp. 50–52.
URL: *http://portal.acm.org/citation.cfm?id=1454266*

Sathish Babu, B. & Venkataram, P. (2009). A dynamic authentication scheme for mobile transactions, *International Journal* 8(1): 59–74.
URL: *http://citeseerx.ist.psu.edu/viewdoc/download?doi=10.1.1.155.4468&rep=rep1&type=pdf*

Shi, E., Niu, Y., Jakobsson, M. & Chow, R. (2011). Implicit authentication through learning user behavior, *Information Security* pp. 99–113.

Su, X. & Khoshgoftaar, T. (2009). A survey of collaborative filtering techniques, *Advances in Artificial Intelligence* 2009: 19.

Toninelli, A., Montanari, R., Lassila, O. & Khushraj, D. (2009). What's on users' minds? toward a usable smart phone security model, *IEEE Pervasive Computing* pp. 32–39.

Uden, L. (2007). Activity theory for designing mobile learning, *International Journal of Mobile Learning and Organisation* 1(1): 81–102.
URL: *http://inderscience.metapress.com/index/EW9VEADD3EUFJHV3.pdf*

van der Heijden, H., Kotsis, G. & Kronsteiner, R. (2005). Mobile Recommendation Systems for Decision Making, *Mobile Business, International Conference on* 0: 137–143.
URL: *http://www.computer.org/portal/web/csdl/doi/10.1109/ICMB.2005.68*

Zhan, J., Hsieh, C., Wang, I., Hsu, T., Liau, C. & Wang, D. (2010). Privacy-preserving collaborative recommender systems, *Systems, Man, and Cybernetics, Part C: Applications and Reviews, IEEE Transactions on* 40(4): 472–476.
URL: *http://ieeexplore.ieee.org/xpls/abs_all.jsp?arnumber=5411745*

Permissions

The contributors of this book come from diverse backgrounds, making this book a truly international effort. This book will bring forth new frontiers with its revolutionizing research information and detailed analysis of the nascent developments around the world.

We would like to thank Dr. Adem Karahoca, for lending his expertise to make the book truly unique. He has played a crucial role in the development of this book. Without his invaluable contribution this book wouldn't have been possible. He has made vital efforts to compile up to date information on the varied aspects of this subject to make this book a valuable addition to the collection of many professionals and students.

This book was conceptualized with the vision of imparting up-to-date information and advanced data in this field. To ensure the same, a matchless editorial board was set up. Every individual on the board went through rigorous rounds of assessment to prove their worth. After which they invested a large part of their time researching and compiling the most relevant data for our readers. Conferences and sessions were held from time to time between the editorial board and the contributing authors to present the data in the most comprehensible form. The editorial team has worked tirelessly to provide valuable and valid information to help people across the globe.

Every chapter published in this book has been scrutinized by our experts. Their significance has been extensively debated. The topics covered herein carry significant findings which will fuel the growth of the discipline. They may even be implemented as practical applications or may be referred to as a beginning point for another development. Chapters in this book were first published by InTech; hereby published with permission under the Creative Commons Attribution License or equivalent.

The editorial board has been involved in producing this book since its inception. They have spent rigorous hours researching and exploring the diverse topics which have resulted in the successful publishing of this book. They have passed on their knowledge of decades through this book. To expedite this challenging task, the publisher supported the team at every step. A small team of assistant editors was also appointed to further simplify the editing procedure and attain best results for the readers.

Our editorial team has been hand-picked from every corner of the world. Their multi-ethnicity adds dynamic inputs to the discussions which result in innovative outcomes. These outcomes are then further discussed with the researchers and contributors who give their valuable feedback and opinion regarding the same. The feedback is then collaborated with the researches and they are edited in a comprehensive manner to aid the understanding of the subject.

Apart from the editorial board, the designing team has also invested a significant amount of their time in understanding the subject and creating the most relevant covers. They scrutinized every image to scout for the most suitable representation of the subject and create an appropriate cover for the book.

The publishing team has been involved in this book since its early stages. They were actively engaged in every process, be it collecting the data, connecting with the contributors or procuring relevant information. The team has been an ardent support to the editorial, designing and production team. Their endless efforts to recruit the best for this project, has resulted in the accomplishment of this book. They are a veteran in the field of academics and their pool of knowledge is as vast as their experience in printing. Their expertise and guidance has proved useful at every step. Their uncompromising quality standards have made this book an exceptional effort. Their encouragement from time to time has been an inspiration for everyone.

The publisher and the editorial board hope that this book will prove to be a valuable piece of knowledge for researchers, students, practitioners and scholars across the globe.

List of Contributors

Larysa Globa and Vasyl Kurdecha
National Technical University of Ukraine "Kyiv Polytechnic Institute", Ukraine

Bidyut Gupta and Sindoora Koneru
Computer Science Department, Southern Illinois University, Carbondale, USA

Ziping Liu
Computer Science Department, Southeast Missouri State University, Cape Girardeau, USA

Marios I. Poulakis, Athanasios D. Panagopoulos and Philip Constantinou
National Technical University of Athens, Greece

Guitao Cao, Jie Yang, Qing Zhou and Weiting Chen
Software Engineering Institute, East China Normal University, Shanghai, China

Pierre T. Kirisci
Universität Bremen (BIK, TZI), Germany

Klaus-Dieter Thoben, Patrick Klein, Martin Hilbig, Markus Modzelewski and Michael Lawo
Universität Bremen (BIK, TZI), Germany

Antoinette Fennell and Joshue O'Connor
National Council for the Blind of Ireland (NCBI), Ireland

Thomas Fiddian
RNID, UK

Yehya Mohamad and Markus Klann
Fraunhofer FIT, Germany

Thomas Bergdahl
DORO AB, Sweden

Haluk Gökmen
Arcelik A.S., Turkey

Edmilson Klen
Universidade Federal de Santa Catarina, Brazil

Mohamed Dbouk and Ihab Sbeity
Lebanese University, Faculty of Sciences (I), Beirut, Lebanon

Hamid Mcheick
Université du Québec à Chicoutimi, Québec, Canada

Dilek Karahoca
Bahçeşehir University Software Engineering Department, Turkey
Near East University Computer Technology and Instructional Design PhD Program Department, Turkey

Adem Karahoca
Bahçeşehir University Software Engineering Department, Turkey

Nilton Serigioli, Edgar Charry Rodriguez and Rodrigo Reina Muñoz
Engineering and Applied Social Sciences Center – UFABC, Laboratory of Integrated Systems of São Paulo University, Brazil

Cicília Raquel Maia Leite
Laboratory of Software Engineering, State University of Rio Grande do Norte, Brazil
Laboratory of Hospital Automation and Bioengineering, Federal University of Rio Grande do Norte, Brazil

Pedro F.R. Neto
Laboratory of Software Engineering, State University of Rio Grande do Norte, Brazil

Glaucia R.M.A. Sizilio, Anna G.C.D. Ribeiro, Ricardo A.M. Valentim and Ana M.G. Guerreiro
Laboratory of Hospital Automation and Bioengineering, Federal University of Rio Grande do Norte, Brazil

João Carlos Damasceno Lima
Federal University of Santa Catarina, Brazil
Federal University of Santa Maria, Brazil

Mário Antônio Ribeiro Dantas
Federal University of Santa Catarina, Brazil

Iara Augustin
Federal University of Santa Maria, Brazil

Cristiano Cortez da Rocha
MobilEasy Technologies Ltda, Brazil